SCHOOL OF
ORIENTAL AND AFRICAN STUDIES

NOMADS IN ALLIANCE

NOMADS IN ALLIANCE

Symbiosis and growth among the
Rendille and Samburu
of Kenya

PAUL SPENCER

Lecturer in African Anthropology
at the School of Oriental and African Studies

0742273

LONDON
OXFORD UNIVERSITY PRESS
NEW YORK TORONTO NAIROBI
1973

68273

Oxford University Press, Ely House, London W. 1

GLASGOW   NEW YORK   TORONTO   MELBOURNE   WELLINGTON
CAPE TOWN   IBADAN   NAIROBI   DAR ES SALAAM   ADDIS ABABA
DELHI   BOMBAY   CALCUTTA   MADRAS   KARACHI   LAHORE   DACCA
KUALA LUMPUR   SINGAPORE   HONG KONG   TOKYO

ISBN 0 19 713576 5

*Printed in Great Britain
by Richard Clay (The Chaucer Press), Ltd
Bungay, Suffolk*

To Rosalind

CONTENTS

MAPS

CHARTS

TABLES

Map 1
THE AREA INHABITED BY THE RENDILLE AND SAMBURU IN 1960

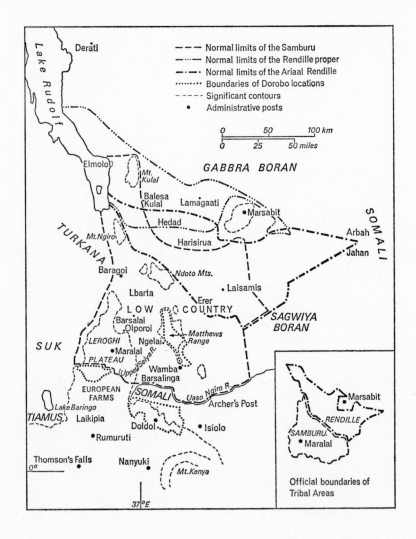

Normal limits of the Samburu
Normal limits of the Rendille proper
Normal limits of the Ariaal Rendille
Boundaries of Dorobo locations
Significant contours
Administrative posts

| 0 | | 50 | | 100 km |
| 0 | 25 | | 50 miles | |

Lake Rudolf

Derati

Elmolo

Mt. Kulal

GABBRA BORAN

Balesa Kulal

Lamagaati

Marsabit

SOMALI

Hedad

Harisirua

Arbah

Jahan

TURKANA

Mt. Ngiro

Baragoi

Ndoto Mts.

Lbarta

LOW COUNTRY

Erer

Laisamis

SAGWIYA BORAN

Barsalai

Olporoi

Matthews Range

SUK

LEROGHI

Ngelai

(Upper Seiya R.)

Maralal

PLATEAU

Wamba

(Upper Seiya R.)

Barsalinga

EUROPEAN FARMS

SOMALI

Uaso Ngiro R.

Archer's Post

Lake Baringo

TIAMUS

Laikipia

Doldol

Isiolo

Rumuruti

Thomson's Falls

0°

Nanyuki

Mt. Kenya

37° E

Marsabit

RENDILLE

SAMBURU

Maralal

Official boundaries of
Tribal Areas

INTRODUCTION

The division of the pastoral nomadic societies of northern Kenya into Cushitic and Nilo-Hamitic is purely linguistic and part of a wider scheme of classification of African languages and hence tribes into major groups. This division separates the Rendille from the Samburu: the Rendille are a Cushitic people whose culture and language bears some similiarity to the Somali further east, while the Samburu are a Nilo-Hamitic people who regard themselves as a branch of the Masai further south. In economic terms, the Rendille depend primarily on camel herding and the Samburu on cattle. In administrative terms, the two officially belong to different provinces of Kenya, the Rendille being administered from Marsabit in the Northern Frontier Province, and the Samburu from Maralal in the Rift Valley Province.

The case for presenting a survey of the two tribes in one volume, is nevertheless a strong one and is based on precisely those reasons that extended my own interest in the Samburu to include the Rendille also. Despite linguistic, economic, and administrative divisions, the two tribes are bound together by strong traditional links of political alliance and by ties of kinship resulting from generations of intermigration and intermarriage, to an extent that they do not share with any other tribes of the area.

In examining their recent history, the accounts of early travellers are characteristically misleading and contradictory. The earliest writer-traveller to the area, von Höhnel in 1888, noted that the two tribes were on the best of terms with each other, but had little else to say on this topic.[1] The next traveller to the area, Chanler in 1893, suggested a somewhat less simple relationship. 'The Samburu, or Burkineji,[2] were originally deadly enemies of the Rendille; but since their defeat at Leikipia by the Masai many years ago and the subsequent destruction of their flocks by the plague, they had been forced into semi-serfdom to the Rendille—watching their flocks, and performing other menial services for them. In return for this they were protected in their persons and possessions ...'[3] Seven years later when Arkell-Hardwick visited the area, the situation appeared to have changed somewhat. 'Now the Burkeneji [Samburu] were perfectly willing to protect the Rendili, but in return they considered

---

1. von Höhnel, 1894, vol. ii, p. 184.
2. These are both names given by other tribes. The Samburu refer to themselves as *Loikop*, rendered variously in the early literature as Laigop, Legup, Leukop, Ligop, Lokkobb, Lokub, and Lukop.
3. Chanler, 1896, p. 316.

that they ought to be allowed the right to help themselves from the Rendili flocks whenever they felt so disposed; and to do them justice they fully acted up to this idea without fear of reprisals. It seemed to me a very peculiar state of affairs. The two tribes lived together; yet the Burkeneji constantly raided the Rendili, and though the Rendili did not seem to like it, they never openly resented the depredations."[4]

From reading these and other accounts one can quite justifiably begin to wonder just who might be protecting whom and whether this would induce the best of terms. Yet there remains one common theme: that these two tribes were closely related in some way. It is this close relationship and the economic factors maintaining their interdependence and yet separateness which is one of the principal themes of this study. Its focus, however, is not on the processes that may have linked the two tribes in the past before administration of this century separated them into two provinces. It is on the processes which were seen to link them in the course of my field work among them between 1957 and 1962, and showed no signs of diminishing.

This study serves a number of other purposes. It provides an opportunity for publishing ethnographic data on the Samburu and Rendille which did not appear in my earlier book on *The Samburu.*[5] There, my principal concern was with the social system of the Samburu, in which case-examples and an outline of the Rendille were used to amplify the processes of that system. Here, I have tried to avoid repetition and to give a more systematic account of the economy (Chapter 1) and the customary observances of the two tribes (Chapters 2 and 3). Where some aspect was only briefly treated, if at all, in the earlier book, it has been given a fuller treatment here; and if it was treated at some length, a briefer mention suffices here. Essentially the two studies are intended to supplement one another, with a shift in emphasis from the analysis of a single system in the earlier work to a discussion of a wider set of problems in the present work.

In elaborating the relationship between the two tribes (in Chapter 4), the Ariaal or southern Rendille, are described. These occupy a position geographically, economically, and socially somewhere between the Rendille *proper* in the north and the Samburu.

At this point, it becomes possible to examine available evidence in order to reconstruct a history of the area and to discern the process of change under modern conditions (Chapter 5). While it becomes

<hr/>

4. Arkell-Hardwick, 1903, p. 241.
5. *The Samburu, a study of gerontocracy in a nomadic tribe,* Routledge and Kegan Paul, 1965, and University of California Press, 1965. This is referred to throughout the present work simply as *The Samburu.*

apparent that a historical perspective does not add substantially to an understanding of the social systems of the Rendille and Samburu in 1960, it does at least throw some light on the nature of the problems that faced the British administration during its forty years in the area. A discussion of these problems with reference to the earlier chapters concludes the main part of the book (Chapter 6).

There is, in addition, an appendix on the Dorobo and Elmolo, the small groups of people who traditionally lived by hunting and fishing. Far from being isolated tribes with a separate existence, they are seen to have specific ties with neighbouring pastoralists (in this context, primarily the Samburu) and they play a vital role in the ecological balance of the societies in the area.

This survey is of a period that preceded Kenyan independence and the disturbances in the north caused by recent Somali territorial claims. In one sense, therefore, it has already been overtaken by events and is a matter of history. In another sense, on the other hand, the societies described here have largely evolved in a situation of political uncertainty and are well adapted to it. Forty years of peace have not dispelled this uncertainty in the minds of the people. Whatever the future may hold for them, all the available evidence suggests that the present is, if anything, confirming their traditional values and impeding any change towards a new form of society. As long as this remains so, this book will, it is hoped, have a current value, especially for those closely concerned with the welfare of these peoples.

It was largely through the support of the Markerere Institute of Social Research, then the East African Institute of Social Research, that I was able to extend my original field work to the Rendille, and in many ways I benefited from their hospitality and encouragement. I would like to take this opportunity of repeating my warmest thanks to the members of the Institute and to all who helped to make this study possible. In addition to those mentioned in my earlier book I must add the Elmolo, the Dorobo from various parts, and especially the Rendille.

As informants, the Rendille were altogether easier to work with than the Samburu. My work among them was no doubt helped by the fact that by the time I became interested in them I already spoke Samburu (Masai) and had a reasonably clear notion of the range of problems I was interested in. But even so, above and beyond this, I found the Rendille in various ways more direct and more consistent than the Samburu when discussing with them the nature of their social system. This enabled me to cover a lot of ground in a comparatively short time, and made this study possible in its present form.

But if this book has a weakness, it must surely be that my knowledge of Rendille society is almost second-hand. Many of the southern Ariaal Rendille and some of the Rendille proper in the north spoke Samburu fluently, and at the level of study I was hoping to achieve, I did not make any concerted attempt to master the Rendille language. Thus, not only did I have to rely on Samburu-speaking Rendille, but also I was unable to corroborate any of their statements with a more direct involvement in the processes of their social system. As I say, their accounts were consistent with each other and with what I understood of the Samburu system but a basic component of anthropological field work was missing.

I feel it is most likely, for instance, that much more could be learnt of the nature of Rendille society at the level of the clan-settlement. All reported incidents seemed to suggest that the relationship between brothers and close clansmen is fraught with strains. Among the Samburu, men faced with these types of situation would resolve the matter by migrating in different directions, whereas among the Rendille, they would remain together in the one large settlement.

There is here an opportunity for further research, for extended case studies of individual Rendille settlements, to an extent that was not possible among the more transient Samburu. This would, I suggest, reveal processes underlying the problems of clanship and camel ownership and the sharp cleavage between settlement and camp. Indeed, there is every reason to suppose that, in the final analysis, a study of the stresses and strains of Rendille settlement life could throw new light on their relationships with the Samburu. If this present book provides some basic material for a future intensive study of the Rendille, then it will have served one more useful purpose.

This book was first drafted in 1961, revised in 1967, and due to be published in East Africa in the same year. There followed a series of delays, and eventually the attempt was abandoned. I am especially grateful, therefore, to the School of Oriental and African Studies for agreeing in 1972 to sponsor the work, thereby helping me rescue it for long overdue publication. I would like to take this opportunity to express my deepest thanks to the Publications Committee of the School, to Mr. J. R. Bracken and to all those who have helped in its production.

1

LIVESTOCK AND ITS MANAGEMENT

The Rendille and Samburu are dispersed over an area of some 16,000 square miles in central north Kenya. To the north and east the land is generally below 2,000 feet in altitude, the climate is dry and hot and the terrain is semi-desert, strewn often with lava boulders. It is here that the Rendille are dispersed with their camels (especially in the north) and small stock (especially in the east). As one journeys south-westwards, so the country gradually rises, the climate becomes slightly less harsh and the semi-desert gives way to desert scrub interspersed with patches of thick bush. On the borders of this country where it is not too dry for cattle or too temperate for camels, the Rendille live interspersed with the Samburu. Still further south-west, one passes the chain of mountains formed by Mount Ngiro, the Ndotos, and the Matthews Range, and then through more Samburu country, and eventually one climbs steeply up to the Leroghi Plateau where the Samburu graze their cattle herds on scattered tree grassland at 6–7,000 feet and the climate is altogether more moderate.

In considering the economy of the area, the pattern of rainfall is of vital importance. In northern Kenya there are two patterns. The western pattern extends to the Leroghi Plateau and the western side of Mount Ngiro and it consists of heavy and generally reliable spring and summer rains. The eastern pattern extends over the remainder of the district—the low country—and it consists of heavy but unreliable spring and autumn rains.

The monthly distribution of rainfall recorded at the various government stations is summarized on p. 6.

These charts show clearly the spring and *summer* rains at Maralal (on Leroghi) and the spring and *autumn* rains at Baragoi, Wamba, and Marsabit (in the low country). The monthly distribution at Doldol has been included here as it illustrates to some extent an area which enjoys both patterns of rainfall (spring, summer, *and* autumn rains): in this respect it is similar to the Upper Seiya area in the eastern foothills of Leroghi.[1]

Chart 1 shows the monthly distribution of rainfall not only as a clear outline representing the average (mean), but also as a

---

1. Further afield, the western pattern of rainfall is shared by Thomson's Falls. Baringo and Eldoret; and the eastern pattern is shared by Isiolo and Moyale.

Chart 1
MONTHLY DISTRIBUTION OF RAINFALL

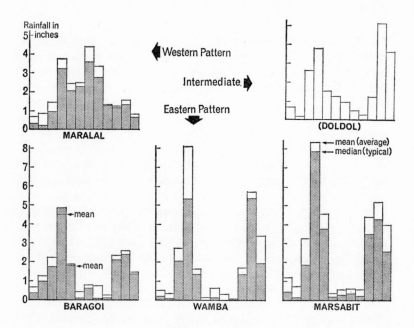

black area representing the typical (median) value.[2] The fact that the median is usually well below the mean value emphasizes the extent to which the average tends to be boosted by local cloud bursts (which may do more harm in eroding the land than good in watering it). The striking differences between mean and median in Wamba and Marsabit especially is a clear indication of the unreliability of the rainfall in these areas. The following table gives further evidence of this.

It must be emphasized that the actual figures are misleading since these stations have been carefully built in places where there is a good supply of permanent water and a reasonable climate. Consequently rainfall tends to be substantially higher than elsewhere. This is particularly true of Marsabit (on top of a mountain) and

---

2. The 'median' value over, for instance, nineteen years would be the tenth heaviest (and hence also the tenth lightest) rainfall figure. The fact that in these charts the median differs from the mean indicates, incidentally, how unreliable a guide for expected rainfall the arithmetic mean value is: it is an *average*, but not exactly a *typical* figure.

Table 1

ANNUAL RAINFALL, 1940–59

Station	Annual average rainfall	Annual median rainfall	Number of months with less than ½" rain
Maralal	24·19"	22·37"	59:240
Baragoi	18·92"	18·85"	84:240
Wamba	26·05"	19·84"	107:240
Marsabit	32·66"	30·45"	92:240

Wamba (at the base of a mountain). It is most likely that areas only 10 miles from Wamba, for instance, had more than 180 months with less than ½ inch of rain during these twenty years, and that this may apply to the low country generally. Typical rainfalls away from government stations could be of the order of 20 inches on the Leroghi Plateau, and well below 10 inches in the drier parts of the low country.

Essential Natural Resources

(a) *Water.* Apart from the Uaso Ngiro river along the southern boundary and Lake Rudolf in the north, all the water in the Rendille and Samburu country comes from rain falling within its boundaries. During the dry winter and summer months in the low country, the only effective supply of water is the rain falling in the mountain areas over 5,000 feet. This is not simply because rainfall is heavier in these areas, but also because vegetation is thicker and water is retained for a longer period: it reaches the low country as it gradually seeps out over a period of weeks and even months. Just a few days of rain in these higher areas, as may be expected in January and in May or June, reduces the harshness of the dry periods considerably. But from August to mid-October there is a general water shortage in these low-lying areas; the only river basins to hold any water at this time tend to be those that are fed by the late summer rains on the Leroghi Plateau, such as the Seiya and the Barsaloi.

Water flows above the surface of the river beds for only a few days or (in places) weeks of the year. At other times it is seeping many feet beneath the sandy surface. However, submerged ridges of non-porous rock in the river beds act as subterranean dams and raise the water level locally where it may be obtained by digging in the sand at a depth varying from three to ten or more feet. I refer to the place where water is obtainable by digging as a *water point* and to the temporary wells which are dug as *water holes*.

(b) *Grass and Browse*. Cattle and sheep prefer grass where this is available in the wetter parts of the district during the wetter months, but all forms of stock in the area can survive on browse. The people tend to accept the sparseness of their environment as one of the facts of their existence. They do not see this as a result of over-grazing which has led progressively to soil erosion. The previous administration regarded this as one of the principal problems of the area, and between 1952 and 1961, grazing schemes were introduced in the areas close to the Samburu government stations. The basic principle of these schemes was that each should consist of four grazing blocks with a limited number of cattle. By rotating these cattle from one block to the next at four-monthly intervals, each block could have a complete year's rest after four months' use, thereby giving the grass a chance to grow and to seed. The success of the schemes, however, was limited partly by the extent to which grazing trespass occurred in the closed blocks and partly by the hazards of the climate, especially in the low country. On the one hand there were not the means to police the schemes adequately, and on the other hand it was sometimes necessary to open blocks to grazing prematurely because a local burst of rain had alleviated the drought that prevailed elsewhere. Between 1959 and 1961 there was a serious rinderpest epidemic followed by a severe drought, killing off many cattle and reducing the pressure on the land. At this point the grazing schemes were abandoned except for the forest areas which were still retained for water catchment purposes.

(c) *Salt*. Salt is important to the stock economy. It is obtainable in salt licks at certain watering points throughout the area. In general it presents no great problem, but it is a factor which constantly affects the nomadic and pastoral activities of both tribes. The Samburu claim that regular access to salt gives their cattle a high immunity to sleeping sickness. This could also be why Rendille camels are generally confined to brackish water points since they generally have a rather low resistance to this disease. The more usual reason given, however, is that lack of regular salt may cause necrotic skin lesions and lameness among camels.[3] Both tribes also maintain that small stock thrive best in an area where there is plenty of salt.

In the indigenous systems of the two tribes, these natural resources are not owned by individuals: different clans may tend to

3. This is confirmed by A. S. Leese (*A treatise on the one-humped camel in health and disease*, 1927, p. 82) and by E. F. Peck (*The Veterinary Record*, No. 14, Vol. 50, p. 409). Neither writer, however, suggests that salt will increase the camels' immunity to sleeping sickness.

use certain tracts of land, but this is a diffuse and often transitory preference rather than a specific claim to ownership. Only a water hole, dug and maintained by a stock owner, gives him prior right to use it over all other Samburu or Rendille. When it is destroyed by a spate of the river or allowed to collapse through disuse, he has no further claim to the spot.[4]

Livestock

(a) *Cattle.* Cattle are relied on by the Samburu mainly for their milk. Oxen may be slaughtered and eaten on certain ceremonial occasions, or when meat is badly needed in the dry season; but they are killed with reluctance, since in the last resort they are a security against a series of harsh dry seasons. When milk is scarce, blood drawn from the neck of a cow may be mixed with milk, or very occasionally it may be taken neat after removing the clot. Calf-bearing females would not normally be killed. Animals that die naturally are eaten, although parts of the carcass contaminated with anthrax or black-quarter are avoided.

It has been generally assumed in government circles that the ecological balance of both human and cattle populations among the Samburu has been completely altered by innovations introduced during the past few decades. The human population has been protected from intertribal warfare and from epidemic and more recently individual diseases; veterinary medicines which were at first spasmodically introduced on to Leroghi in the 1920s have been very popular; as the total number of cattle in the country has soared so there has been increasing pressure on the available grazing leading to soil erosion and a general deterioration of pastureland; stock (mostly male) has to be sold at periodic cattle sales; work is available outside the district and cash can be used to buy alternative forms of food. These changes must affect the ecological balance in different ways, and it is not easy to assert whether they have led to a net increase in the ratio of cattle to human populations or to a

4. In the *Kenya Land Commission Evidence*, a good geographic description of Maralal District is given in pp. 1451–3, a generally depressing account of its grasslands is given in pp. 1562–9, and the distribution of water points is given in pp. 1713–15. Owing to considerable speculation today on the deterioration of the land due to overgrazing, this account of 1933 is important and presents a situation surprisingly similar to that of 1960.

Nowhere in these accounts, however, is there a summary of the principal saltlicks in the area. The following have been recorded. On the Leroghi Plateau they are: Kisima, Saguta Marmar, and Kelele. In the low country they are: the upper Seiya, Nagoruweru, Ilkisin, Losikirechi, Lkidoloto, Lalbarsaloi, Sekera, Swiyan, Swari, Lokumugum, Langatangiteng, Sachati, Naisesho, Larosoro, Kom, Serolipi, Kauro, Laisamis, Lodosoit, Lamagaati, and Lake Rudolf.

Table 2

EARLY AND RECENT ESTIMATES OF SAMBURU
CATTLE STATISTICS

	Early estimates	Recent estimates
Cattle per herd	81·4 (1925)	80·1 (1958–9)
Cattle per person	15 (1922); 9·5 (1928)	11–12 (1958–9)
Proportion of female cattle to total	{66·3% (1933) {74·5% (1939)	{74·6% (1958–9) {65% (1962)
Proportion of total cattle in milk	41·7% (1950)	

net decrease. Table 2 comparing early with more recent estimates is therefore of considerable interest.[5]

Perhaps the most striking aspect of these figures is the consistency between early and later estimates. They suggest that regardless of the introduction of new medicines, etc., there is a reasonably constant ratio between the stock and the human population, which, allowing for fluctuations, is essentially stable.

A useful and authoritative account of the breeding characteristics of Samburu cattle and their rate of maturing has been given in the *Kenya Land Commission Evidence*.[6] Information collected directly from the Samburu was quite consistent with this: they claim that a healthy and fertile cow would bear between seven and ten calves at ten-monthly intervals from the age of 30 months. As the period of gestation is nine months, this would imply pregnancy shortly after giving birth. It is harder to collect exact information as regards the milk yield because of the variation from one animal to another and from one season to another. Two udders (i.e. about one-half of the milk) are given to the calf while the other two are milked for human consumption. The milk for consumption could typically vary from

5. The figures for 1922, 1925, and 1928 are based on early veterinary records. The figures for 1933 is quoted in the *Kenya Land Commission Evidence*. The figure for 1939 was estimated when it was proposed to cull Samburu stock. The 1950 figure is estimated from the number of calves inoculated against rinderpest in a year when it was reported that the scare was sufficient to persuade the Samburu to bring nearly all their cattle for inoculation. To suggest that each calf represents one cow in milk assumes that those calves that survive the deaths of their dams are roughly balanced by those who die while their dams continue to give milk: the Samburu use a tulchan (the stuffed hide of the calf) to induce her to give this milk. The 1958-9 figures are based on herds that were entered into new government grazing schemes. There is good reason to suppose that each entry corresponded more or less with the herd of one stock owner; instances where two men had entered their herds under one name or one man had divided his herd were both recorded, but broadly appeared to cancel each other out. The 1962 figure was the estimate of the veterinary officer at a time following a long period of drought when herds were generally depleted.

6. *Kenya Land Commission Evidence*, 1933, pp. 1657 ff. The breed under study were Boran cattle which had been obtained from tribes in the area. Samburu cattle are predominantly of this type.

a half-pint per milch cow in the dry season to one or even two pints in the wet season. The only selective breeding practised is to avoid castrating the male calf of a good milch cow on the assumption that it could become a useful bull. To attain this position, however, it would have to outfight three or more mature rivals before it could assert its mastery of the entire female herd.

A greedy young ox that tends to search for new grass ahead of the herd is suitable for the bell-ox of the herd: the other cattle are conditioned to follow the sound of the iron bell tied round his neck; as he constantly searches for fresh ungrazed ground, so they follow him instead of spreading out and straying in a private search for patches of grass. In this manner the herd keeps moving together and time is not wasted unnecessarily in poorer grazing land. Once a boy is old enough to herd cattle, he does so without a day's respite except through illness. Older men will continue to take an active interest in the herding, but focus their energy more on watering the stock and tracking down strays.

The cattle are milked by the women twice a day: early in the morning as soon as they wake up and early in the evening as soon as the cattle return from the day's grazing. In the wet season when there is grass close to the settlement, the cattle may, however, be grazed locally before being milked in the mornings.

(b) *Camels*. The Rendille regard their camels in much the same way as the Samburu regard their cattle. There are several important differences between the two types of stock, however. Samburu cattle herds are typically four times the size of Rendille camel herds, although the amount of milk produced by one camel far exceeds that produced by a cow. Secondly, camel herds increase at a much slower rate than cattle herds. In fact, Rendille have remarked that the total growth of their herds, if any, is imperceptible: any slow increase in the herd of one man is offset by the losses in the herd of another. The slower rate of growth is not necessarily due to the infertility of Rendille camels: they claim that their she-camels calve as many times as Samburu cattle. It is due rather to the higher incidence of disease among their camels and to their more leisurely rate of calving: a camel would be six years old before bearing her first calf and would subsequently calve every other year. The period of gestation is thirteen months, and so there is a longer interval between birth and pregnancy than among Samburu cattle.

Thus to the Rendille, each camel is worth much more than a cow is to the Samburu, in the first place because its milk yield is much greater and secondly because it is harder to replace.

That the Rendille cannot make more of their camel economy may be due to limitations in their husbandry. According to their own statements, they do not water their camels more often than one day in ten even in the harshest dry seasons, they live in rough stony areas where camel flies are common, and disease (especially anthrax) is endemic. Whereas according to Leese, the Somalis water their camels every third to seventh day in dry weather, and breeding should only be carried out in stone-free plains country and places where disease and disease-bearing flies are absent.[7] Again, while all authorities agree that camels need regular supplies of salt, during the wet season when the Rendille do not take their herds to water at all it is possible that they suffer from a salt deficiency.

On the whole, the areas which best suit the Samburu cattle are those which least suit the Rendille camels. There are three main reasons for this. The first is that the camels do not thrive so well in the rather cooler climates to the south-west; the second is that they readily eat a particular poisonous plant (*Capparis Tomentosa Lam*) found in the higher altitudes; and the third is that they have a low resistance to sleeping sickness which tends to be prevalent in areas of thick bush associated with so many parts of Samburu grazing areas. Thus, it is in the north where the Rendille proper live, especially around Lamagaati, that camels thrive best. Further south where the Ariaal Rendille live interspersed with the Samburu, the land is generally acknowledged to be less good for camels.

When a camel dies naturally or is killed ceremonially, it will be eaten. However, the camels are kept for their milk rather than their meat. Female camels only give milk for a year after calving and they do not bear a calf for at least another year. At a guess, those actually giving milk might produce about 8 pints of milk a day for human consumption, and assuming that 60 per cent to 70 per cent of the herds are females, this would imply that the milk produced by an average herd of about twenty Rendille camels would be similar in quantity to that produced by an average herd of eighty Samburu cattle in the height of the wet season However, in the dry season, when cattle tend to dry up, camels continue to give moderate supplies of milk, and in this way they are superior beasts. The Rendille assert that two camels in milk are sufficient to feed a man, his wife, and several small children.

Herding camels is a rather more arduous task than herding cattle. It entails practically all young men as it cannot be done by boys under about 14 years or by women. Thus Rendille herdsmen tend on average to be several years older than their Samburu counter-

7. Leese, op. cit., pp. 84–5, 95, 101. This is the most detailed and competent work on the camel that I have found. The Rendille believe that camel flies carry anthrax.

parts. It is the herdsmen who milk the camels and this is undertaken three times a day: once in the morning and twice at night. The older males who actually own the camel herds do not normally take an active part in the herding, but a large portion of their time is often spent searching for stray beasts from the herd. Searching for just one animal, looking for tracks, and inquiring at distant settlements in the hope that the stray has joined another man's herd may take a week or even longer. The animal may be found up to fifty miles from the spot where it left the herd originally.

Male camels are used as pack-animals. They can travel 20 or 30 miles a day and carry a load of 150 to 200 lb. When used for fetching water (a woman's task) one camel will carry up to 16 gallons in four large containers. The Rendille do not ride their camels; possibly the breed is unsuitable and the terrain is altogether too rough to train them for this purpose.[8]

(c) *Small stock* (sheep and goats). Sheep and goats are managed and herded together, and are kept primarily for their meat. They are killed as little as possible during the wet season so that they can be kept as a reserve for the rigours of the dry season when milk is scarce. In general goat meat is regarded as more sustaining than mutton, but mutton has more fat and is more easily digested by invalids and small children. In addition, goats tend to kid at the height of the dry season (four months after the wet-season impregnation), and the milk that they give for the following month is particularly useful for the Samburu cattle economy as supplies of cattle milk are then at their lowest ebb.

Small stock, because they are small, are not difficult to manage, but care of a different kind is necessary. If the flock does not keep together when grazing, then an odd stray is easy prey to a lurking hyena or jackal. Sheep in particular tend to go astray and one stray sheep may be followed by others: goats tend to remain with the herd. On the other hand, when a sheep bears a lamb in the bush, it will bleat and draw the attention of the shepherd who will carry the lamb, whereas goats may do nothing and after having kidded about four times, they tend to desert their new-born kids in the bush. In the wet season, the hooves of both types of animal become soft and pick up thorns and foot infections which need individual treatment by an experienced adult. Tending to small stock requires concentration: spotting which animals are lame with foot sores (especially in the wet season) and which goats are likely to kid (especially in the dry season); and finally keeping the flock together at all times (especially the sheep).

8. See Leese, op. cit., pp. 123–4.

Many of the sheep and goats are in the eastern areas of the low country where the Samburu have flocks of up to 100 head: here the dry season is at its harshest and the alternative form of food most in demand. In this area they are predominantly white in colour, and the earlier nickname for the Samburu, *Loiborkineji* or *the people of the white goats*, may derive from a time when they were mostly living in this area between about 1850 and 1900.

At first sight, the Rendille with camels giving good supplies of milk in the dry season have less need of small stock. But there are, especially among the Ariaal Rendille in the south, a considerable number of poorer men who may prefer to build up their own flocks of small stock rather than herd the camels of others. The area inhabited by the Rendille proper further north is generally too harsh for small stock, especially around Lamagaati and Balesa Kulal where camels thrive so well.

With careful herding, a flock can increase at possibly four times the rate of cattle to a point when it becomes an unmanageable size. However, the lesser food value of small stock is not thought to justify the energies of active young men who might otherwise be engaged in herding large stock. Most of the herding is carried out by rather younger boys.

Available evidence suggests that the advantages of large stock over small stock are exaggerated by the two tribes. Social values and relationships tend to be concentrated on the former. Prestige through wealth is measured primarily with reference to the herds of camels or of cattle, and as will be seen in Chapters 2 and 3, it is the characteristics of these animals and their management which plays a major part in the social systems of the two societies. There is every reason to assume that the economic value of small stock is underrated in more purely social activities.

(d) *Donkeys and horses*. The Samburu keep donkeys as pack animals only. As compared with camels, they can only carry meagre loads at an ambling pace for a relatively short distance. Every second or third day, the women take them to fetch water at the nearest water point, and at times of migration, every five weeks or so, it is the women who pack their huts and all personal belongings on to these donkeys. Altogether, the Rendille are better served with their baggage camels: they can fetch enough water to satisfy all domestic requirements for one or several weeks, and at times of migration these camels are generally less trouble to manage and can travel at a faster pace.

The Rendille have recently acquired a few horses for riding, but the animal is still comparatively rare. With veterinary medicines to improve its immunity to endemic diseases, it could conceivably transform the economic pattern of Rendille (and for that matter Samburu) life.

The Pattern of Grazing

The basic principles involved in grazing and herding stock are elaborated through the development of a geometrical model. This model applies in the first instance to a hypothetical herd of cattle belonging to a completely isolated settlement in a uniform environment at the onset of the dry season.

Let us suppose that a man's cattle are in such a condition that they are capable of travelling a distance of $2r$ in one day in the course of daily grazing. Around his settlement a circle of radius r may be drawn. The perimeter of this circle is the theoretical limit of grazing since, if he drives his herds outside this area, then the total distance travelled on his return home must exceed $2r$. The land lying inside the perimeter is the *effective grazing area*, that is, the area which his herds can effectively graze. The grass close to his settlement is inevitably grazed more often than that further away (Chart 2, Figure a), and when a large settlement stays in one area for an extended period, good grazing becomes increasingly hard to find.

This model does not take into account the need to water cattle

Chart 2
A MODEL FOR THE PATTERN OF GRAZING

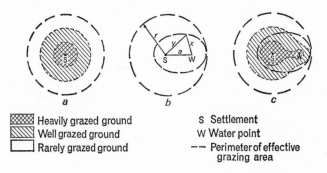

▨ Heavily grazed ground   s Settlement
▧ Well grazed ground   w Water point
▢ Rarely grazed ground   — — Perimeter of effective
                                       grazing area

regularly at the water point. If (as is frequently the case) there is only one convenient water point at, say, distance a from the settlement, then the effective grazing area is diminished since the cattle cannot on one day visit *both* the water point *and* distant land lying in the opposite direction. The new effective grazing area is no longer a circle of radius r, but an ellipse of which the settlement S and the water point W are two foci (Figure b, where the ellipse is defined by the equation: $x+y=2r-a=constant$).

Under these conditions, the path between the settlement and the water point, and the ground surrounding both the settlement and the water point are heavily grazed. The zones of grazing are now modified as shown in Figure c.

This leaves little ground that is rarely grazed inside the new effective grazing area (bounded by the perimeter of the ellipse); and as the dry season advances the cattle go to the water point only every other day in order to exploit more of the rarely grazed zone. On the days that they do not go to water, they may be driven in the opposite direction towards the rarely grazed ground and on these days the effective grazing area is again a circle rather than an ellipse. In this way, the cattle can have adequate water and adequate grazing on alternate days, and two stock owners can share one water hole by agreeing to water their cattle on different days.

As the dry season advances yet further, the cattle become physically weaker and give less milk: part of the fall in milk yield is due to the energy expended in trekking these long distances. In the driest parts of the district, they may even be watered only every third day. The distance they can travel in one day ($2r$) now decreases, the ratio $a:r$ increases and the ellipse and circle representing the effective grazing areas contract in size. Thus the effective grazing is constantly being reduced.

Ultimately, the only good grazing is too far from the settlement and it must move. When other settlements are using the water point (as invariably occurs in practice), then this move tends to be away from the water. In this way the distance a increases, and the effective grazing area is reduced yet further on the days that the cattle go to the water as the ellipse becomes more elongated.

With the arrival of the wet season, the situation is eased, grazing is ubiquitous and water is more easily obtainable. Heavy local showers of rain may leave pools of water for the cattle to use; the water point is now superfluous and for a few days the effective grazing area is once again a complete circle, which grows larger as the cattle regain their strength.

Such an ideal pattern is modified in practice not only because of the presence of other settlements in the vicinity, but also because of environmental variations in the countryside, and because water may be available to one settlement at a number of points. Settlements prefer to move to fresh areas and new water points some time before the grazing in one area is completely exhausted. Each man herds his own cattle as he sees best under the existing circumstances, but there is considerable difference of opinion as to what is best. On certain days, the distance $2r$ may be exceeded so that the cattle can reach a salt lick or graze for a rather shorter time on some especially fresh grass. In general, however, if this distance is exceeded, the cattle cannot graze sufficiently to justify the extra effort and they may not be able to travel as far as $2r$ for a number of subsequent days if their milk yield and physical condition are to be maintained.

The distance a during the wet season is typically between 2 and 3 miles, and it increases to 5 or 6 miles in the dry season. The distance r may be of the order of 8 miles in the dry season, but it is not easy to estimate this during the wet season as cattle need not be driven to the limits of their capacity at this time of year. It seems likely that with their improved physical condition in the wet season, they have strength to go much further than 16 miles in one day. In very rough and broken country, the distance travelled in one day is severely curtailed.

*   *   *

This basic model needs slight modification to apply it to the grazing of other stock. Camels require water far less frequently than cattle and they have the additional advantage of being able to travel much greater distances. The effective grazing area is not now limited by their capacity to travel a given distance in one day, as by the capacity of the camel herdsmen to travel this distance (on foot). A daily journey of 25 miles in the hottest and driest parts of the country is about as much as a man can endure, and this limits r to $12\frac{1}{2}$ miles. On the majority of days in which the camels do not go to water, the effective grazing area is a complete circle and they can exploit areas which are as much as 20 miles from water. Moreover, camels jog to their daily browse at a steady 3–4 miles an hour, which gives them more time when they reach a suitable spot and is also less tiring for the camel herdsmen—so long as they have the herd under control. Cattle on the other hand tend to spread out and in herding them, the herdsman must at times zigzag behind them to keep them together: not only does this mean that he travels further than they do in the course of the day, but it also limits the amount of time left for grazing in richer areas. Camels also have an advantage over cattle in that they can carry containers of water (when it is available) round their necks to refresh the herdsmen.

In the dry season sheep and goats can stay without water for four consecutive days, and in the wet season this increases to ten days, a fortnight, or even longer. They cannot travel long distances in search of browse (i.e. r is small), but they are at least better able to live off wasted land than cattle, and can therefore be herded closer to the settlement by younger children who are not yet able to herd large stock. Calves are treated in much the same way: they need less water and grass than cattle as they are smaller and are fed by their dams every morning and evening. It is also necessary to keep them apart from the adult herd except at feeding times or they would continually rob the settlement of its milk supply.

Baggage camels (among the Rendille) and donkeys (among the Samburu) do not go out to browse with the other large stock on days when they are needed for fetching water. Donkeys, when they do go out with the cattle, are kept to the rear of the herd so that the cattle can have the pick of any fresh grass or browse.

Settlement, Camp, and the Pattern of Nomadism

In order to appreciate the organization of the two societies into settlements on the one hand and more mobile camps on the other, it is first useful to distinguish three types of grazing area based on the general availability of the natural resources. The first, *type A*, is an area where there is a semi-permanent water point and a salt lick, usually at that point. The second, *type B*, is an area where there is a semi-permanent water point, but no salt. And the third, *type C*, is an area where there is neither semi-permanent water nor salt, but conditions allow grass or browse to grow. (Logically, the completely barren regions of the district form a fourth type of area, but they are only significant in their negative aspect of limiting the grazing and inhibiting communication.) Type A grazing areas are generally the most heavily grazed: this is primarily because sheep and goats need salt regularly and tend to be concentrated in these areas. Type C grazing areas, on the other hand, because of their limited water supplies, are the least heavily grazed. Chart 3 summarizes the distribution of water, salt, and grass (browse) in these areas in the dry and wet seasons.

(a) *The Rendille*. The Rendille herds and population are divided between settlement and camp for the greater part of the year, especially during the dry season. In the settlement live the women, small children, and most married men, and they keep only enough milch camels for their immediate needs. In the camps, the older boys and the young active men look after the remainder of the herds.

Chart 3
THE AVAILABILITY OF ESSENTIAL RESOURCES IN DIFFERENT GRAZING AREAS

	Water	*Grazing*	*Salt*
Type A grazing area			
Dry season	Present	Bad	Plentiful
Wet season	Plentiful	Tolerable	Plentiful
Type B grazing area			
Dry season	Present	Sparse	Little or none
Wet season	Plentiful	Reasonable	Little or none
Type C grazing area			
Dry season	None	Plentiful	None
Wet season	Unpredict-able	Abundant	None

These camps are situated in areas where living is rough but browse is adequate (i.e. type C grazing areas), whereas the settlements tend to be sited in areas that may be easier for the humans, but are less ideal for the camels (i.e. type A grazing areas where there is salt but browse is sparse during the dry season). The rigours of camp life with a general shortage of water are offset by the abundance of milk: it is not simply that browse is plentiful (it may not always be), but also that all milch camels surplus to the requirements of the settlement are at the camps, and only a portion of the human population are there to live off them. The ability of camels to cover up to 30 miles or more a day in a two-day trek to and from the water point opens up a large part of the district to camps during the dry season.

Settlements can also be relatively independent of a suitable supply of (brackish) water for the same reasons, but the settlement itself needs some more convenient source for domestic needs and thus there is less choice open to it. If it chooses to live in a type B grazing area where there is no salt, then it may be necessary for the small stock to be separately herded in a small camp in some more suitable area. This would be managed by a few older men and a number of girls and younger boys old enough to herd the flocks.

Twice a year following the spring and autumn rains, the camps may briefly rejoin their parent settlements. The norm, however, is for the dry season arrangement with the two quite separate. The camel herds, no doubt, benefit from this degree of flexibility, but in other respects, it is worth noting that the Rendille avoid other choices open to them. It is quite conceivable, for instance, that camp and settlement could be united for a larger portion of the year if the settlement itself were to divide into smaller more flexible units. As it is, settlements are large, containing quite often 80 or even 100 families (huts), and they remain large until the rigours of the dry season may force them to disperse into smaller units some months after the camps have left them.

A number of reasons are given for this. In the first place a large settlement is less vulnerable to attack: this is not as outdated an argument as it might at first appear: as recently as 1952, seventy-six Rendille were massacred in their settlement during a raid. Secondly, camels are more docile and easier to handle in larger numbers: the smaller the settlement, the fewer and more restive the camels. Both of these arguments are, however, inconclusive, since there are more active men for defence and more camels for company when the camp rejoins the parent settlement: there appears to be an equally sound argument in favour of keeping the camp with the settlement.

One is led to conclude that a third reason—that the Rendille are accustomed to and prefer life in larger settlements associated with their clans—is the strongest argument and that the more economic reasons are to a very large extent rationalizations of this essentially social choice. The Rendille approve of large gatherings where the pressure of public opinion is strong and where there is a pronounced sense of respect for the consensus of opinion, and they prefer that their younger men and poorer dependants should be away from the settlement living with the camp. The diagram opposite shows the plan of a Rendille settlement as compared with a quite typical Samburu settlement drawn to the same scale.[9]

(b) *The Samburu*. The Samburu have altogether smaller settlements containing typically four independent families living in six or seven

9. Rendille clan settlements tend to be associated with certain migratory tracts without implying ownership of the land. These tracts are as follows. Orare, Urwen and Nahagan clans tend to inhabit the more northerly areas of the district parallel to the shore of Lake Rudolf. The other clans of the Rendille proper tend to be concentrated in the dry season on Lamagaati. In the wet season, Gavana and Galdeelan stay in this vicinity, Nebei, Tubsha, and Dibshai move in a north-westerly direction towards Mount Kulal and Lake Rudolf; and Uiyam, Matarpa, Gobonai, and Rongumo tend to migrate westwards into the Hedad. The Ariaal Rendille tend to migrate in the wet season as follows. Ilturia move westwards from Laisamis towards Arbah Jahan more or less followed in the same direction by Lorogushu. Lokumai and Masula in the vicinity of Erer move out towards Harisirua, and Longeli situated further north follow a parallel path into the Hedad. Thus, the general movement of the southern Rendille is eastwards in the wet season, while that of the northern Rendille tends to be westwards.

It must be emphasized that these general movements are essentially variable; they are typical preferences of these clans rather than strictly defined territories. The Rendille have often been reported many miles outside their district ranging from Derati (40 miles to the north), to the foothills of Leroghi (during a particularly severe dry season). Their tracts adjust themselves as opportunities for browsing change from one season to the next.

Map 2
PLAN COMPARING A RENDILLE AND A SAMBURU SETTLEMENT

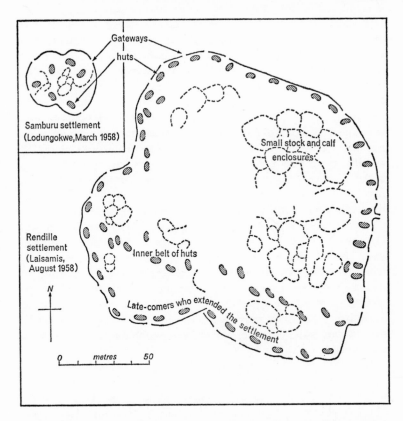

Samburu settlement
(Lodungokwe, March 1958)

Small stock and calf
enclosures

Gateways

huts

Rendille
settlement
(Laisamis,
August 1958)

Inner belt of huts

Late-comers who extended the settlement

N

0   metres   50

The Samburu settlement (top left), drawn to the same scale, is altogether smaller. In both societies, each stock owner (generally a married elder) has his own gateway through which his stock enter and leave, and each married woman has her own hut. However, because of the high degree of polygamy among the Samburu there are rather more huts (women) than gateways (married men); whereas because of the essentially monogamous nature of Rendille society there are (ideally) as many gateways as huts. It can be seen that the inner belt of huts on the southern side of the Rendille settlement is an exception to this ideal. At one time, in fact, these huts had their own gateways, but when the settlement was joined by a set of late-comers, the latter built their own huts and gateways to the south, and the earlier gateways of the inner belt were dismantled.

huts. A settlement with as many as fifteen huts is a large one by their standards. The fact that families are essentially independent is significant. It introduces a flexibility into the organization of the settlement, and as the seasons change, so individual elders may choose to migrate with other families or separately. In general, they will prefer to remain in association with their clan, but because of the smallness of the settlements and the extent to which each clan is widely dispersed, there is a wide choice. The social advantages of large settlements are to them less important than the economic disadvantages: cattle do not go as far afield to graze as camels, consequently the land around a large settlement will be soon exhausted and it will be necessary to migrate more often. Even individual herds may become too large and unwieldy to manage, and under these circumstances, an elder will often divide his herds and family into two economically independent units. These may even live in different settlements and in different vicinities.

This is rather different from the division between settlement and camp which are essentially two parts of the same basic economic unit. This division among the Samburu is regarded as a temporary measure to tide over the worse parts of the dry season even although in practice it occasionally divides up the family and herd for six months or more at a time. Because distances are not always great, an active elder can often pay an overnight or even a day visit to his surplus cattle at the camp, and thereby maintain its link with the settlement.

In many respects, this pattern differs from the Rendille. In one sense their larger settlements are less viable; on the other hand, because of the greater interdependence between families, a surplus of active youths in one family can usefully be absorbed by a surplus of camels in another, and the precise balance between the size of the herd as a food-giving unit and the size of the family as a labour force is less critical. The division between camp and settlement is more institutionalized among the Rendille than among the Samburu where it tends at times to be almost an *ad hoc* arrangement; and as the distances between camp and settlement are greater, the link is more tenuous. And finally, the greater economic dependence among the Rendille corresponds with stronger social pressures, especially within the clan. Values, if anything, are slanted more towards conformity and dependence on the settlement.

Altogether the situation in which the Samburu find themselves in managing their cattle is easier than the Rendille with their camels. Cattle are easier to handle and herding can be done by a far wider range of people: younger boys, older men, and even occasionally by the more active women. The demand for active young men among the Rendille is such that they are tied to camel herding to a far greater extent than are young men among the Samburu. This varies of course from one family to another according to the size of the herd and of the active labour force. But it is characteristic of Samburu society that a considerable proportion of young men (the traditional warriors, or *moran* as they are more usually called) are able to free themselves from herding duties and to enjoy a more socially and less economically oriented existence.

While this is especially true during the wet season, even in the dry season the problems of many families are not so much to find adequate labour for herding as to find sufficient food. When the food problem among young men (*moran*) becomes more acute than the herding problem, a group of them may join together to eat an ox somewhere far from the settlement—often in the forested mountains. Having literally begged, borrowed, or stolen a particularly fat ox, they drive it to this remote part, gorge themselves for several days, and make soups from the meat and from certain roots and herbs in the area. This is known as *loikar*, and the customary repayment for the ox (if it has been borrowed) is four male calves. It tends to be practised when milk is really scarce and when some of the young men are weak with the pangs of hunger.

The constant need of cattle for water tends to confine Samburu settlements and camps to type A and type B areas. The heavy overgrazing in type A areas where salt is to be found does not encourage migration in this direction during the dry season. The movement of cattle tends to be towards type A areas (salt but heavily grazed) in the wet season and towards type B grazing areas in the dry season.

There are three ways in which this may be achieved. In the first, the settlement moves to a type B area in the dry season and back to a type A area in the wet season: this does not involve splitting the herd between camp and settlement, but it is not always practical with older sick people. In the second, the settlement stays for a prolonged period in a type B area and sends its surplus cattle to a type A area when they need salt, especially in the wet season: typically they may go to a salt lick for one day every week or so, for four days every month, or for one month in six according to the nearness of the lick and the requirements of the cattle. And in the third, the settlement stays for a prolonged period in a type A area and sends its surplus herd to a type B area in the dry season when grazing becomes difficult: settlements with large numbers of small stock often prefer this arrangement as it suits them to remain as long as possible in an area where there is salt.

The movement towards type A areas in the wet season and type

B areas in the dry season concerns cattle rather than people and camps rather than settlements. When it rains in the wet season and there is water almost everywhere, this opens up the type C areas and the surplus cattle are often sent off with camps to take advantage of it.[10]

Conclusion

The principal differences between the wet and dry seasons may be summarized in Chart 4.

This chapter has considered the adaptation of two stock-owning tribes to semi-desert conditions which preclude any form of agriculture and encourage nomadism. This nomadism is not limited by any developed concept of land ownership but by largely practical considerations. The Samburu, with their cattle and small stock, are obliged to live in smaller settlements, but they can at least assert considerable independence of one another and to some extent the need to remain flexible in their economic organization forces them to do so. The Rendille, on the other hand, with their camels and small stock, are able to live in larger settlements and are obliged to collaborate to a greater extent. From the point of view of food production, there is little doubt that the camel economy is more satisfactory, and the more collective economy makes it easier for poorer men to lend their services to richer men in return for food. But the camel in Rendille hands is a scarce beast and this leads to serious property problems described in the next chapter. A large

10. These three forms of nomadism are most plainly discernible in the eastern areas of the low country beyond the Matthews Range: here, type A and type B grazing areas, each centred on a water point are separated from each other by stretches of waterless type C grazing areas.

When the Samburu are not encumbered with imposed grazing restrictions, there tends to be a seasonal migration between the Leroghi Plateau (a type B area with plenty of water but little salt) and the low country areas adjoining it (type A areas, with plenty of salt licks in the south). Because of the congenial conditions for living on the Leroghi Plateau, the second form of nomadism was often preferred: the older men with their families tended to stay on the plateau, while the younger men would take away the surplus cattle to the salt licks when there was rain in these parts. For those who put the well-being of the herd above their own comfort, however, there was much to be said for living in the vicinity of salt and tolerating the greater heat of the low country: the cattle appeared to thrive better.

The pattern of nomadism in the low country relies heavily on the rivers watered from the Leroghi Plateau: the fact that there is a summer wet season on Leroghi when the low country to the east has its four most serious months of drought is of great importance. As the dry season advances, the settlements converge on the water points along these rivers, or closer and closer to the foothills of other mountainous districts (such as the Ndotos and the Matthews Range). These parts are over-grazed and the thick bush adds risks from wild animals and tsetse fly. As soon as the drought breaks, the settlements may disperse once again to other less heavily grazed areas.

Chart 4
SUMMARY OF THE TWO ECONOMIES

	Wet season	*Dry season*
1. *Seasons*		
Leroghi Plateau and West Mt. Ngiro	Apr–May (spring rains) June–Aug (summer rains)	Sept–March (comparatively mild)
Low Country	March–May (spring rains) Oct–Dec (autumn rains)	Jan–Feb (mild) June–Sept (harsh)
2. *Stock performance*		
Camels	Not watered at all, copious supplies of milk	Watered every 10–14 days, moderate supplies of milk
Cattle	Watered every day, adequate supplies of milk	Watered every 2nd or 3rd day, limited supplies of milk
Sheep and goats	Watered every 10–14 days, left to breed	Watered every 4–5 days, useful for meat and (goats) milk
3. *Social implications of economy*		
(a) Collaboration: Rendille Samburu	Comparatively high Comparatively low	Very high Comparatively high
(b) Settlements: Rendille	Very large and widely scattered	Smaller and concentrated on brackish water points
Samburu	Small to moderate and generally scattered	Smaller and concentrated on certain water points
(c) Camps: Rendille	Start to join settlements towards end of season	Leave for remoter areas and remain for long periods
Samburu	May occasionally leave settlements to exploit type C areas	*Ad hoc* arrangements, often not too far from parent settlement

portion of the society are unable to build up adequate herds of camels readily, and turn their energies in particular to rearing small stock as an alternative. Thus what for the Samburu are essentially regarded as reserves for food in the dry season serve another purpose among the Rendille, especially the Ariaal Rendille in the south.

Appendix: The Monetary Economy

The two tribes depend predominantly on their indigenous economic systems. Nevertheless, they have adapted themselves marginally to the introduction of a monetary economy into the area. This is particularly true of the Samburu where cattle sales are held as regularly as quarantine restrictions permit, and where for a time grazing schemes were introduced. The following balance sheet shows how a typical Samburu stock owner living in a grazing scheme in 1959 might gain and spend his annual income.

Table 3

ANNUAL BALANCE SHEET FOR A SAMBURU STOCK
OWNER IN A GRAZING SCHEME

	Credit	Debit
	Shs.	Shs.
Sell 3 steers	300	
Sell unwanted hides and skins	90	
Tax and African District Council fees		
(for self and adult male dependants)		75
Scheme grazing fees		150
Fines for cattle trespass and other offences		20
Veterinary medicines		5
Luxuries (blankets, cloths, tobacco, tea, sugar, maize-		
meal for child-bearing wives)		140
TOTAL	390	390

2

AN OUTLINE OF RENDILLE SOCIETY

In the previous chapter, it was shown how among the Rendille and the Samburu, different types of stock are associated with rather different patterns of economic activity and that this is a basic difference between the two tribes. This is not to suggest that the economic activities of the two societies are altogether determined by their environments and by their choices of stock; but it does at least imply that this is true to some extent and has certain social implications. In so far as one can speak of economic determinism, it is that there are sound practical reasons why Samburu techniques of cattle management are not all extended to Rendille camel management and vice versa. But it does not follow that either tribe could not adopt some other form of management which would have beneficial effects on their economies and secondary implications for their social activities and structure.

In the next two chapters, differences between the two tribes are explored in greater detail and where possible these are related to the basic economic differences already discussed. The present chapter is primarily concerned with an outline of the Rendille proper, and the next chapter with a similar description of the Samburu.

1. Social Structure

The Segmentary Descent System

The segmentary descent system of the Rendille proper has four levels distinguishable primarily by associated modes of behaviour. A man normally inherits his position in this system through his father, although the belief in common ancestry for the more inclusive levels is only diffuse. The segments recorded in the upper three levels are shown in Chart 5, and associated customs are as follows:

(a) *The lineage group*. Rendille agnatic lineages extend typically to the informant's grandfather and no further: the older men can therefore generally trace their ancestry back one generation further than the younger men. While there is always a precise knowledge of the order of seniority between different lineage groups, there

Chart 5
THE SEGMENTARY DESCENT SYSTEM ON THE RENDILLE

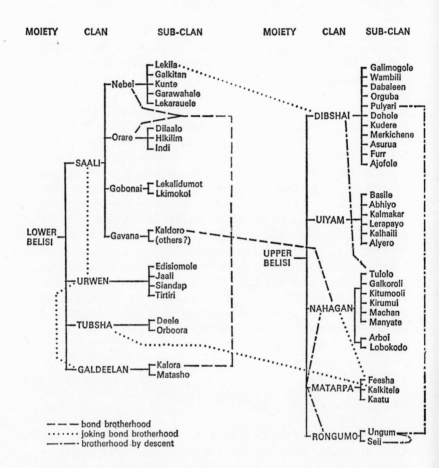

| MOIETY | CLAN | SUB-CLAN | MOIETY | CLAN | SUB-CLAN |

Lower Belisi moiety:

- SAALI clan
  - Nebei sub-clan: Lekila, Galkitan, Kunte, Garawahale, Lekarauele
  - Orare sub-clan: Dilaalo, Hlkilim, Indi
  - Gobonai sub-clan: Lekalidumot, Lkimokol
  - Gavana sub-clan: Kaldoro, (others?)
- URWEN clan: Edisiomole, Jaali, Siandap, Tirtiri
- TUBSHA clan: Deele, Orboora
- GALDEELAN clan: Kalora, Matasho

Upper Belisi moiety:

- DIBSHAI clan: Galimogole, Wambili, Dabaleen, Orguba, Pulyari, Dohole, Kudere, Merkichene, Asurua, Furr, Ajofole
- UIYAM clan: Basile, Abhiyo, Kalmakar, Lerapayo, Kalhaili, Alyero
- NAHAGAN clan: Tulolo, Galkoroli, Kitumooli, Kirumui, Machan, Manyate, Arboi, Lobokodo
- MATARPA clan: Feesha, Kalkitele, Kaatu
- RONGUMO clan: Ungum, Seii

- - - bond brotherhood
...... joking bond brotherhood
- · - · brotherhood by descent

tends to be a vague uncertainty of the manner in which collateral lineages of a sub-clan are descended from one putative ancestor. There are two customs generally associated with the lineage group. The first occurs at the marriage of one of their daughters where all the more important members of the group should be first consulted, and one of them is allotted a heifer-camel from the bridewealth. The second is associated with the death of any man of the group when all the men should shave off their hair. However, in neither respect is this a strictly defined group. As it grows larger, common ancestors tend to become forgotten, members dispersed, and it tends implicitly to fragment into smaller units.

(b) *The sub-clan.* A Rendille sub-clan typically consists of thirty adult males. Norms of behaviour between members of a sub-clan are partly determined by generational differences between them and partly by their relative seniority within the segmentary descent system: these are described more fully in a later section.

(c) *The clan.* Rendille exogamous clans are corporate groups, to a very large extent living in the same settlements, tending to rely on one another economically rather than on other Rendille, mobilizing local pressures, and arriving at important decisions by debate and mutual consensus. Typically there are 100 or more adult males in a clan: enough for one large or two typical settlements. Where members of other clans live with them, these are frequently in the process of being assimilated.

As will become evident in Part III of this chapter, the seniority between clans determines the order in which different families participate in certain ceremonies. Apart from a certain prestige attached to this, however, there is no further significance in this order. Certain features associated with individual clans are noted in Part IV.

(d) *The moiety.* The Rendille moieties, *Upper Belisi* (*Belisi Bahai*) and *Lower Belisi* (*Belisi Beri*) consist respectively of five and four clans. In one context Upper Belisi can claim ritual superiority because it is first to perform in the age-set ceremonies and Disbhai clan choose the incumbents for certain ceremonial offices in each age-set. But in another context, Lower Belisi can claim superiority, because the most senior of these incumbents, the ritual leader, must always be chosen from Saali clan. Outside these ritual contexts, the moieties have no significance.

Intersegmentary Ties

Cross-cutting this segmentary structure and linking specific segments are two kinds of tie, referred to here as *brotherhood by
descent* and *bond brotherhood*. The more important of these ties
only are shown in Charts 5 and 6.

Brotherhood by descent assumes that the linked segments of
different clans are descended ultimately from one ancestor, and
have since been separated by inter-clan and inter-tribal migrations.
Apart from the fact that as 'brothers' these segments do not intermarry, this tie tends very often to have little social significance.
At most it is regarded as a distant tie of kinship which is rather less
binding than that of clanship. It should perhaps be stressed that
sub-clans of a clan do not always claim a common ancestry, and
that for the Rendille it is the community and corporateness of the
clan that is socially binding rather than any belief in the common
descent of all its adherents.

Bond brotherhood is a rather special form of brotherhood by
descent, where behaviour is prescribed by custom and it is believed
that any breach of this would lead to severe misfortune. A man has
powers of moral coercion over his bond brothers who should not
refuse him any request.

In addition there are certain other customs which vary from one
bond brotherhood to another. In some bond brotherhoods, a constrained formality should be observed on all occasions. In others,
there is a permissive joking verging at times on ribaldry. But even
with the joking bond brotherhoods there is an element of constraint:
if either party loses his temper with the other instead of taking the
matter as a joke, then misfortune will follow. This joking is ex-
tremely apt between the sexes. A man might creep up to a joking
bond sister (or vice versa) daub her head and body with a paste
made from ash, sand, and red ochre, and then run away. In retaliation the other might give chase, grab his cloth (or her skirt),
and then run away with it. In a more extreme instance, this horse-
play may lead to the rape of a young girl, although bodily violence
on her should be avoided once her breasts have developed, and
after her marriage joking should be confined to swearing and hurl-
ing abuse. The various customs associated with different ties of
brotherhood are summarized in the following chart.

There is in this chart a basic consistency: as one descends the list,
so there is a cumulative number of customs associated with specific
brotherhoods. It is also worth noting that the last three customs
(3, 4, and 5) are all associated with marriage. The permitted inter-

Chart 6
CUSTOMS ASSOCIATED WITH OTHER FORMS OF BROTHERHOOD

Segments involved	Type of brotherhood	Associated Customs*				
		1	2	3	4	5
(a) (See Chart 5)	Brd by descent	no	no	no	no	no
(b) Kalora/Saali (Nebei and Orare)	Formal bond brd	yes	no	no	no	no
(c) Nahagan/Kaldoro Uiyam/Longeli (Samburu—see Chapter 3)	Formal bond brd	yes	yes	no	no	no
(d) Tubsha/Galdeelan	Joking bond brd					
(e) Seii/Ungum	Formal bond brd	yes	yes	yes	no	no
(f) Urwen/Saali Feesha/Nahagan	Joking bond brd	yes	yes	yes	yes	no
(g) Dibshai/Lekila Longeli/Urwen Tirtiri/Galdeelan	Joking bond brd	yes	yes	yes	yes	yes

*Key to associated customs:
1. Reciprocal powers of moral coercion backed by mystical beliefs
2. Avoidance of blood and red meat in each other's presence
3. Intermarriage permitted
4. Marriage by capture and lover/mistress relationships permitted
5. Avoidance of each other's wives.

marriage (3) may be regarded as a preferred form (as between Seii and Ungam or between Urwen and Saali) or as a rather inferior form (as between Dibshai and Lekila). Under these conditions, a request in marriage would have coercive implications and should not be refused. Most Rendille feel that as a general principle, marriage with a bond sister should be avoided since it is never certain that the mutual respect entailed by the relationship will be sufficient to avoid domestic strains and ultimately mystical misfortune. In addition it could imply that a man jokes with his relative-in-law, whom he should normally respect above all others. Marriage by capture (4) whereby a joking bond 'sister' is abducted, circumcised, and married by force is invariably regarded as inferior and to be avoided if possible because of the high feeling it may arouse. The final custom of avoiding the wives of a joking bond brother (5) contrasts with all other bond brotherhoods where the wives tend to be treated with a privileged familiarity verging often on joking: in a sense there is an inversion in the relationships of the formal bond brotherhoods (b, c, and e) on the one hand and the final joking bond brotherhood (g).

Segmental and Generational Seniority

Within the segmentary descent system of any sub-clan, the Rendille may be classified according to their generation or their line of descent. This gives rise to two forms of seniority, referred to here as *generational seniority* and *segmental seniority*, which govern their behaviour towards one another. Within the sub-clan, each man should show a marked respect for all members of his father's generation and for all those of his own generation who are segmentally senior, whether they are his own elder brothers or the more senior members of the sub-clan. He may treat the wives of these men with a privileged familiarity. Conversely, he expects a marked respect from all members of his son's generation and from those of his own generation who are segmentally junior to him. The wives of all these men are addressed as his sons' wives and he should avoid them altogether. Between alternate generations, there is a reciprocal joking relationship which is not affected by differences in segmental seniority. This joking is extended to both the man and his wife and is especially marked among coevals.

There is no acknowledgement of segmental seniority *between* the sub-clans of a clan except for ceremonial purposes. However, there is a modified recognition of generational seniority. A man will show at least a nominal respect for clansmen of his father's generation, and he will at least avoid the wives of his sons' generation sexually. Within the same generation and between alternate generations, clansmen may treat each other's wives with a privileged familiarity.

Thus relationships between sub-clansmen contrasts with that between sub-clans. Within the sub-clan there is no truly reciprocal relationship apart from the joking relationship between alternate generations. Certainly, I have the impression that the Rendille often look beyond the sub-clan for their closest friends to the wider clan where relationships are less constricting and they are not constrained either to show respect, or to demand it, or to joke.

The linking together of alternate generations of the clan as a whole produces what may be called *alternations*:[1] each man automatically belongs to the opposite alternation to his father and his sons. In the age-set system which is described below, these alternations have a ceremonial significance.

1. Following Gulliver, 1951, p. 127.

The Age-set System

An *age-set* consists of all those men (*age mates*) who have been initiated during a certain period of time and they tend, therefore, to be approximately of the same age. Among the Rendille proper, all members of one age-set should ideally be circumcised at one time and there is a period of perhaps eleven years before they can marry and fourteen years before the succeeding age-set is initiated. The Samburu age-set system is of some importance to the Rendille, not simply because it resembles it in certain ways, but also because the Rendille look to the Samburu age-set cycle for a cue to initiate a cycle of their own. The following chart shows the last ten Rendille age-sets and their Samburu equivalents.

Chart 7
SUCCESSIVE RENDILLE AND SAMBURU AGE-SETS

Reference	Rendille age-sets	Samburu equivalent age-sets	Estimated initiation years Rendille	Samburu
(1)	Irpaandif	Kipayang	c. 1825	c. 1823
(2)	Kipeko	Kipeko	c. 1839	c. 1837
(3)	Lipaale	Kiteku	c. 1853	c. 1851
(4)	Dibkuto	Tarigirik	c. 1867	c. 1865
(5)	Dismaala	Marikon	c. 1881	c. 1879
(6)	Irpaankuto	Terito	c. 1895	1893
(7)	Difkuto	Merisho	c. 1916	1912
(8)	Irpaales	Kiliako	c. 1923	1921
(9)	Lipaale	Mekuri	1937	1936
(10)	Irpaandif	Kimaniki	1951	1948

Three features are apparent from this chart. The first is that by constructing it in this manner, with three successive age-sets forming a cycle, certain names tend to repeat themselves at corresponding points of the cycle among the Rendille: age-sets (1) and (10), and (3) and (9) have identical names, and there is a difference of only one consonant (and no tonality) between (4) and (7). The three series of linked age-sets that emerge are referred to here as *age-set lines*; thus age-sets (1), (4), (7), and (10) form an age-set line. The second feature is that the name of the Kipeko age-set (2) is identical for both societies. It is said that this age-set had another name among the Rendille at one time, but after some misfortune (possibly the death of its ritual leader), its name was changed to that of the Samburu. Be this as it may, it does seem to confirm that the age-set systems of the two tribes have been in step since at least the time that the Kipeko were initiated, and that this is not a recent innovation. And the third feature is that while there is a certain irregularity in the time span between successive initiations among the Samburu, those estimated for the Rendille are multiples of seven years. The Rendille seven-year cycle and evidence confirming its observance in practice are discussed towards the end of this chapter.

A Rendille should strictly avoid the daughters of members of his age-set, and on no account could he marry one of them. Ideally, he should be circumcised into the third age-set after his father (i.e. into the same age-set line). Thus, if his father was of age-set (3), then he should be of age-set (6). If, however, he was very young when age-set (6) was initiated then he must wait for initiation until the next age-set (i.e. 7) is formed and must wait for a further twelve years or so before he can marry.

This basically straight-forward system is complicated by a custom which in effect serves to encourage a difference of exactly three age-sets between generations. It achieves this by permitting certain boys who have been circumcised late to marry early. The custom is known as 'climbing' an age-set (*alakuche*). To do this, it is necessary for the latecomer to have performed as an uncircumcised boy in a particular age-set ceremony (*galgulumi*) of the preceding age-set into which he intends to climb. But he may only do this if it would have been appropriate for him to be circumcised into this preceding age-set had he been old enough. Thus, if an uncircumcised boy whose father is of age-set (3) performs in the *galgulmi* of age-set (6), then once he has been initiated into age-set (7), he can marry more or less immediately. In a sense, he is now a member of both age-sets having been circumcised into one and having performed *galgulumi* and married with the other. He cannot marry daughters of either age-set, but so far as his own sons are concerned, he is a member of age-set (6) and they can be circumcised into age-set (9). If he has not performed in the *galgulumi* of age-set (6) then he cannot climb into age-set (6), but this does not prevent his sons, when they have been circumcised into age-set (10), from climbing into age-set (9) providing again they have performed *galgulumi* with that age-set. In other words, any man can climb an age-set so long as he can justify this in terms of his rightful age-set line in relation to some agnatic ancestor.

In a sample of sixty-eight elders of a sub-clan, eight had climbed an age-set. The fathers of three of these eight had previously climbed age-sets in their own youths, and the father of two others had been in a position to climb, but had failed to do so; in these two cases, therefore, the sons had climbed to within two age-sets of their own fathers. In this way, adjacent generations of males tend to be separated by exactly three age-sets, and this custom limits the age span of a generation in any sub-clan. Thus, among these same sixty-eight elders in the sample, only *one* man stood as a member of the grandparent's generation to any of his contemporaries and enjoyed a joking relationship with them.

The linking of every third age-set has some relevance also for the marriage of women. One of the three age-set lines is known as *teeria*: this is the series Kipeko (2)—Dismaala (5)—Irpaales (8), etc. All the daughters of a member of a *teeria* age-set and of elders that have climbed up to it are circumcised privately one year after the initiation of the subsequent *teeria* age-set (i.e. ideally that of their own brothers), but they cannot be married until members of this age-set marry some ten years later. These girls are known as *sapade*. Thus, at the time of my field work in 1962 it seemed likely that the next *teeria* age-set, the 'sons of Irpaales' (corresponding to the Samburu Kishili) would be initiated in 1965, and that the *sapade* who were daughters of Irpaales elders would be initiated in 1966 but they would not be allowed to marry until about 1976. The fathers of these girls started to marry in about 1935, and hence by the times that they are allowed to marry some of them will be 35 years old or more with the larger part of their child-bearing years behind them. The Rendille say that if they were to marry such girls prematurely then their stock would suffer misfortune, and that a number of *sapade* who feel that they are unlikely to obtain suitable husbands because of their age run away to neighbouring tribes to become concubines or sometimes wives. *Sapade* wear a special hairstyle and short beaded skirt similar to Turkana women.

Inevitably, the custom of delaying the marriage of *sapade* cuts down the potential growth rate of the Rendille as a tribe: women who might otherwise marry and bear children are prevented for a time from doing so. The Rendille claim that at one time this custom was more prevalent and that two of the three age-set lines were *teeria*, with the result that only one-third of the women were not actually *sapade*. However, this led to a dwindling in numbers for the whole tribe, and one of the two *teeria* abandoned the custom.

Between alternate age-sets there is a well-defined relationship whereby the senior of the two is responsible for the moral education of the junior and the inculcation of a sense of respect. It is a relationship, however, which is more significant among the Samburu and will be considered further in the next chapter. It is sufficient here to point out that Rendille youths are confined for long periods to camel camps and that the need to inculcate a sense of respect is not regarded as a major problem in their society.

Finally in this brief outline of Rendille structure it is useful to summarize the relationship between elders and the wives of others. This tends often to contrast an avoidance in one instance with a privileged familiarity verging on discreet sexual licence in another. Thus within his own generation and sub-clan, an elder would tend to avoid the wives of those segmentally junior to him, but could be on familiar terms with the wives of those senior to him. He would avoid women *married* into his wife's clan, but could be familiar with her 'sisters' *born* into it and married elsewhere. He would avoid the wives of certain bond brothers, but could be familiar with those of others (see Chart 6). He would avoid women married into his son's generation (with whom his father might be familiar) while he would be on terms of exceptional familiarity and licence with the wives of his mother's 'brothers' (whom his father would avoid). Under all circumstances he would strictly avoid the daughters of all his own age mates, but he would be moderately familiar with their wives. In these ways, the structure of Rendille society may be seen to polarize certain relationships, especially between the sexes and between generations.

II. The Principles and Practice of Camel Ownership

The previous chapter showed that in Rendille hands, the camel is a somewhat delicate beast. Herds are hard to manage and they grow relatively slowly, apparently more slowly than the human population. Inevitably, this leads to personal economic problems of building up and of maintaining herds: it is unlikely that a Rendille will be able to build up a much larger herd than he inherits, and frequently a moderately rich man may be reduced by misfortune to poverty.

Rights in Inheritance

Under these circumstances, it is understandable that one of the dominant principles of Rendille camel ownership is that each herd should remain intact as far as possible and be owned by only one man: to divide the herd would be to create a smaller and less viable unit. This principle is invoked when it is held that the first son of a man's first wife should be his sole inheritor, and the rights of the younger sons are strictly limited to nominal gifts from the herd at their circumcisions, their marriages, and to one female beast at the death of either parent.

When a Rendille marries for a second time, it is frequently because his first wife is barren, and hence the ultimate inheritance of his herd by the eldest son of the second wife is assured. It does happen, however, that very rich men take on second wives for other reasons, which entails the first wives having to surrender certain of their rights (or more strictly the rights of their eldest sons) to at least a few camels from the herd. This is generally only achieved by the elders of the settlement gathering to coerce her to give up these rights while she invokes the general principle that the herd should not be divided. To a large extent, younger sons of the first wife and all the sons of the second wife have to be content with few camels and flocks of small stock. When a younger brother dies before getting married, his herd is inherited by the eldest brother and so, once again, there is a return of stock into the principal family herd.

The Shared Beast (mal)

At first sight, the rules of inheritance would appear to produce a society of propertied first sons and impoverished younger sons. Any such neat and unambiguous pattern, however, is rather confused by a custom of sharing certain beasts and by the extent to which this is done. Any stock owner may approach another for a heifer-camel to share. Initially he would offer a number of small gifts and favours before making the request. It is unlikely that he would be refused by even an only moderately rich man: to have shared out camels from one's own herd is a mark of prestige for the Rendille, and it signifies among other things that in this society where everyone is to some extent dependent on others, one is the giver rather than the receiver and to be regarded as a worthy man (*mejil*).

The man who begs the shared beast in effect pledges his honour to observe certain rules. These are as follows: (*a*) whenever this camel bears a female calf he will put the brand mark and ear-clipping of the original owner's clan on it; (*b*) when it bears a male calf he may put his own clan's brand mark and ear-clipping and treat it as his own property entirely; and (*c*) the female calves in their turn become shared beasts and their offspring are treated in the same way. In time and with luck, a small herd of camels is built up within the borrower's total herd in which each beast is marked with the insignia of the original owner: these are the female descendants of the originally shared beast by an unbroken uterine line, and may be referred to as *the shared herd*. In the last resort nothing is lost or gained by transferring rights in the male descendants: it is the fertility of the female line that determines the growth of the herd.

The original owner can always claim that this shared herd bears the insignia of his clan and is therefore his own, and as it stands, this custom is a very neat way in which a man can create a set of obligations and lend out his camels without losing any lasting rights over them. However, the camels are shared, and the original owner (or his inheritor) cannot assert an incontrovertible right to claim them back from the borrower (or his inheritor). He in turn is bound by certain conventions: (d) he should never ask for the return of the originally shared beast; (e) he should never try to bring the relationship to an end by begging back the last surviving camel of the shared herd; and (f) he should to some extent avoid the homestead of the borrower, never asking directly about the welfare of the shared herd: if he wishes to know how the herd is increasing and how well it is being treated, he must limit himself to making discreet inquiries among friends and kinswomen in the borrower's settlement or to a casual appraisal from a distance. It is only when he wants to ask for the return of a heifer-camel from the shared herd that he may broach the matter directly with the borrower, and he may still be refused on the grounds that the herd has not yet grown adequately (e.g. to more than five camels) or has not yet recovered its size owing to previous return gifts to the original owner. In other words, the original owner seems at first sight to have prior rights in the shared herd, but in practice the borrower is in the stronger position. Once a particular heifer-camel has been returned to the original owner, however, it becomes his own unshared property.

The Rendille maintain that it would be unpropitious for a man to try to cheat others by putting his own ear-clipping and brand mark on the female calf of a shared camel. His neighbours and clansmen would certainly find out what he has done and criticize him for it; and the previous owner would be likely to find out sooner or later.

When the shared herd increases at an exceptionally fast rate under the borrower's management, it is regarded as auspicious and the honour and prestige entailed in his relationship with the original owner would be enhanced. Under these circumstances, it is possible that the borrower would be offered a new heifer-camel to start a second shared herd and so develop the relationship further.

This system of sharing can be elaborated further. If the herd has increased propitiously, then a third person (C) may approach the borrower (B) for a shared beast, and he may be given a heifer from the herd that is already shared with the original owner (A). In this case, C becomes a secondary borrower from A's herd, and he must observe the same rules of behaviour towards B as B observes towards A. Females of this shared herd, as it is built up by C, still bear the insignia of A's clan, but A cannot approach C for the return of any beast: only B can do that. If, after B has re-shared out some heifers from his shared herd this herd dies out, then his relationship with A does not come to an end as he can still build it up once more from returns he obtains from C and from other secondary borrowers. The relationship should only come to an end when the last surviving camel of the shared herd dies without leaving any living shared female descendant.

The secondary borrower (C) may in his turn lend a beast from the shared herd to a tertiary borrower (D) and so on; and the ramifications of the originally shared herd become even more complex. The Rendille themselves point to the incongruity of the situations which sometimes arise. They say that among the richest of their camel-owners are men who do not have a single beast in their own herds which bear their own brand marks and ear-clippings: they are all shared beasts to which other Rendille have some claim. On the other hand, there are paupers who in theory can point to vast herds of camels of which they are the original owners, yet they are unable to assert their rights in these animals. If they are really poor and the primary borrowers are really rich, then they should be able to obtain at least some return from their shared out herds, but it is quite possible that the wealth of these herds lies in the hands of secondary or tertiary borrowers and that the primary borrowers may have enough camels of their own not to want to build up their shared herds by asking for returns from the secondary borrowers.

Thus, in any one herd there may be a mixture of brands and ear-clippings. If the owner puts his own clan's brand and ear-clipping on a camel, it indicates that it is his by right; if he puts some other clan's brand and ear-clipping, it indicates that it is a shared beast; and if he puts his own clan's brand but some other ear-clipping, then it indicates that a part of his herd previously suffered misfortune and he has tried to change his luck by altering the ear-clipping.

When a Rendille approaches a kinsman for the gift of a heifer-camel, as when he wishes to marry, he may be offered an animal which is already shared. This would be inferior to an outright gift and the offer might not be accepted. Sharing is incompatible with the ties of kinship and if he accepted it he would share the animal not with his kinsman but with the previous borrower (or owner) and he would be under the same obligations to him. For similar reasons, the eight camels of the Rendille bridewealth should never include any beasts which are still shared as they would be inferior to the outright gifts expected at a marriage.

Giving away a shared beast is a form of investment, but the value of the shared herd which it founds depends on the subsequent behaviour of the previous owner, whether he is a borrower or the original owner. If he (or his descendants) continually beg for the return of heifer-camels, then it will become known that they are greedy and in future people will avoid approaching them for beasts to share: it would be considered that they do not give the camels they lend a chance to increase in number, and in effect the interest demanded on their loans is too high for there to be a satisfactory net profit. The Rendille consider it an honour to be approached for an animal to share as it is an indication that they are considered worthy; moreover, it provides an opportunity to create an obligation. It is likely that they will make the loan if they can possibly afford to do so and if they are satisfied that the borrower is competent enough to build up some kind of a herd from one beast, given sufficient luck. Prestige in camel ownership derives not simply from the actual size of a man's *de facto* herd, but also from the extent to which this herd is the source of shared herds elsewhere, rather than the beneficiary.

Dependence and Independence of Poorer Men

The situation in which there are a considerable number of unusually rich men and also of unusually poor men leads to a system of clientship in which the poorer men are attracted to the service of the richer to help them herd their camels. Poorer men would normally be expected to manage the herds of their closest agnatic kinsmen who would often be their elder brothers. Herding the camels of a senior kinsman is regarded as an obligation of kinship and no payment would be expected except at the circumcision and marriage of the herdsman. But even at these times some Rendille are not prepared to give more than one nominal beast. For this reason, continued poverty quite often induces younger brothers and junior kinsmen to migrate to other Rendille clans, such as those of their mothers' brothers. In herding the camels of another clan they have more right to expect some form of payment for their services. Apart from small stock which may be given them frequently, the standard payment they can expect every other year of their service is a heifer-camel from a shared herd. It is unlikely that they will be offered any camels as outright gifts, although this could happen where an unusually competent herdsman allies himself to an unusually generous and rich patron.

If a herdsman is not paid for his services to some other clan, there would be no public pressure or coercion applied to his patron.

His only recourse is to leave and to ally himself as a client to a more worthy man. This is a major factor which inhibits the initial migration of a younger son: among his own agnatic kinsmen at least, he can rely on a certain popular pressure on his behalf at times of circumcision and marriage. If he is a resourceful and energetic herdsman then it is more than likely that his own kinsmen would feel obliged to acknowledge their diffuse obligation and less likely that he would feel tempted to migrate elsewhere.

When a younger son or a man made poor for some other reason wishes to build up his own herd and to assert his independence, it is to small stock that he should turn. The country to the south suits them well and they can increase rapidly. There is little prestige attached to relying almost solely on small stock: the emphasis in social values is fully concentrated on the ownership of camels. But at least there is certain dignity in maintaining an independence from any form of patronage. A resourceful man can seek out a rare opportunity to exchange a large number of small stock for a female camel and from there, he can attempt to build up a herd of camels of his own.

III. The Life Cycle and Associated Customs

Birth and Infancy

The Rendille celebrate the birth of a boy by cutting the throat of a billy-goat known as *morr*. The *morr* is then eaten by women, and the elders put its fat on their heads, chew tobacco, and bless the infant four times. The afterbirth is buried in the camel-calf enclosure. The mother drinks blood taken from a male camel for four days and abstains from milk for four months. These and other associated practices are similiar for the birth of a girl except that the frequent use of the number four is substituted by the number three; in addition the *morr* is a ewe and the afterbirth is buried in the small-stock enclosure. When the mother stops drinking blood, two further animals are killed: the first (*helem*) is a ram which is eaten by the mother, and the second (*nefitubaali*) is a castrated goat eaten by everyone else. The mother sleeps on the father's side of the hut (to the right of the entrance) for nine or ten nights according to whether the father is of Upper or Lower Belisi moiety respectively. She then leaves the hut to open her husband's gate and to re-enter into the daily routine of the homestead. The following night she moves over to sleep in her own half of the hut and the father returns to sleep in his.

Weaning may take place between six and eighteen months after the birth. A boy should be weaned in the heavy spring rains that follow the first autumn rains after his birth, and a girl should be weaned in the lighter autumn rains that follow the first spring rains after her birth. Thus a boy born in October, just before the onset of the autumn rains may be weaned six months later in the following spring, whereas a boy born in December, just after the autumn rains, must wait a further year before he is weaned.

A hair-style in the form of an elegant crest (*doko*) is proudly worn by all Rendille wives whose first-born is a boy. This draws attention to the importance of the first son in so many contexts in Rendille life. The *doko* is finally shaved off on the death of the husband (or the son).

Certain infants are thought to be unpropitious and would be aborted or killed at birth. These include children of forbidden genitors (of a segmentally senior lineage, of the father's age-set or alternation, of blacksmiths, or of boys), first-born twins, boys born on a moonless Wednesday or after their eldest brother has been circumcised. There is some evidence that the last two customs are not always observed but the Rendille would still insist on their going to some foster family, such as among their maternal kin. It is maintained that a boy born on a moonless Wednesday is liable to be jealous of the superior privileges of his older brothers and would resort to any means, even sorcery, to kill them in order to gain their inheritance. Eldest sons born on a moonless Wednesday are held to have a similar attitude towards the father, but as it is only a matter of time before they inherit his herds they are thought less likely to manoeuvre his early death. When a Wednesday's boy is allowed to live, the *morr* killed at birth is a ewe instead of a billy-goat (cf. a girl).

It is unpropitious for an uncircumcised girl to conceive and brings also dishonour to the family. After the abortion has been carried out, the family head may drive her from his home. Such girls generally settle down as concubines with Samburu or drift towards the townships. Even if the family head does not drive her out it is unlikely that any Rendille would want to marry her as his first wife. Her lover would not perform in any of the Rendille age-set ceremonies. It is said that in the past, both the girl and her lover would be killed by setting them blindfold on a camel and driving it over a sheer precipice.

Childhood

The customs associated with inheritance and birth repeatedly draw attention to the importance of the eldest son of each Rendille family. The rules of the society are not oriented towards younger sons or second marriages, but rather towards maintaining the herd in one unit within the family. The homestead, however, is not an isolated unit: it is dependent to a very large extent on other homesteads in the settlement, and hence on the clan. In this context, each family conforms with a stereotyped pattern, and the children grow up, not in the confines of an isolated family unit with its own characteristic stamp, but rather in a wider society which encourages conformity and in the last resort is prepared to interfere with a man's domestic affairs in order to protect its wider interests. This takes the education of the children to a large extent out of the hands of their parents and into those of the total society. In particular, both boys and girls are expected to show respect where it is due: for the elder brothers and for the elders (especially of the father's age-set).

Underlying the respect due to elder brothers, there is also a suppressed hostility. The Rendille themselves point out that the customs and beliefs associated with certain forms of infanticide are related to the secret jealousy of all younger brothers who can never wholly accept the total inequality of their inheritance. Stories concerning the jealousy between brothers are not one-sided: there are also cases of elder brothers who have resented their younger brothers outshining them in warfare and have driven them from their homes. It is said that when a Rendille dies, his brother cries with one eye and counts the stock he hopes to inherit with the other.

At first young children are made to help in the herding of small stock. From the age of 13 or 14, boys join in the herding of camels and until the time of their marriage more than ten years later, they spend nine or more months in every year away from their parents' settlement in the camel camps, where they are expected to devote themselves to the welfare of the herds. The older sons, of course, have a more personal interest in these herds; but the younger sons cannot afford to be disinterested since they are aware from an early age that they depend on the goodwill of their closer kinsmen for building up even a small herd. Thus the conformity of boys and youths with the expectations of the wider society is linked with the realities of the camel economy into which they are drawn.

One custom associated with boyhood which is perhaps unique among the Rendille must be noted. When they are about eight or nine, the father or some other male cuts into the skin round their navel. This is done in a series of snicks over a period of months until the circle is complete. As the wound heals, the skin contracts over the navel until it is covered by a hole only one-quarter of an inch in diameter and is barely visible. The Rendille are proud of this disfigurement provided that it has healed successfully. But if the healing is only partial or leaves some other disfigurement, then it is known as a *bajo* and is a matter of shame and derision. A man with a *bajo* will always wear his cloth high so as to cover his navel and he will want to fight any person who makes any reference to it. The worst insult possible would be to say to him: 'You commit incest with your sister—you have a *bajo*.' The Rendille do not elaborate on this point: they deny that a man who commits incest necessarily develops a *bajo* or vice versa, and they deny any mystical significance in the custom. They do not relate it in any way to cutting the navel-string at birth or to any later social separation between a boy and his mother. It is a custom which seems to suggest any of these possibilities. At most one can say on present evidence that committing incest and having a *bajo* are both matters of shame, and that it is the shame that is emphasised by informants.

A Rendille girl who is approached by a youth who wishes to be her lover may ask to see his navel to reassure herself that the operation has been performed and that it is not a *bajo*. It is said that when a man with a *bajo* lies dying, his hand goes to his navel to cover up the ignominious disfigurement rather as if his last living act must be to conceal it.[2]

Rendille girls are expected to acquire a more pronounced and an earlier sense of respect than boys. In the case of members of their fathers' age-set and generation, this should amount almost to an avoidance. To appreciate the full significance of this ideal one should bear in mind the implicit competition for worthy husbands: monogamy and the delayed age of marriage among men implies that potentially there are more men wanting to marry off their daughters well than suitors looking for first wives. It is in this context that the Rendille lay a stress on the deep sense of respect expected among their womenfolk. A wife with a sense of respect is not only an asset to a worthy lineage, but she will also pass this sense on to her daughters who will make good wives and be sought after.

Once again, this is an ideal which points to conformity in the society and to pressure from beyond the family in cases where less than a full sense of respect is shown. In the context of everyday life in the homestead, it is the growing children who inevitably show less understanding of respect and the girls in particular from whom it is expected: the boys are mostly at camel camps and do not marry or enter into the full life of the homestead for many years. It is

2. cf. the general belief among Rendille and Samburu that when a woman dies her hand may grope to conceal her vulva: a part of her anatomy which out of decency and respect no man should see.

largely, therefore, by the standards of behaviour among its children and especially its girls that a lineage and in the last resort a whole clan is judged by outsiders. At each stage in their development they are encouraged or if necessary coerced to show the respect due.

The extent to which youths and girls can meet one another is inevitably hampered by the fact that the youths spend so much of their time at camel camps in the remoter areas of the country, However, a circumcised youth and a girl may become lovers provided they are discreet in their more intimate behaviour. There is a custom that *sapade* (p. 35) should only be the mistresses of youths in *teeria* age-sets. Thus many of these girls will be as old as twenty years before these youths are actually circumcised. In such circumstances, and only then, the Rendille permit these youths to have *sapade* as mistresses *before* their circumcision, and they can conceivably remain as lovers for fifteen years or more. A *sapade* is given a special carved staff by her *teeria* lover which she should look after very carefully.

The Initiation of an Age-set

It is in the initiation of an age-set in particular that the Rendille follow the lead set by the Samburu. After the Samburu have performed the ceremony of killing the boys' ox, the Rendille boys perform a similar ceremony known as *herhladaha*. A bull calf is begged from the Samburu Nyaparai phratry and killed in the bush. The right-hand side of the carcass is shared by boys of the Upper Belisi moiety and the other half by Lower Belisi boys. Inedible parts are entirely burned.

The initiation ceremonies (*khandi*) follow two or three years after the Samburu. Ideally all Rendille clans should circumcise all their initiates in the same month and there should be no subsequent circumcisions. Each clan has just one circumcision settlement inside which a large initiate's hut (*mingidakhan*) has been built. Within each family, the senior son should be circumcised first and no boy should be circumcised before an elder brother, but beyond this restriction, there is no prescribed order of circumcision with regard to, for instance, segmental seniority.

The operation is always performed outside the settlement by a man of Tubsha (Deele) clan. Only one initiate is circumcised at a time, and he sits on a stone while the others queue up to await their turn. By custom, the eldest son of each wife is given a heifer-camel by his mother's eldest brother, while younger sons are each given one heifer-camel by their fathers or guardians. However, each initiate has a right to expect further gifts from his richer kinsmen and the exact amount is undefined: this is one of the two occasions of his life when he can expect gifts of camels from his senior kinsmen. When the operation is completed, he at first refuses to rise, for on rising he forfeits any further right to expect more camels until his marriage which is the second occasion. This is said to be the cause of considerable delay and excitement during the operation as the next initiate cannot be circumcised until the previous one rises. Other elders may shout at him to rise or shout at his kinsmen to give him another beast. Unrelated elders will support him against his kinsmen if they consider that he has shown respect and has herded their camels well, and that these kinsmen can afford to give him more camels. But these same elders will support the kinsmen and urge the boy to get up once they feel that he has been given as much stock as he can justifiably expect. He eventually rises and the next initiate takes his place to be circumcised and to extort camels from his kinsmen. Gifts may include certain shared beasts and the objection of a stubborn initiate may not be that he would like more camels but that he is dissatisfied with having to share some of them.

After the operation, the initiate goes to the circumcision hut to recover. Here the elders make all the boys of one alternation sit down on one side of the hut and those of the other alternation on the other side. They then explain to them what the principle of alternations signifies, and from this time they are expected to behave towards each other in accordance with it. This is the only occasion on which this principle is ceremoniously expressed by either tribe.

From this point, the initiates are under two specific ritual avoidances: they may not hold any piece of iron (e.g. a spear or a knife) and they may not touch meat with their hands: any food of this kind therefore has to be prepared for them. The period of initiation is brought to an end by a subsequent ceremony (*lahaoloroge*) which the Rendille acknowledge as deriving from the Samburu equivalent (the *ilmugit of the arrows* ceremony) although it is essentially a simpler ceremony and does not have quite the same significance or importance.

Subsequent Age-set Ceremonies

Galgulumi is a ceremony performed in one vast settlement on the eastern shore of Lake Rudolf. If possible it is held in the year following circumcision, and is the occasion on which each age-set is given its name.

The mothers of the youths of the age-set and anyone else who

wishes to participate build their huts in a clockwise order of segmental seniority in a gigantic ring (theoretically a circle). Clans of
the Upper Belisi moiety build in the northern half of the settlement
and of the Lower Belsi moiety in the southern half, so that to an
observer facing the lake, the senior moiety (Upper Belisi) is to the
right and the other to the left. Informants describe the settlement as
more than two miles in diameter. The thorn fence surrounding it
often encloses not only stock and huts, but also gazelle and other
small game trapped there by accident when it was built. Many
people, especially small children, completely lose their bearings
inside it and cannot find their own huts for hours on end. Camels
tend to wander about freely and are temporarily lost to their
owners: it may take several days to sort out the various herds at
the conclusion of the ceremony.

Every Rendille male should perform in this ceremony once only.
Those of the newly formed age-set who previously performed as
boys in order to climb an age-set do not participate, while those
boys who intend to climb up to it after their own circumcisions in
twelve years time do participate.

On the evening after the settlement has been built, all the participants take off two feathers worn as a head-dress and throw them
away in a thorn bush. During the night, the two moieties form
separate parties and, wearing white loin-cloths and all their orna-
mental beads, they bathe in Lake Rudolf and wash these trappings.
They then return to the settlement and drive a few camels into their
respective halves. Each youth then collects a stone which is used to
make a large circle (*naapo*) in the centre of the settlement. The
elders then bring along bowls (*basiki*) of mixed milk and water and
place them in a circle inside the stone circle. The youths must drink
the milk and water without touching the bowls, and to do this they
improvise drinking straws.

Each stage of the ceremony is accompanied by singing, dancing,
and shouting. Once the above formalities have been completed, men
of all age grades join in and the dancing may last until the following
day and continue intermittently for several days. In these dances,
each youth has two staves, one of a light and one of a dark coloured
wood. Women may watch the celebrations and girls may take these
staves and oil them.

It is during the *galgulumi* ceremony in particular that youths
wander around and dance with their loin-cloths held low so that
they can display their perfectly healed navels. Any man with a
disfigured navel (*bajo*) is said to perform the initial part of the
ceremony at night and then to hide himself in the bush, hoping
that his absence will not be noticed.

In the course of the ceremony each clan chooses a number of youths to fill an age-set role known as *hosoop*: the exact number chosen varies from clan to clan and there is generally a tradition of electing one *hosoop* from each of certain sub-clans. *Hosoop* acquire a potent blessing and curse. At the same time, they are subject to certain ritual prohibitions: they must not sleep on anyone else's headstool; they must not wear sandals made of camel hide; they must not eat meat of any animal that has died naturally or oil their heads with its fat; they must always drink milk before drinking a mixture of milk and blood; they must only drink milk from certain types of container, and they should only do this when the camel herds are inside the settlement. Once they have married, they lose their ritual powers and these prohibitions are relaxed. Any relaxation before this time would, it is thought, lead to general misfortune to the clan and especially its camel herds.

When *galgulumi* is delayed for several years, as does appear to occur sometimes, a number of minor circumcisions may be undertaken. However, there can be no further circumcisions once *galgulumi* has been performed.

Orelogoraha is another ceremony performed by the youths. It should be performed every seventh year starting with the fifth year after circumcision. Thus, age-sets which settle down to elderhood within twelve years of their initiation may only perform it once, whereas others may perform it twice, and an age-set which remains as youths for a long time (as did Irpaankuto) may actually perform it three times. It is performed by as many youths of the tribe as care to attend in a camel camp in which each gateway is built in a clockwise order of segmental seniority, although being a camp, there are no huts. The year in which it is performed is held to be an unpropitious one (p. 67), and the overt purpose of the ceremony is to prevent any widespread misfortune that could come in such a year. Dibshai clan organize this ceremony, and provide a bull-camel for slaughter. Uiyam clan hold the head of the animal, and Dibshai its tail and spatter it with milk. Each participant puts his hand into the beast's mouth, on his own forehead, and touches its hump with his two staves. Then members of Dibshai clan throw it to the ground and members of Saali (Nebei) cut its jugular vein to kill it. Each man dips his staves into the blood and puts some of the blood on to his own forehead. A fire is built up for which every man provides a stick. The carcass is completely destroyed in this fire, and no part of it is eaten.

In the centre of the settlement all the *hosoop* have one enclosure of stones and on their respective sides each moity has its own enclosure. The camels are milked and each clan brings some milk to the enclosure of the *hosoop*, who then bless the stock. Everyone retires to his enclosure to drink milk and to sleep. This milking and blessing are repeated on three subsequent nights.

In a series of less important *orelogoraha* ceremonies, Nahagan clan provide the bull-camel once every seven years starting with the year that follows circumcision (i.e. ideally the same as *galgulumi*); and in any year of severe drought or epidemic, Tubsha clan may be called on to provide a bull-camel for an extra performance of the same ceremony.

There is no notion that the bull-camel is in any way sacrificed. It is made unpropitious by the ceremony and is destroyed to rid the tribe of possible misfortune especially from drought and enemy raiders. No settlement would be built to the west of an *orelogoraha* camp, as it is thought it might be destroyed by raiders. A youth who has made a girl pregnant should stay well away from the camp.

Shortly before the youths of an age-set perform their final cere-money, *naapo*, four members of the age-set are chosen for certain auspicious and inauspicious roles. These are, in the order in which they are chosen, the *man-of-the-fire* (*nebelakapire*), the *man-of-the-feather* (*oeyabokhote*), the *ritual leader* (*kudur*), and the *man-of-the-horn* (*arapelekete*).

The man-of-the-fire is the most despised of all these roles. The youths of Dibshai clan secretly decide who the victim is to be, and a member of Rongumo clan must be the first to seize him. Without warning, he is seized, his right sandal is taken off and placed on his right lap; a fire is then kindled on top of this sandal and his captors burn his loin-cloth, sandals, and ear-rings in the fire. His bead neck-lace is cut and instead he is given a necklace made of a strand of elephant tail with two dark-coloured beads previously worn by an old woman. Then, singing, they run away and leave him. It is gener-ally held that he will suffer severe misfortune for the remainder of his life, and he may go mad or die early.[3] The only explanation given for this custom is that it protects the remainder of the age-set from a similar fate. The victim should ideally have a personal name which has a propitious association, such as 'the milking of camels' (*Gal-masho*) or 'wet season' (*Rrobile*).

It is said that when the time approaches to choose a man-of-the-fire, many eligible youths become nervous: some leave their homes and others even go on a protracted visit to Samburu country to avoid possible seizure. Youths of Dibshai clan counter these

3. The victims chosen by Difkuto and Irpaales age-sets died without getting married. The victim more recently chosen by Lipaale married but died only ten years afterwards: he spent some of this time in prison for having made a violent attack on those who had installed him. I have no information on the type of man who is liable to be chosen in the first place.

precautions by pretending that they have no immediate intentions of performing the ceremony or making conspicuous sorties in some direction to give other Rendille a false impression of where the victim they have chosen lives.

Dibshai clan also choose the man-of-the-feather, who is always a member of Lekila (Saali Nebei) sub-clan. He is seized and a feather is stuck upright into the ground in front of him; he must then pick it up. There is only mild and temporary ridicule attached to this role; it is quite compatible with the joking bond brother-hood between Dibshai and Lekila (the choosers and the victims) and is sometimes quoted as an example of this relationship.

The ritual leader is chosen on the eve of the *naapo* ceremony, and he is always a member of Saali Gobonai or of Saali Gavana Kaldoro sub-clan. This is an auspicious role and when the incumbent is informed of the decision, he is expected to accept it calmly. Once he has been chosen, he should not shave his hair until a new ritual leader for the subsequent age-set has been chosen: if he does this or is killed before then, it is held that his whole age-set would suffer misfortune. The ritual leader has a powerful curse over his age-set, and is the first to marry. In his relationship with the wife of any age mate, it is as though he were a member of the senior generation. When he visits her hut, he may leave his shoes outside the entrance; once she has taken them in, he will put milk on them and sit on them. She should then give him some oil to rub in his hair and he blesses her and her hut. He marries by a form of coercion and is given a herd of camels by each of the Rendille clans.[4]

The man-of-the-horn, is a relatively unimportant role and on the whole slightly inauspicious although he is not expected to be dogged by misfortune. He is installed in an almost casual manner: Dibshai Wambili sub-clan have an ivory horn whose high-pitched sound is said to carry for miles. Immediately after the first night of the *naapo* ceremony, some member of Wambili blows on this horn and calls out the name of the victim. If, for some reason, the victim is not present at the ceremony, he may only learn of his new appoint-ment quite by chance: it is no one's duty to inform him and most people would prefer to avoid doing so anyway. However, whether he realizes it or not, he is the man-of-the-horn from the moment that the horn of Wambili is blown and his name called out.

The *naapo* ceremony is performed immediately after the appoint-ment of the ritual leader. As with *Orelogoraha* this is performed in a camp with the gateways arranged in clockwise order of segmental

4. This herd is made up of the following number of camels from the various clans: Dibshai 10, Saali (Gobonai and Gavana) 10, Rongumo 8, Galdeelan 8, Tubsha 8, Saali Nebei 4, Saali Orare 4, Urwen 4, Nahagan 4, Matarpa 4, Uiyam 4.

seniority. No more camels than are required for subsistence are brought to the camp, but each youth must provide a billy-goat for slaughter. What can best be described as a game is then played. Each youth builds a 'hut' in his own part of the camp: the 'hut' consists only of a circle of stones, and sitting in his 'hut', he tells his 'wife' (a stone) to give him some tobacco and some milk. And then, leaving her to look after their 'child' (a smaller stone), he kills his goat (a real one). Again, in the order of killing goats, strict segmental seniority should be observed. At this point, the most senior representatives of each lineage go to the ritual leader's stone enclosure (naapo)[5] to which every youth has contributed a stone, and they discuss what stock they shall give him, leaving their junior kinsmen to cut up their goats. They then return to their 'huts', and each youth pairs off with one of his immediate neighbours to exchange a back leg of his goat. After this anyone can go to another's 'hut', even in his absence, to eat some of his meat.

The next morning, the man-of-the-horn is chosen, and after sleeping in the camp for three more nights, they all disperse.

The ritual leader marries shortly after this ceremony and he is followed in the subsequent year by most of his age-mates. Those who do not marry then, tend to be younger sons and members of poorer families.

The naapo ceremony may be performed three or four years before the next age-set is due to be initiated, and thus there is actually a period in which there are only uncircumcised boys and eligible elders, but no youths as such.

Warfare among the Rendille

The customs associated with warfare deserve some mention here. It is not so much that they are currently in use as that there is still some uncertainty in the minds of Rendille as to what the future may bring, and periodic disturbances in the area remind them of their dormant traditions. There is every reason to assume that in a tribe that still retains its indigenous organization, any return to inter-tribal warfare in northern Kenya would involve (at least in the present) a return to these earlier customs.

The Rendille adopted a defensive policy in their relations with other tribes and generally preferred to attack only in retaliation. However, the ferocity of their fighting in attack or defence has earned them a considerable reputation among surrounding tribes.

5. The term naapo as an enclosure in the middle of the camp or settlement is common among the Rendille and it is not certain that in the present context it bears any significant relation with the name of the ceremony, naapo. On the other hand, it is worth noting that the Samburu ilmugit is both the name of the ceremony and of the moran enclosure in the bush (p. 89).

They had an economic explanation for this. They valued their camels highly, and would be prepared to go to almost any length to defend them against attack: a man who lost his camels in a raid could not hope to replace them easily. They prized their reputation as fierce fighters: it was felt to act as a deterrent to other raiders. When they raided in retaliation, it was both to regain their camels and to reassert their reputation.

The tradition of defensive fighting was as follows. When enemy raiders were reported in the vicinity, all the camels would be confined to the settlement or camp, and it would be surrounded by a defensive ring of young men (older boys, youths, and younger elders). Each would stand guard outside the gateway of his own family, with a bull-camel tethered between himself and the gateway. Ideally, he was expected to stand his ground or to die in the attempt. A man who ran behind the camel would be branded a coward for the remainder of his life: if he died, his body would be speared by other Rendille and his teeth smashed in with their kicks; if he lived, he would openly be scorned, made to carry out menial tasks, and others would use his loin-cloth to wipe their mouths after eating. A man who killed an enemy, on the other hand, would bring honour to his family. The body of the enemy would be castrated and its genitals would be hung round the neck of the tethered bull-camel until they eventually rotted away.

When, on occasion, the Rendille did go on raids, it was often in company with Samburu. Once again, there was honour to be gained through killing an enemy. A man who had killed would slit open the right side of the victim's stomach, castrate him, and lay him open on his right side with arms and legs bent together. He would then observe a number of prohibitions and sing a song known as *meraat*. On returning home, he and other Rendille that had actually killed would build a special wigwam-shaped hut (*mingi meraat*) and sleep in it. The genitals of the victims would be hung from the framework of this hut in full view of their settlement. None of the killers would shave their hair until a member of a certain lineage (Lereya, Dibshai) had come and thrown the genitals to the ground.

Preparation for Marriage

It is not easy to reconcile the accounts of the Rendille who on the one hand stress the large-scale marriage of youths that takes place in a very short time after the *naapo* ceremony, and on the other hand also emphasize the difficulties experienced by the younger brothers in acquiring camels to marry with. However, three points are worth noting. The first is that all sons are entitled to marry at this time and have an acknowledged claim on their closer kinsmen if they do not have enough camels to provide the bride-wealth. Secondly, marriage negotiations may be conducted before the *naapo* ceremony, and so the younger sons may have succeeded in overcoming these difficulties at an earlier stage. And thirdly, marriage among the Rendille entails a shortage of young men looking for their first wives rather than a shortage of girls suitable for marriage, and so even a poor younger son, provided he is acceptable in other ways, may be acceptable as a suitor. It seems likely that any Rendille who has difficulty in marrying immediately after *naapo* may have difficulty for a number of years.

It is fortuitous that in the 1930s, when the Irpaales age-set would have performed their *naapo* ceremony (probably 1934), annual censuses were made in the district which could indicate the extent to which younger sons were able to marry promptly. (At the same time, one should accept these figures with considerable reservations, as did the district commissioners at Marsabit who sponsored them: the censuses were made easy by the fact that the Rendille lived in a few large settlements, but the results had to rely on dubious information collected in an unsystematic manner.)

Table 4

RENDILLE CENSUS FIGURES 1932–9

Year	Official census figures		Percentage annual increase	
	Elders	Women	Elders	Women
1932	1,070	1,185	—	—
1933	1,172	1,226	9·6	3·5
1934	1,143	1,377	2·3	12·4
1935	1,501	1,699	31·5	23·5
1936	1,536	1,962	2·3	15·5
1937	1,584	1,994	3·1	1·5
1938	no census		} 1·5 (av.)	} 0·2 (av.)
1939	1,633	2,011		

Accepting these figures at their face value, they show a sudden and dramatic increase in the numbers of 'elders' (married men?) in 1935, which could suggest that a large number of youths had no difficulty in finding wives. Subsequent increases appear to be marginal.[6]

6. The District Report also notes widespread marriage in this year. There is no simple explanation to the more sustained increase in 'women' other than deficiencies in the census techniques. However, it is just possible that the daughters of Dismaala age-set, who as *sapade* could not marry until this point, suddenly flooded the marriage market, and many of them, unwanted because of their age, waited and then had to be content to become the junior wives of older men.

Apart from circumcision, marriage is the only time when a Rendille can expect his closer kinsmen to supplement his camel herds. If his wife dies, however, then he has no claim to further camels to help him marry again. Again, the extent to which they help him will depend on the extent to which he has helped them in the past to manage their camels and the extent to which public pressure can arbitrate between a kinsman who feels there is no further obligation and a suitor who feels that there is. A wealthy kinsman might offer him a heifer-camel as an outright gift, a more distant kinsman or a poorer man might offer him a female that is already shared, thus placing him under an obligation to some other person. A really poor kinsman could quite reasonably refuse his request. In the last resort, the burden of ensuring he has enough camels for his bridewealth lies with his father or his father's heir (i.e. his senior brother). Ideally, he would be given the requisite number of camels as outright gifts. However, it is also possible that he will be directed to obtain the return of some camels that are shared out elsewhere. It is said that exceptionally irresponsible younger brothers who find their claims thwarted may take the law into their own hands and approach these primary borrowers of their own initiative. In the right circumstances, this could be a good way of raising public opinion within the clan: even if the elders criticized him for asserting himself against his elder brother, they might also criticize the elder brother for his meanness and encourage him to make concessions.

The Wedding Ceremony

The bridewealth (*gunu*) is invariably four female camels (known as *deyeheo*) and four ox-camels (known as *foolas*). The father of the bride is given two of each, her mother's senior brother one of each, and a member of the father's lineage group is given the fourth female camel. The fourth ox-camel is the *birnan* killed on the third evening of the ceremony (see below). It is a matter of negotiation as to whether the female camels should be heifers or not: a camel that has calved once or twice may be preferable in some respects to a heifer camel that could prove barren; on the other hand a camel that has calved four or five times might not produce many more and might be less acceptable.

The ceremony itself extends over eight nights. The more important details of the elaborate procedure are outlined below.

The bridegroom, at first wearing a white cloth on his head in the form of a turban, and an entourage of clansmen enter the bridal settlement and kill a ram, *guru*. This is eaten by the women who throughout the ceremony sing a song known by this name.

(1st night)

The bride is circumcised on the following morning in her mother's hut.   (2nd night)

A billy-goat, *galmorsi*, is killed inside the settlement and a blacksmith runs away with it to his own hut and eats it. At this point, negotiations are held between the groom's party and bride's senior kinsmen concerning the exact nature of the bridewealth. The number of camels is of course fixed, but their quality may be the subject of further discussion. It is only when the bride's clan elders and her mother's brother are satisfied with the offers or are prepared to defer negotiations and payment to a future occasion that they give permission for the marriage hut (*mingidakhan*) to be built on the spot where the *galmorsi* goat was killed. The hut is then pulled down and rebuilt. This is repeated three times, and when the hut is built for the fourth time, it is allowed to remain standing. Elders of both parties go to the circumcision hut (i.e. that of the bride's mother) and the bride is ceremonially handed over to the husband and reminded sternly of her duties. A young ox-camel of the bridewealth, the *birnan*, is killed in front of the marriage hut by a blacksmith who claims one of its flanks, while the remainder of the beast is divided among other people (except the groom's party). The bride is led to this hut from the circumcision hut, and accompanied by some other girls she sleeps there.   (3rd night)

Next morning, the groom and best man enter this hut. Their finger and toe nails are pared and mixed with those of the bride. A small girl with milk and a boy with the hump of the *birnan* ox-camel (both members of the bride's clan) enter the hut and address the groom as their affine. The groom's party are then given some meat previously cooked by the bride's mother (any meat) which they taste and then return to be given to small boys to eat. The bride and girls again sleep in this hut.   (4th night)

The groom's party are again given meat to taste and the bride and girls sleep in the same hut.   (5th night)

The groom's party are again given meat to taste and the bride and girls sleep in the same hut.   (6th night)

The groom's party are given meat to taste for a fourth time and they kill a male goat (*waharoko*). They cook and taste it, and then give it away to be eaten by members of the bride's settlement. An apron is made from its skin for the bride to wear. That night, the bride, groom, and best man sleep in the marriage hut. (7th night)

The bride, groom, and best man also sleep there on the following night.   (8th night)

On the final morning, the groom and best man kill a ram (*helen-kidafareedh*) and give the bride its fat to eat. Anyone can eat the meat.

There is a slight variation to this ceremony if the groom is of Saali clan. On the third night, when the bride is led to sleep in the marriage hut, she is led by the best man through a hole in the side of the hut while the groom leads another wife of a Saali man through a hole in the opposite side. This is preceded by a special song, *ileyaho*, which eight men of Saali sing eight times: two of these men are behind the marriage hut, two in front, two in the entrance, and two (the groom and best man) inside.

Each Rendille clan has its own song (*kinaan*), which can be sung by the lovers of girls when they are married. This amounts to a mild curse against the bridegroom, and it would not be sung if he was of a lineage or an age-set which the lover should respect or (ideally) of his own moiety. When the lover comes to sing this song with other members of his clan, the bridegroom may offer them a heifer-camel to keep quiet, or he may perform a small ceremony with them subsequently by giving the lover and his group a ram to eat in return for their blessing and then offer them the heifer-camel. The *kinaan* song of Uiyam clan is popularly thought to be an especially potent curse, and hence their mistresses tend to be avoided in marriage. It should be noted, however, that most marriages take place after *naapo* when the lovers themselves are getting married and the situation of a thwarted lover cursing the bridegroom does not commonly arise.

Two irregular forms of marriage are by capture between certain clans in a joking bond brother relationship, and by coercion when the elders support a clansman who is experiencing some difficulty in marrying and threaten to curse the family of the bride if she is withheld.

If a wife dies when still young, her husband may be able to obtain a younger sister in her place, depending on the cordiality of his relationship with his affines.

If the husband dies before they have had any sons, then his eldest brother looks after his stock and his wife goes to the household of his next youngest brother (or for some other close kinsman with whom she is on terms of privileged familiarity). Any sons she bears are jurally those of her dead husband and they inherit his stock. Widows do not remarry.

A preferred form of marriage is into the same clan as a distant ancestor (preferably a great-grandfather). This is known as marrying the 'bones of an ancestor' (*lafuashi*). A man may marry into his mother's natal clan, though this is regarded as less than ideal and he would not marry into her sub-clan.

There are a number of beliefs surrounding marriage to certain sorts of women: *sapade* would be unpropitious to the camel herd if married before the permitted time, women born on Thursdays tend to be barren, women from certain families are thought to be unpropitious and their husbands might die young, divorced women who are taken on as second wives are thought to be unpropitious for the family of the first wives, and first wives who wear iron coils round their legs (i.e. all Samburu women and those of several other tribes) are thought to be disliked by the camels who will not increase. For such women, getting married may present a problem. Typically, they would be married rather late by the younger sons of poorer families who were themselves finding difficulty in getting married, or by the Samburu who tend to take a more casual view of whom they marry. Consistent with these beliefs, it is also maintained that divorce is rare and that the Rendille do not look to the Samburu to provide them with wives.

The variety of belief that surrounds marriage and the unpropitiousness of certain circumstances draws attention once again to an aspect of Rendille life in which there is a comparatively high degree of uncertainty and concern. In considering birth, it was the whole future of family survival which was seen to be at stake. At marriage, the same is true and it is worth noting that these beliefs do not just concern the future of the family, but extend to the future of its all too brittle camel herd.

The Periodic Festivals

The ceremonial activity of Rendille elders is largely confined to two periodic festivals which draw attention to settlement life, and in particular to the individual families. Because each settlement tends to be of one clan, this also involves the corporateness of each clan.

The first and more important is *soriu*. This is celebrated four time a year in two sets of two: the January festival is linked with the one in February; and the June festival is linked with the one in July. Both of these are periods following the rains when the camel camps can normally rejoin the settlements. All the boys and youths should return with their herds to join in the celebrations. When possible they will stay for at least the intervening month between two linked festivals, but if the rains have failed, drought conditions may make it necessary for them to leave after only a few days. In general these are the only periods of the year when boys and youths are expected to be living in the settlements in any large numbers.

Ideally, everyone should participate in these festivals; although a man may, if he wishes, forgo one festival provided he participates in the one linked with it a month earlier or later.

Soriu is a family festival. Each participating family provides an animal for slaughter: these would normally be ox-camels, but in a drought, poorer families and junior members of a lineage may prefer small stock. The type of stock would essentially be adapted to the likely demand for meat. On this occasion, the huts of the settlement are not built in any order of segmental seniority, but still the animals are slaughtered in this order: consequently this means that the elders witnessing the killing of each beast in turn have to traverse the length and breadth of the settlement a number of times in the course of the festival. As each animal is slaughtered, these elders dip their staves in the blood and mark parts of their own bodies with it. In addition camels are daubed with blood and small stock are spattered with a mixture of blood and sand. Ultimately all the stock in the settlement should have been thus marked. Women and girls may not see this part of the ceremony and should remain inside their huts.

No stock go out to browse on this day. After the killings have been completed, blacksmiths cut up the camels and youths cut up the small stock. Parts of the camels are divided between different sectors of the community: youths have the humps, elders the chest parts, boys the ribs and heart, girls the backs, women the stomach parts, a blacksmith has one flank, and the owner of the beast the other flank. Other parts of the camels and all parts of any small stock slaughtered are not divided in any specific way.

As soon as an eldest son marries, he performs *soriu* on behalf of his father and family, even when the father is still alive. This is a unique instance among the Rendille where the eldest son deputizes for his living father: in all other respects and on all other occasions, the father retains control over his household and herds so long as he is able.

The second festival, *olohdalmhato* or simply *almhato*, is held annually in April with the onset of the heavy rains. This festival does not entail unmarried youths or boys away at camp and is in some respects much more elaborate in detail than, for instance, the *soriu* festivals. Whereas with *soriu* there is a greater emphasis on family solidarity and well-being, with *almhato* there is a certain suggestion of averting misfortune (cf. *orelogoraha*, p. 48), and it tends more to involve the different age-sets. Of particular importance is the elder's enclosure in the centre of all Rendille settlements, *naapo*, where discussions are held and a fire is always kept alive.

At this festival, a drinking trough and a milk container are placed just outside the *naapo* enclosure. The elders bring some fresh camel milk for a collective blessing and then pour some of it into the trough and container. They return to the *naapo* and the women come to add more milk and grass to these containers, to put some herbs on the *naapo* fire, and to give the elders some tobacco for a blessing. This is pronounced age-set by age-set in order of seniority. The boys of the settlement are then called to drink as much of the milk as they want and the elders go to their own huts to continue their blessing. The same ceremony is repeated seven days later, but sour milk is used instead and the most junior age-set of elders do not provide their own milk. Seven days later, for the first time since the ceremony began, all the elders shave their heads and the wives prepare a herbal brew. The elders go to their own or their age-mates' huts and may drink some of this, but most of it is given to the boys. A procession then takes place led by the wives, and concluded by the elders: between them came all the stock not away at camp. This procession starts between two fires lit to the west of the settlement and moves eastwards to the settlement itself. Horns are blown continuously. Two days later the procession continues in this direction through two more fires: this time the stock lead the procession and the *whole* settlement (including huts, etc.) follows to pitch itself a short distance away. During the ceremony, no one should give away any stock or household article.

Death and Disposal

The Rendille have no developed belief in the survival of the soul or in any form of afterlife. Insomuch as there is any explanation surrounding their customs associated with death as with so much of their other ceremonial activity, the explanation given is to avert further misfortune. Ideally, a man's head should be shaved before his death. If this has not been done then some wholly unrelated member of another clan should be asked to do it; this is thought to entail considerable risk of misfortune, and he would be offered some stock from the dead man's herd. The dead man is then carried, with his senior son holding his head, to a grave, about 3 feet deep, immediately opposite the entrance to his hut. He is laid in this grave on his right-hand side with arms together and knees tucked right up (this may or may not be a pre-natal position, but it is certainly one of the most effective ways of fitting a body into a small hole). Each member of the settlement then places a stone and some earth on top of the corpse; his shaved hair is strewn on top of this; and finally the spot is covered by a dead thorn branch.

After two nights, a pregnant ewe is killed near the grave, and its head, stomach, and foetus are left there while a blacksmith takes the remainder of the carcass for himself (or else it is burned in the bush). The hut of the dead man is then rebuilt in another part of the settlement just outside the main enclosure, a new fire is kindled and a ewe is killed and cooked. This is, in effect, a ritual cleansing of the hut, and the main enclosure of the settlement is enlarged to include it.

From the time of death, the close agnates of the dead man should not slaughter any stock, eat red meat, drink blood, or celebrate *soriu*. However, they can eat meat that has been well cooked by other people, and in the depth of the dry season they can avoid these restrictions by begging a goat from some outsider, killing it in front of their huts, and smearing their right heels with its blood. Other members of the sub-clan (or clan) would simply avoid killing a camel at any *soriu* festival and would not daub their heads with red ochre as they might normally do at times of celebration.

These restrictions are lifted in a small ceremony shortly after the next new moon. In this ceremony, a female goat is slaughtered, and the elders share the right-hand side and the wives the left-hand side. A man shaves the hair of those closely related to the dead man, a girl marks the faces of members of his clan with chalk, while another man holds a propitious green sprig. Each of these three is given a ewe from the dead man's herd. This day is known as *buubakhapa*.

When a woman dies, her head is held by her eldest son and she is buried to one side of the entrance of her hut, lying on her left-hand side. Only her husband and children shave their heads.

*   *   *

By tradition, a Rendille who killed another accidentally became almost an outcast of the society. He would not be able to marry and no one would eat food with him. The only people prepared to shave his hair for him periodically would be other homicides in the same ritual and social state.

When the killing was deliberate, however, the murderer—if he had not already fled to some other tribe—would be bound and then stoned to death by other Rendille. This method of killing would ensure that no one person could be held responsible for the second death, and incidentally, it would serve to prevent the first killing from developing into a feud. Again, as with the killing of a pregnant girl and her lover, it is difficult at this time to know whether this is more an unfounded myth of the past or a firm, well-established tradition. But, certainly, informants claim that these customs were observed until the establishment of the administration in the area, and the older men quote instances that could well have taken place in their lifetime.

Since the arrival of administration in the area, fines have been imposed on the clan of a homicide in order to compensate the family of the dead man. This stock has been regarded as exceptionally unpropitious by the Rendille, and following the compulsory payment of compensation, they have deliberately dispersed it by virtually giving it away to other unrelated Rendille.

IV. Customs Associated with Various Lineages and Segments

Totemic and Other Similar Relationships

There are a large number of Rendille lineages claiming a mystical association with specific objects, which on the one hand may endow them with certain powers and on the other hand may entail certain avoidances.

Prominent among these are the *iipire*, who claim to have a particularly potent power to bless or to curse: altogether about two-thirds of the Rendille are *iipire*. The remainder are known as *wakhumur* (=thunder; *Wakh*=God). The attitude towards the *iipire* appears to be essentially ambivalent. On the one hand, the power of a strong curse is regarded as dangerous and even almost inauspicious. At the purification ceremony on *buubakhapa* after a death, only a *wakhumur* may hold the propitious sprig while the mourners have their hair shaved. Moreover, there are certain *iipire* lineages that are recognized as 'bad': these are thought to have a rather vicious and easily provoked curse, and even 'good' *iipire* would avoid marrying their daughters. On the other hand, the *iipire* can enjoy a considerable immunity not accorded the *wakhumur*. At a social level, they would be less likely to be slighted for fear of their curse; and at a ritual level, they would never be chosen for an inauspicious age-set role: only *wakhumur* are chosen as the man-of-the-fire and the man-of-the-horn.

Different *iipire* lineages have different types of curse with different associations. Besides the broad division between 'good' and 'bad' *iipire*, there is a difference between those whose curse may take effect over a long period, and those whose effect is thought to be immediate. While the second category have a particularly potent curse, it is thought that if the cursed man manages to survive one day then the curse is unlikely to have any future effect.

Another difference between *iipire* lineages is their association with different dangerous totemic animals, objects or diseases which to a large extent forms the basis of their power. The totemic relationship with animals in particular has close parallels with bond brotherhood: an *iipire* should avoid harming his totemic animal while at the same time he would claim to have power to coerce it: by cursing an adversary he would be in effect coercing (or invoking) his totemic species to come to his aid. And when, for instance, a man of Saali goes to marry by coercion, it is said that one of his 'brother' rhinoceroses may be seen nearby adding his own weight to the pressure of coercion.

There is, however, more to the powers of an *iipire* than simply his relationship with a dangerous species or disease. His curse or his blessing may be more diffuse and related to general bad or good luck. His powers are only retained through the appropriate ceremonial activity. A ceremony that should be performed by his family each month when the new moon is first seen is as follows. When the camels come home in the evening, the *iipire* puts cedar shavings into the fire in his hut, puts his hands and then a piece of carved ivory into the smoke, on to his forehead and chest, and pronounces a blessing. This is repeated for each member and guest of the household, and each marks his right brow and arm with chalk or red ochre. Different lineages have variations of this ceremony.

In order to transmit his powers to his sons, an *iipire* summons the elders who place honey beer (or just honey) and then poison (from a poison arrow tree) on the infant's lips and invoke in it the power to bless and to curse respectively. The father or some other *iipire* then spits in the child's mouth.

Certain details of these beliefs and practices suggest some phallic interpretation. Thus a 'bad' *iipire* is said to have 'bad urine' (sperm?); there is a general tendency to associate *iipire* and their curses with poisonous snakes—it is commonly said that *iipire* and snakes were once twins although only certain *iipire* lineages are totemically associated with snakes; and the piece of carved ivory used in the monthly ceremony is phallus-shaped as the Rendille themselves point out, and it is kept safely hidden at all other times.

Iipire are thought to be quite distinct from witches (*ndederie*, *buudh*) who in other tribes inherit evil powers without any associated ceremony, or sorcerers (*tibaato*) who resort to the malicious use of magical formulae. The latter are loosely associated with diviners (*moro*) who also have a knowledge of the use of magic. At first sight, the Rendille do not appear to rely on the powers of such men; but certainly one diviner, mentioned in some of the early literature of the area, Laogom, appears to have been quite influential in his day, and his son was appointed the senior chief of the tribe by the administration.

In a sense, blacksmiths (*tumaal*) have certain parallels to *iipire*: they have a power to bless and to curse especially in relation to dangerous iron objects, circumcision razors, spears, etc. There is a general notion of pollution attached to blacksmiths: their food and hospitality is generally avoided, and the Rendille prefer not to intermarry with them. Thus they form, in a sense, an endogamous caste within the tribe. Nevertheless economically and ritually they are an integral part of the total society. Economically, the tribe depends at all times on their ironwork; and ritually they have a prescribed role in the slaughter of stock at each marriage, after each death and at the *soriu* festivals. It is said that blacksmiths have only recently begun to acquire large stock: previously, they had to rely on other Rendille for much food in return for their services.

Certain lineages avoid certain objects which are thought to be associated with some past disaster. These are known as *dor*. Thus Kalkitele (Matarpa clan) avoid goats' meat, Ajofole (Dibshai clan) avoid milk from their own camels, and Kudere (Dibshai) have certain camels which must not go near a spot where a woman has recently given birth to a child.

Notes on Rendille Clans[7]

Upper Belisi Moiety

(a) *Dibshai* (250). Claims to be senior phratry ritually because of the lead given in the *galgulumi* ceremony, in the principal *orelogoraha* ceremony, and in choosing youths for three of the four age-set roles: Wambili sub-clan own the horn used for choosing the man-of-the-horn. Wambili, Galimogole, Dabaleen, and Orguba are considered bad *iipire*: they have a potent curse by which they can invoke lions and illnesses which emaciate the body, Pulyari as brothers by descent of Rongumo share the same *iipire* powers, but they can in addition invoke or cure jaundice through their curse or blessing. Lereya lineage of Dibshai play an important part in lifting a man's ritual prohibitions after he has killed an enemy in war. The unpropitious beliefs surrounding Arbah (Wednesday and every seventh year) do not affect Dibshai: they do not therefore kill boys born on moonless Wednesdays and they act as hosts in the *orelogoraha* ceremony performed every seventh year by the youths. Dibshai are one of the two Rendille clans to have a segment of blacksmiths.

7. In order of segmental seniority; the figures in parentheses are the numbers of men registered as tax-payers at Marsabit in 1958—officially all youths and elders. See also Charts 5 and 6 (pp. 28 and 31).

(b) *Uiyam* (62). This clan is slightly despised as atypical. It is the only Rendille clan that does not have any alternations or any *iipire*. However, its *kinaan* song, sung as a curse by a youth when his mistress is married, is held to be particularly potent, and it is said that no one would want to marry such a girl: when a Tubsha man did so and the Uiyam lover sang *kinaan*, a whole family of Tubsha clan were annihilated by a raid from Ethiopia. Before 1948, Uiyam belonged to Lower Belisi moiety, but became Upper Belisi by asking Dibshai for patronage because both the man-of-the-fire and the man-of-the-horn had been chosen from Uiyam for Difkuto age-set and they wanted to avoid being chosen on future occasions.

(c) *Nahagan* (101). Machan and Kirumui sub-clans are *iipire* and can curse with respect to lions and general bodily illnesses. Kirumui are considered bad *iipire*, Manyate sub-clan provide the bull-camel when Nahagan act as hosts in *orelogoraha* a year after a new age-set is initiated.

(d) *Matarpa* (73). At one time, they were closely associated with Nahagan clan and shared the same settlement; they still remain brothers by descent. Kaatu sub-clan are thought to have a potent diffuse curse as *iipire*. Feesha sub-clan are thought to be ritual specialists remembering past phenomena and perceiving the significance in the repetition of sequences of events.

(e) *Rongumo* (140). The only Rendille clan to have a bond brotherhood between its constituent sub-clans: youths may not have bond sisters from their clan as mistresses, but they may marry them: this is in fact a preferred form of marriage. Only Garguile lineage of Ungum sub-clan are not potent *iipire* with a curse relating to puff adders and anthrax. If members of this clan wish to marry when the star nebula, the Great Megellanic Cloud, is not visible, they should first take certain ritual precautions. A member of Rongumo clan should be the first to seize the man-of-the-fire when he is chosen.

Lower Belisi Moiety

(f) *Saali*. A clan which is so large that its constituent sub-clans might almost be regarded as autonomous clans in their own right. All members are *iipire* and have a curse through their totemic 'brothers', rhinoceroses, through any form of wood that can pierce a person, and through a wind that may bring deadly diseases with it.

Nebei (83). Otherwise known as *Fofeengaldayan*. The man-of-the-feather is always a member of Lekila sub-clan. This sub-clan is also thought to have certain sorcerers (*tibaato*).

Orare (92). Otherwise known as *Lesarge*. Closely associated with Nebei. Indi and Hlkilim have certain associations with the Ariaal Rendille (Chapter 4).

Gobonai (120). This segment is generally respected primarily because the ritual leader is usually chosen from it.

Gavana (107). Otherwise known as *Gavanayu*. Closely associated with Gobonai and is the only other segment which may provide the ritual leader. Kaldoro sub-clan are thought to be ritual specialists with an ability to read a meaning into the patterns of clouds.

(g) *Urwen* (94). Closely associated with Saali with whom they have a joking bond brotherhood. As *iipire*, Edisiomole sub-clan have a curse with diseases in general, and especially with headaches severe enough to cause death. Laogom, an influential diviner, regarded by early travellers as the most powerful man in the tribe was of this clan.

(h) *Tubsha* (113). The Orboora sub-clan are *iipire* and have a totemic relationship with elephants. Deele sub-clan are always the circumcisers at Rendille boys' initiations. After a severe drought or epidemic, Tubsha may be called on to provide a bull-camel for an extra performance of the *orelogoraha* ceremony.

(i) *Galdeelan* (105). This clan are thought to be the most recent immigrants to the tribe. Kalora sub-clan migrated from the Marle tribe and Marasho more recently from some Galla (Boran) speaking tribe. The clan has certain customs peculiar to itself and derived it is thought from their previous tribal associations: they have, for instance, their own customs following a death. Kalora are *iipire* with a general curse. This is the only other Rendille clan with a segment of blacksmiths.

V. Customs Associated with the Rendille Ritual Calendar

This calendar is based on four cycles: a seven day weekly cycle, a seven-year cycle (*Serr*, named after the days of the week), an annual cycle (based on twelve lunar months), and a lunar cycle. The days of the week have names closely similar to those in Somali.

The Seven-day Weekly Cycle

(a) *Gumaat* (*Friday*). The first day of the Rendille week and a most propitious day; ideal for the circumcision of boys, and the only day of the week on which a settlement should move after celebrating *soriu*. It is thought that a boy born on a Friday will be generally lucky and well liked by everyone; he should accumulate large herds and would never be killed in battle on a Friday. Girls may not be circumcised on this day.

(b) *Sabdi* (*Saturday*). Associated with cattle. No cattle should be given away on this day, and a man born then will always be successful in rearing cattle if he turns his hand to it (i.e. emigrates to the Samburu). A Rendille raid on a cattle settlement would always be successful on a Saturday.

(c) *Ahat* (*Sunday*). Associated with camels. On Sundays, no camels should be begged or given away, none should be taken to water where there are palm trees or they will run away, no camel settlement should move in a westerly direction or there will be a drought, and any (Rendille) raid on a camel settlement would be successful. A man born on a Sunday would tend to accumulate large camel herds.

(d) *Alasmin* (*Monday*). Associated with sheep and goats. The beliefs concerning cattle on Saturdays (above) are identical with those concerning sheep and goats on Mondays.

(e) *Talaada* (*Tuesday*). There is a diffuse belief that boys born on Tuesdays tend to be obstinate and even quarrelsome. Girls may not be circumcised on this day.

(f) *Arbah* (*Wednesday*). The most unpropitious day of the week. Ideally a younger son born on a moonless Wednesday should be killed at birth or at least be brought up by his mother's brother away from his father's home. No camel settlement should move at all on a Wednesday. Dibshai clan, however, claim to be immune from the unpropitiousness of this day and do not observe these customs. Girls may not be circumcised on this day.

(g) *Khamis* (*Thursday*). There is a diffuse belief that girls and female stock born on Thursdays tend to be barren. Girls may not be circumcised on this day.

The Seven-year Cycle

The Rendille age-set system is ceremonially based on a seven-year cycle. These years have identical names with those of the days of the week. There is also a diffuse correspondence between the associated beliefs which tend to emphasize 'Friday' as the most propitious year, and 'Wednesday' as the least propitious year (again except for Dibshai clan). Each year ends with the spring rains when the *almhato* festival is held.

(a) *Gumaat* (*'Friday'*). Ideally, the age-sets should be spaced apart by two seven-year cycles (i.e. fourteen years) with initiations taking place always in January of a 'Friday' year. Alternatively, it would also be propitious to initiate a new age-set seven or twenty-one years (i.e. one or three cycles) after its predecessor. In fact it seems likely that there were three seven-year cycles between the Irpaankuto and the Difkuto initiations and only one seven-year cycle between the Difkuto and the Irpaales initiations (Chart 7). It is the span of the Samburu age-set cycle, working quite independently of the Rendille seven-year cycle, that determines the precise span between successive age-sets. Thus, ideally, the Rendille initiate a new age-set during the first 'Friday' after the Samburu initiations.

(b) *Sabdi* (*'Saturday'*). The year in which *galgulumi* should be held and *sapade* be circumcised. If it proves impossible to hold galgulumi in this year, then a complete seven-year cycle should elapse before it is held, again in a 'Saturday' year. It is also in 'Saturdays' that Nahagan should act as hosts in the minor *orelogoraha* ceremonies.

(c) *Ahat* (*'Sunday'*). No associated customs recorded.

(d) *Alasmin* (*'Monday'*). Ideally, the *naapo* ceremony should be held in a 'Monday', although failing that a 'Saturday' would also be permissible. Logically, one might expect the *naapo* of an age-set to be held in a 'Monday', ten years after its 'Friday' initiation, or failing that it could take place in a 'Saturday' eight or fifteen years after initiation or even in a 'Monday' seventeen years after.

(e) *Talaada* (*'Tuesday'*). Youths should marry in the year following their *naapo* ceremony, and consequently many marriages tend to be in this year.

(f) *Arbah* (*'Wednesday'*). Associated (as in the weekday) with general misfortune from which Dibshai are immune. It is Dibshai who act as hosts in the principal *orelogoraha* ceremony which is always held in this year to avert misfortune, especially raids from other tribes.

(g) *Khamis* (*'Thursday'*). No associated customs recorded.

This is the ideal pattern of the seven-year cycle. Whether or not it is strictly observed in practice, on the other hand, is open to question. It is possible, for instance, that the Rendille observe it within certain limits, but occasionally adjust it to suit the convenience of their age-set system, making an initiation year a 'Friday', rather than waiting until a 'Friday' for their initiations. It is worth noting, therefore, the extent to which official Marsabit records give direct and indirect evidence which supports the existence of a regular and strictly observed seven-year cycle since at least 1917. From entries in these records, the following table may be constructed.

Chart 8
AGE-SET CEREMONIES AND THE SEVEN-YEAR CYCLE

Name	Year							Associated ceremonies
'Friday'	1916c?	1923c?	1930	1937c	1944	1951c	1958	Circumcision (c)
'Saturday'	1917g	1924g?	1931	1938	1945g	1952g	1959	Galgulumi (g)
'Sunday'	1918	1925	1933	1939	1946	1953	1960	
'Monday'	1919	1926	1933	1940	1947n	1954		Naapo (n)
'Tuesday'	1920	1927	1934n	1941	1948	1955		
'Wednesday'	1921	1928	1935	1942	1949	1956		
'Thursday'	1922	1929	1936	1943	1950	1957		
Age-set	Difkuto	Irpaales		Lipaale		Irpaandif		

Specific reports for circumcision (c) in 1937 and 1951, for ceremonies that could only have been *galgulumi* (g) in 1917, 1945, and 1952 occur in the official records. Reports of widespread marriage in 1935 and 1948 suggest the performance of *naapo* in 1934 and 1947 respectively. From these reports and from more definite evidence for the Samburu initiations, the circumcisions of 1916 and 1923 and the *galgulumi* of 1924 have been conjectured here. It should be noted that only the *naapo* of 1934 appears to have occurred during the wrong year—a 'Tuesday' instead of a 'Monday'—and even here, the evidence is so indirect that it could still be that the ceremony was in fact performed in 1933 ('Monday'), but for some reason, the mass marriages were postponed a further year or noted officially a year later. The Lipaale age-set's *galgulumi* is shown to have been quite correctly postponed for a full seven years, so that it took place during a 'Saturday' in 1945. Incidentally, 1938 was a year of severe drought.

The Annual Cycle

The annual cycle is based on lunar months. The dates below refer to the full moons in 1959, taking this more or less as a typical year.

Sonder, 24 January. *Soriu* celebrated, and the ideal month for the initiation of a new age-set and for the marriage of elder sons.

Sonder, 23 February. *Soriu* again celebrated, and the ideal month for *lahaoloroge* which should follow one month after circumcision.

Soom, 24 March. No ceremonies should be performed in this month, and members of Odoolah segment (see Chapter 4) should not shave their hair or cut any wood. For this reason, it is sometimes referred to as the 'month of Odoolah'.

Furam, 23 April. No directly associated custom, but as this is the time of the spring rains, the *almhato* ceremony is likely to be held during this month and a new year of the seven-year cycle begins.

Dipial, 22 May. Again no directly associated custom, but about this time the Great Magellanic Cloud nebula (thought to resemble a camel in shape) can no longer be seen for a month and while it is invisible members of Rongumo clan may not marry. They can, however, circumvent this by tying a handful of earth inside their garments before the Great Magellanic Cloud has disappeared.

Harafa, 20 June. The most important of the *soriu* festivals, but no camels should be killed in it and no other major ceremony should be held.

Daga, 20 July. *Soriu* again celebrated and this is the most suitable one in which to kill a camel for the festival. It is the ideal month for the *orelogoraha*, *galgulumi*, and *naapo* ceremonies, although either of the *Sonder* months half a year later would also be appropriate.

Ragarr, 18 August. The worst part of the dry season; no ceremonies should be performed in this month, no stock should be given away or ear-clippings be put on stock (*soriu* months are, in fact, ideal for clipping ears), and no man who has killed an enemy should end his ritual prohibitions during this month.

Ragarr, 17 September. Same as above.

Haitikelee, 16 October. An only child of either sex should not marry in this month.

Haiborboran, 15 November. No specific customs recorded.

Haiborboran, 15 December. No specific customs recorded.

The Lunar Cycle

It is more pertinent to think of nights of a lunar cycle than of days. The first night of the Rendille 'month' begins in the late afternoon when the new moon is first visible and it continues until the following morning; the second night begins that afternoon, and so on. Note that early in the month the vague association of unpropitiousness with odd numbers is reflected in the performance of *almhato* and *buubakhapa*, and the propitiousness of even numbers is reflected in the performance of *naapo*.

1st night: *iipire* perform their ceremonies in the evening and no settlement should move next morning.

2nd night: no associated custom record.

3rd night: suitable night to begin an *almhato* ceremony or to shave one's hair after death (*buubakhapa*).

4th night: suitable for starting a *naapo* ceremony.

5th night: again suitable for *almhato* or *buubakhapa*. Moving a settlement in the morning could lead to an attack from enemies or wild beasts.

6th night: suitable for starting a *naapo* ceremony.

7th night: suitable for *almhato*.

8th night: suitable for *naapo*.

9th night: Upper Belisi moiety hold their *soriu* festivals (cf. association of this moiety with nine at birth). Also suitable for *almhato* or *buubakhapa*.

10th night: Lower Belisi moiety hold their *soriu* festivals (cf. again the association with ten at birth).

11th night: suitable for *buubakhapa*.

12th night: no associated belief.

13th night (*lkadet*): suitable for male initiations, and building a *galgulumi* settlement.

14th night (*haguder*—full moon): also suitable for male initiations.

Those performing *galgulumi* should go down to bathe in Lake Rudolf. The best time of the month to perform *orelogoraha*.

15th night (*goobaan*): those performing *galgulumi* should spend the night singing and dancing.

16th night onwards (*mukhedhe*): no longer the most propitious part of the month and no further associated customs. From this point boys born on Wednesdays, especially younger sons, are thought to be unpropitious.

3

AN OUTLINE OF SAMBURU SOCIETY

I. Social Structure

There are many close similarities between the Samburu and the Rendille social structures. However, rather than repeat much of what has already been written in Chapter 2 and at even greater length elsewhere,[1] here I merely outline the significant areas in which the structures of the two societies are clearly in contrast.

There are seven distinguishable levels in the segmentary descent system of the Samburu. They are the lineage group, the hair-sharing group, the sub-clan, the clan, the phratry, and the moiety. Of these, the clan is by far the most significant in terms of social cohesion and shared interests. In contrast to the Rendille whose clans tend to be concentrated in one or a few large settlements, the Samburu clans tend to be scattered over much of the tribal territory in interspersed clusters of small settlements. A number of Samburu clans are segments of more inclusive units, which I refer to as *phratries*.[2] While the phratry is not a particularly cohesive unit socially, the principle of exogamy is extended to it and it has a ritual significance in the age-set system, each phratry having its own ritual leader.

Brotherhood by descent and bond brotherhood are as common among the Samburu as among the Rendille. All bond brotherhoods are of the type referred to as 'c' in Chart 6: joking in this context only occurs in the relationship between a man and his bond brothers' wives. In addition, the Samburu may form new ties of bond brotherhood following some homicide: the Rendille do not do this.

Within the Samburu segmentary descent system, segmental seniority is of ceremonial significance only, prescribing the order in which participants should perform. Certain sub-clans have *alternations*, but the relationships that this involves correspond to those observed at the level of the *clan* among the Rendille (and not the sub-clan). In

1. See, *The Samburu*, especially Chapter 4 and the chart of segmentary descent system on pages 72–3.
2. These *phratries* are referred to as *Sections* by the Samburu administration. I have avoided this term because of the confusion it is liable to cause when compared with *Sections* among the Masai. Masai Sections are territorial units and are cross-cut by a number of clans so that any one clan may be represented in several Sections: They are not therefore a part of a segmentary descent system as is the case among the territorially dispersed Samburu Sections/phratries.

other words, between alternations (i.e. adjacent generations) there should be a mutual sense of respect which tends to be accentuated in the presence of each other's wives and tends to be modified among coevals and close friends. It follows from this that relationships between members of a sub-clan are far less constrained by custom among the Samburu. Within the Rendille sub-clan, the only truly reciprocal relationships that can be enjoyed are the joking relationships between alternate generations: all others entail either showing or being shown a respect that amounts at times almost to an avoidance. This combination of avoidance and joking between all members of a Rendille sub-clan, implying constraint and even tension, contrasts with the cordial relationships that tend very often to be formed between Samburu sub-clansmen and a greater sense of equality. Later in this chapter, it will be seen how these differences are consistent with the different rules of stock ownership in the two tribes, and that for the Samburu, tensions that are built up tend rather to be *between* clans rather than within the clan.

Examined in its wider social context, the age-set system of the Samburu appears to be more significant than that of the Rendille. The various customs which permit the Rendille to climb an age-set, to delay the marriage of certain daughters, to marry off their sons promptly on reaching elderhood have the effect of blurring the age-set system and they are absent among the Samburu. Consequently, owing to this earlier marriage of Samburu daughters and later marriage of their sons, there is a more striking division of the society into different age grades and a much higher degree of polygamy than among the Rendille who are typically monogamous. The age grade of unmarried young men, who are known as the *moran*, is altogether more striking and the centre of more ceremonial activity. They are sharply in contrast with boys on the one hand or elders on the other, in their appearance, their code of behaviour and their values. Among the Rendille the age grades tend to merge with one another and it is not always possible at first sight to distinguish between a fully grown clothed boy and a circumcised youth, or between a youth and an elder. Among the Samburu, the age-set system and the division of males into three age grades is distinct and clear-cut. The following diagram illustrates this contrast between the two societies in terms of the proportions of married to unmarried persons of each sex.

It is tempting to regard the Samburu system as the purer more extreme form, while the Rendille age-set system, with its mitigating customs, emerges as a derivative form with a lesser social significance. In this context, it is worth noting that by custom, it is the Samburu who determine the periodic length of the age-set cycle,

Chart 9
A COMPARISON BETWEEN AGE GRADING AMONG THE SAMBURU AND RENDILLE

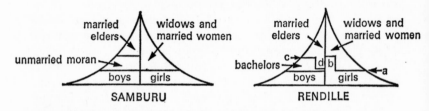

[Note factors that among the Rendille tend to produce a greater balance in numbers between married men and women. These are:

(a) The relatively later age at which girls generally marry.
(b) The excessive delay in the marriage of certain girls (*sapade*).
(c) The relatively earlier age at which young men are permitted to marry.
(d) The custom of allowing certain men to marry young by climbing an age-set.]

and the Rendille who take the cue for their own ceremonial cycle from this.

The Samburu share with the Rendille the custom of having a well-defined relationship between alternate age-sets, whereby it is the senior age-set that is responsible for the moral education of the junior and the inculcation of a sense of respect. Among the Samburu this is known as the *firestick relationship* (*olpiroi*) and the elders responsible for the current age-set of moran are known as the *firestick elders*. Altogether this relationship is more strongly stressed among the Samburu, especially in its more negative aspects of intimidation through the power of the curse of the firestick elders; the more positive role of the firestick elders as educators tends to be somewhat spasmodic. The prime reason for this further contrast between the two societies is not hard to find. Among the Rendille, control over the younger men is largely achieved through the potential threat of economic privations from their senior kinsmen; whereas among the Samburu, the easier economy does not provide the same effective means, and control over the young men becomes a major social problem, exacerbated of course by the fact that they tend to face an even more prolonged bachelorhood than the Rendille and the adultery with the wives of elders is a recurrent source of strain between *moran* and elders.

Customs linking every third age-set are present, but they are not so pronounced among the Samburu as among the Rendille. There is no climbing from one age-set to another and no attempt to belong to the same age-set line as an ancestor. Indeed, because polygamy is more common among the Samburu, many men are the younger sons of second and even third wives and would not be old enough to be circumcised until four or five age-sets after their fathers. For the Samburu, the issue of prime importance is that no man and his father should be of alternate age-sets or they would be in a firestick relationship with one another. Beyond this, it is of lesser importance exactly how many age-sets a man is below his father.

II. The Principles and Practice of Cattle Ownership

The Family and the Herd

The cattle economy of the Samburu has its own hardships, risks and problems of management. Nevertheless, as compared with the Rendille, they do not face the same problems of stunted growth. Any diligent and resourceful Samburu can expect to build up his herds substantially through his lifetime and is less likely through sheer bad luck to suffer any lasting misfortune. If he takes on a pauper as a herdboy, then he can afford to give him a heifer every other year (the generally recognized payment) as an outright gift. At this rate and with luck, the herdboy will have the nucleus of a herd of his own in a matter of ten years. This could not be contemplated by the Rendille with their camel economy.

This essential difference between the two tribes accounts for many of the differences in their customs of stock ownership. There is, for instance, no Samburu tenet that a herd of cattle should remain intact correspondingly to the Rendille tenet for camels. Consequently, there are frequent gifts of cattle between clansmen, especially to assist one another in marriage. The marriage payments are quite different also: among the Rendille there is an initial payment of eight camels as bridewealth, and it is quite understood that any demands for further gifts from the wife's kinsmen will only be for small stock. Among the Samburu the bridewealth payment is eight cattle, but there is no convention as regards further gifts, and throughout his lifetime the husband is plagued by a wide range of affines who are constantly begging more cattle from him and holding their power to curse his children over him if he should refuse them unreasonably. Even after his death, these affines may approach his children as their 'mother's brothers' and expect yet more gifts. Altogether this tends to produce more mistrust between men and their affines (or maternal kin) among the Samburu than among the Rendille where the obligations are constrained by custom, and where only really close kinsmen of the bride would expect further gifts in any case.

The potential growth of a cattle herd also permits it to be split up progressively within the family as this develops. When a man first marries he takes a portion of his *total herd*, allotting it to his wife (her *allotted herd*) and retaining a smaller portion (his *residual herd*). As he marries further wives and builds up several families with several allotted herds, certain rules prevail. These are as follows: (*a*) no one save the husband can alienate any beast from the total herd; (*b*) the husband cannot take an animal from the allotted herd of any wife and give it to any other wife or return it to his own residual herd; (*c*) offspring of any female cattle in a wife's allotted herd remain in her allotted herd; (*d*) a wife can give any cattle from her allotted herd to any of her sons and these cattle remain effectively in her allotted herd so far as these rules apply, and of course they remain effectively inside the total herd.

Having allotted the bulk of his cattle to his first wife, a man starts marriage at a disadvantage. Moreover, he is vulnerable to the demands of her kinsmen in their requests for further stock. There are, however, certain loopholes in the rules which a shrewd man can exploit if he wishes to build up his residual herd in order to marry a second time. Whenever his own close clansmen or those of his wife ask him for a cow, he can take one from the allotted herd of his wife as an outright gift (rule *a*); on the other hand, when he in his turn approaches his own clansmen or the husbands of his clanswomen for gifts, there is no compulsion for him to give them to his wife and so his residual herd benefits. In this manner he can build up his residual herd at the expense of his wife's allotted herd without actually infringing the rules, and maintain at the same time the goodwill of his own clansmen and affines. If he does actually infringe the rules, then he is endangering his own marriage and his clansmen will put pressure on him to make amends to his wife; otherwise she might run away to her parents' home and have their support.

A Samburu initially builds up his herd from the stock allotted to his mother by direct agreement with her. Thus custom precludes direct competition between half-brothers since their mothers have separate allotted herds, but it does not at first sight prevent full brothers from competing for the same cattle. However, once again it is here that social pressures within and if necessary beyond the family come into play: each son is expected to show respect for his elder brothers and to avoid competing with them in building up a herd. These pressures ensure that each boy at any time has a substantially larger herd than his next youngest brother. By the time he has reached an age for marriage, he can expect to have a large enough herd to assert some degree of independence and from this moment he ceases to ask his mother for further cattle. So long as his father is alive, however, his herd remains inside the total herd of the father and no cattle should be alienated without his permission.

At the death of the father the eldest son of his first wife inherits his residual herd; though the other sons may expect the gift of a heifer from that herd. From this moment each of the married sons of the dead man becomes fully independent and can alienate cattle from his total herd as he sees fit. Unmarried sons, however, are still under the patronage of their married elder brothers until they too become married. The rules of inheritance and society essentially favour the eldest son, but it is altogether a more generous economy than among the Rendille, and younger brothers are freer to assert their independence. There are few customs or beliefs which suggest either to the observer or to the Samburu that this is a relationship fraught with strain as occurs among the Rendille.

In her old age, a woman is generally expected to accompany her youngest son after he has in effect pre-inherited the remainder of her allotted herd on his marriage. If, however, she dies before this point, then it is he who has the right to inherit *all* those allotted cattle that have not been reallocated to any of his elder brothers.

Cattle and the Clan

The reciprocal nature of gifts among clansmen and the non-reciprocal gifts by a man to his wives' kinsmen naturally lead to different forms of social relationships within the clan and between clans. Between clans, especially those of different phratries, there is mistrust, and this is constantly reinforced by the tension between affines in their attempts to exploit each other's herds to the utmost. Within the clan, there is a spirit of co-operation. In the first instance a man regards his total herd as his own. But he openly acknowledges the reciprocal rights that his clansmen have to gifts from it, and it is this element of reciprocity which creates the assumption of a larger herd belonging to the whole clan. It is their interests in this larger herd and in the general welfare of the clan which prompts clansmen to interfere in one another's domestic affairs, persuading one man not to jeopardize his marriage by infringing the rights of his wife in her allotted herd, and persuading another man to maintain the good name of the clan by respecting his elder brothers. Clansmen are in a sense in collusion in order to exploit the allotted herds of their wives, and in order to uphold their own interests *vis-à-vis* other clans with whom they have numerous ties of marriage.

Clanship is not based on any fiction of descent from a common ancestor, it is based on social obligations of mutual help and trust, so that the stock owner, far from being quite independent and autonomous, is in reality enmeshed in a web of diffuse ties that are expressed in a complex set of rights over cattle. Between clans where there tend to be strains kept alive by disputes over existing and proposed marriages, the uneasy relationship can be expressed in terms of the undefined rival claims they have in one another's herds for further marriage payments, and the ultimate sanction they have in their powers to curse.

The Dispersal of the Herd

The Samburu do not have the custom of sharing beasts with other stock owners. They either make outright gifts of them (as to clansmen and affines) or else they create a debt (*sile*). A debt is normally the gift of a fat ox in return for the promise of a heifer: in a harsh dry season, a man may wish to feed his family or he may have to provide an ox for some ceremonial occasion. For the receiver, the ox is a makeshift solution to his immediate problems, whereas for the giver it is an investment. When asked why they hold their oxen in such high regard, the Samburu claim that it can be exchanged for a heifer which in turn might become the founder of a whole herd. 'A debt', they say, 'can never die.' Thus, if a man temporarily borrows a milch-cow from a friend to help him feed his family and the animal dies, then he is under no obligation: but if he receives an ox as a debt, then he must repay it as promised. If a man takes an ox from his wife's allotted herd as a debt, then the debt must be repaid to that herd.

Milch-cattle may be lent when clansmen need them to feed their families. A similar loan may be made from a herd of cattle that have strayed to any man who has rounded them up and has looked after them well. There is no question as to the ultimate ownership of these cattle or the right of the owner to ask for their return at any time. He may, however, occasionally offer a female calf as an outright gift to the borrower in which case the borrower's ear-clipping would be put on it.

Thus, in various ways, the herd of a Samburu tends to be dispersed: by splitting the homestead as described on page 22 when the stock owner retains full rights in his stock; by creating debts when the stock owner invests in other men's herds; and by outright gifts (to clansmen and affines) when the investment is in terms of fulfilling and creating diffuse social obligations. These are also investments in another sense in that they are means whereby a man can insure himself against sudden loss through epidemics, raids, or confiscation: having dispersed his herds and created specific or diffuse obligations, he is in a strong position to recoup his losses.

The dispersal of the camel herd on quite this scale among the Rendille, however, is not practised. They may share out certain beasts, but the principle that the herd should remain intact prevails. It is worth considering briefly why the Samburu and Rendille should not follow each other's customs.

The Samburu would find it difficult to share their cattle in the sense that the Rendille share their camels since the practice would be very hard to keep under control: cattle increase at a much faster rate than camels, there are many more of them, and individual stock owners tend to migrate from one local clan group to another. East man would certainly know the uterine pedigree of his own cattle, but it is less likely that others would know this and hence it would be easier for him to ignore the rules behind the custom and claim shared female offspring for himself. The custom of sharing a beast is essentially a custom associated with a greater uniqueness of each beast and a desire to keep the herd intact: the original owner always has a claim in the borrower's shared herd. But the rate at which cattle can be and are transferred from one owner to another among the Samburu would play havoc with this custom.

The Rendille do, it is true, occasionally create debts by borrowing ox-camels for slaughter in return for the promise of a heifer-camel, but the practice is felt to be somewhat ludicrous: food is generally available, the need for ox-camels for slaughter is rare, and the value of a heifer-camel is priceless. Because of this, the Rendille are very reluctant to repay such debts which may be handed down from one generation to the next. At least one debt is claimed to go back more than a century to the time when the Kipeko age-set were youths. Sharing camels is in many ways an unreliable form of investment against misfortune, but at least it is a custom which seems to be well adapted to the scarcity of camels and the slow growth of camel herds, just as the customs of making gifts and creating debts among the Samburu are well adapted to the relatively quick growth of the cattle economy.

In both societies, social relationships tend to focus on rights in large stock almost to the exclusion of small stock. To a certain extent it is possible to examine the different forms of relationship between brothers, clansmen, affines, etc., and to relate these to the physiological differences between camels and cattle (coupled perhaps with different techniques of management). This point of view altogether underrates the economic importance of sheep and goats in both societies: among the Rendille these are especially important for the poorer sector of the society, and among the Samburu they are an important source of food in the dry season. Paradoxically, it is precisely because sheep and goats multiply freely and do not present the problems of large stock that they seem not to be the focus of important social relationships. Because they are easy units of the economy, they have less importance; and because they have less importance, their value in expressing, forming or moulding social relationships is muted. They can be the focus of everyday expressions of friendship, but not the subject of bitter disputes and rivalries or the discharge of heavy debts as in the gift of a daughter in marriage. The Rendille who are thought by the Samburu to be so niggardly in not giving away camels are also praised highly for their generosity with small stock.

III. The Life Cycle and Associated Customs

Birth

Custom permits a woman to have discreet sexual relations with men other than her husband, in particular those of his age-set or alternation. However, from the moment that her pregnancy is established, she should only have intercourse with her husband and this too should be curtailed in time. As she loses her appetite for milk she is fed increasingly on meat, and, today, maize-meal.

Preferably a child should be born in the homestead rather than the bush. During the final stages of labour, the mother squats with her feet open, her face turned downwards and her hands grasping the supporting post of the hut. Only married women attend her; the most experienced among them acts as midwife and uses her fingers to assist delivery while the others help to steady her. The umbilical cord is placed across the father's right shoe (or the mother's when the baby is a girl) and is cut with a knife. The afterbirth is buried by two small girls in the calf enclosure and the hole is covered with a flat stone.

The elders kill a goat (*morr*) in front of the hut, and this is eaten by wives and rather small girls. If the child is a boy, the *morr* is a male and the father directs that blood should be drawn from the neck of a male calf for four consecutive days: this blood is the only food taken by the wife during this period, and the calf is then given to the baby boy as the foundation of his herd. If the child is a girl, then the *morr* is a virgin female, and a female calf is bled but not given to the child. Until the fourth day, the midwife sleeps beside the mother and the father sleeps elsewhere. On the fourth day, the father kills an ox (*buutan*) and other elders and wives in the vicinity may come to eat it. The mother eats some of the chyme of the *buutan* and herbs to make her vomit. She and the sleeping hides of the hut are washed well, and the father returns to sleep there.

After perhaps another three days, the wife opens her husband's gate one morning and then resumes her domestic duties within the homestead. At this point, if the infant is a boy, the husband directs her to give it a particular heifer of the allotted herd and he may voluntarily add to this another heifer from his own residual herd.

For the next two (a girl) or four (a boy) months, the mother drinks no milk and again is fed on meat and, today, maize-meal. This period tends to make heavy demands on the father's flock of small stock.

Beads are placed around the neck and waist of the infant after about two months. Those around the waist are discarded as the child grows up.

Until the infant is weaned, the mother wears a broad leather belt which should never be thrown away until it is too old to wear again. The child sleeps at night inside her apron and is only denied her breast when it is particularly obstinate or bad-tempered: on such occasions it will be left to cry. Cow's milk may be introduced into the child's diet after only one week, and within a few months it will form the bulk of its food. Weaning is said to be done after only eight months, but twelve to fifteen months appears to be more typical, and at the discretion of the father it is carefully delayed until a good wet season when there is plenty of milk available. At this point and without forewarning, he orders the mother to cover up her breasts. There is no return to the breast: the child may cry and scream for the first two or three days and may try to claw at the cloth covering the breasts at night. Within a week, however, the flow of milk will have dried up and the child will accept the new situation. The cloth covering the breasts is then loosened, and the child may even be allowed to sleep once more inside the mother's apron.

Limited sexual intercourse may be resumed prior to weaning; however, pregnancy should if possible be avoided and a pregnancy by some man other than the husband would be regarded as unpropitious.

In relation to these customs of weaning and their possible significance on the child's later personality, it is perhaps pertinent to point out firstly, that from a dietary point of view it is largely a gradual transfer from one form of milk (from the mother) to another (from the herds), secondly that from a social point of view it is not accompanied by any other change in behaviour towards the child or in its position within the family, and thirdly that from the point of view of the immediate impact of weaning, children appear to accept the sudden transition from unlimited access to the breast to complete denial comparatively easily after the initial tantrums.

Apart from these customs which accompany a normal birth, there are others that may accompany it in certain circumstances.

If the father by chance happens to be absent from his homestead when his wife gives birth to a son, she is expected to leave the settlemen as soon as she hears he is approaching. He then threatens her with a bow and arrow, and she returns to the homestead. He then takes a heifer from her allotted herd and adds it to his own residual herd. The Samburu explain this custom by saying that when the mother tries to leave the settlement it is because she feels her husband has deserted her at a critical stage, and that the husband takes the heifer for his own because in giving birth to a son in his absence, the mother has behaved as though he were no longer alive: only this payment can avert misfortune.

There are several customs to cure barrenness or to avert misfortune. *Remori* is a ceremony performed for barren women. The uncircumcised boys in any locality may decide among themselves when and where it should be held. They present the wife with a doll made out of cow dung, and she nurses it for four days as if it were a child, giving it milk and putting fat on its body. Several weeks or months later, the husband kills an ox and spends a whole day cooking it. In the evening, the boys come to bless the couple and eat a part of the meat in the calf enclosure. That night, some of the boys sleep beside the husband and his wife in their hut, and next morning again they give their blessing. The ceremony is supervised by local elders who give their blessing.

A woman who has had one or several children that have died shortly after birth may be persuaded to have her next child in the hut of a blacksmith or of a *lais* (the Samburu equivalent of *iipire*). If this appears to succeed in averting further misfortune, she will bear all her subsequent children in the same place. Alternatively, the husband may call other elders of his locality and clan and ask for their blessing, in return for which he slaughters an ox to feed them. Or he may consult a *laibon* (diviner) who may be able to perceive some inner reason for the misfortune and devise a ceremony to counteract it. In searching for some ritual formula that will change their luck, the wife may be advised to leave off wearing certain ornaments until the circumcision of her children, or the children may be made to adopt some particular hairstyle.

Another custom that may be adopted under these circumstances is for the wife and child to grow their hair for the first six months or so after birth. Finally their hair is shaved in a small ceremony in which the husband slaughters a sheep which is eaten by the wives and small children. If this particular custom apparently reverses the luck of the married couple and their children live, then their sons will observe it when they marry and it will become a custom of the lineage they found. This is quite widespread among a number of lineages.

Breech deliveries and the birth of twins are thought to bring luck to the homestead. When such children are perhaps 11 years old, their lower incisor teeth are removed, the lobes of their ears are pierced, and a sheep is killed (or two for twins). The father provides honey beer and milk for the elders to drink and the wives dance. The elder who removes the incisors and pierces the ears of each child is given a ewe by that child and becomes his (or her) close friend (*sotwa*). All other children have their lower incisors removed and their ears pierced when they are rather younger and there is no ceremony involved.

First-born twins, however, are not propitious and they are killed at birth. It is thought that to ignore this practice would lead to the extinction of the family. Similar beliefs are attached to the births of certain other children, such as those begotten by a member of the wife's father's clan or age-set, of the husband's father's alternation, a junior *moran*, an uncircumcised boy, a *lais* or a blacksmith. If the mother is uncircumcised, the child is also thought unpropitious and will be aborted, although the Samburu are slightly more tolerant in their attitude towards the parents themselves than the Rendille.

Killing such children at birth is carried out by putting tobacco in their mouths and leaving them in the bush immediately after birth, and certainly before feeding them. Abortion may be achieved by other wives feeding the woman on fat and then forcing the miscarriage by manipulating her abdomen with their hands and knees. A woman who is seriously ill before giving birth may be given a bitter herbal drink to induce a miscarriage. No form of hysterotomy is practised. When the choice has to be made, the life of the mother would be saved in preference to that of her child.

The Samburu show the greatest concern for their children. The complex and varied ceremonial activity associated with child-birth is an indication of this attitude and of the hazards which accompany building up a family.

Childhood

To the Samburu, children are more than a security for their parents against the coming of old age. They are a focus of interest and attention. Their presence is the only certain thing that can stabilize marriage. They enhance the status of the parents, and the more there are of them the more propitious the family is thought to be. With a number of children, especially sons, a man can hope to build up his herds and in time to lead a less active life in herding and a more active life in the gossip groups of the elders and (if he wants) in their more formal discussions. While his daughters, after their marriages into worthy families, are an asset to him and his closer kinsmen: he can look to their allotted herds for an added source of revenue.

Basically, there are very close parallels between the Samburu and the Rendille so far as childhood is concerned. The differences, however, are both significant and illuminating, especially as both tribes will point them out. They stem primarily from three facts of the cattle economy: that it is better suited to smaller and socially more viable settlements, that it offers greater opportunities for growth, and that this in turn encourages polygamy.

The smaller and more viable settlements imply a lesser intensity of social life and hence less consistent pressure on individual families to conform with the generally expected standards of respect. These standards are acknowledged but the means available to take a deviant family to task are less pronounced. The opportunities for growth of a cattle herd imply that a boy has less to lose by antagonizing his closer kinsmen: even if they are in theory able to curtail the growth of his herd, this would not necessarily prevent him building up a herd later in his life as it would among the Rendille. Once again this serves to encourage a degree of deviance among boys. The preference for polygamy implies that wives are in more constant demand and that their inherent value is higher than among the Rendille. Consequently, there is less need for the Samburu to apply pressure on their girls in order that they should acquire the qualities ideal in a wife: their future is more assured.

Such arguments, however, can only be carried so far. Thus, the fact that the competition is for wives rather than husbands also implies that young men are constrained to conform to the ideals of worthiness in a potential suitor. The fact that cattle herds can be successfully built up at a later stage in life is not to imply that boys are uninterested in starting to build up herds of their own as soon as they are able. The fact that practically any girl can be married off does not lessen the fact that marriage into a rich and worthy family is altogether preferable for both the girl and her kinsmen. And the fact that there is less opportunity to apply pressure from outside the family in no way implies that there is no pressure. On balance, however, both tribes agree that, while their ideals of respect and conformity among children are essentially identical, the standards achieved by the Rendille are higher.

If Samburu boys show insufficient respect, the elders may ridicule them and threaten to delay their circumcision, on the pretext that so long as they behave as boys they do not deserve to become *moran.* As a means of coercion, this may have a profound effect among boys over the years. Not only will they want to be thought prepared for *moranhood;* they will also apply pressure on one another to conform. It may well be significant that no one suggested that such coercion was necessary among the Rendille.

A major difference between the two tribes is the extent to which girls are expected to avoid elders. Among the Rendille, they would tend to avoid members of their father's age-set and generation. Among the Samburu, this avoidance is extended to all elders. Consequently, when a Samburu girl is married to an elder, it is into a world that is totally unfamiliar to her. Thus while Rendille wives are popularly held to have a more pronounced sense of respect than Samburu wives, this would be offset to some extent in the early stages of marriage by the awe that the latter have for the elders.

The Initiation of an Age-set

The Samburu have a custom not shared by the Rendille, that full brothers and sisters should be circumcised in order of birth. For the girl this is normally a preliminary to her marriage; whereas for the boy it is his initiation as a *moran* into an age-set. Thus, after one age-set has been 'closed' (i.e. to further recruitment through circumcision) there is a growing number of boys of a suitable age waiting for circumcision into the succeeding age-set and *also* a growing number of marriageable girls who must wait until their elder brothers have been circumcised before they can be married. In particular, the children of the current age-set of firestick elders may be well above the normal age for circumcision and by custom must wait until the new age-set is formed. There is a growing pressure from various directions for initiating a new age-set which is by no means confined to the boys themselves: many different persons have an interest in unfreezing the situation which a 'closed' age-set can give rise to. As against this, there may be a general desire to keep the current age-set of *moran* from marrying and so to restrict competition for marriageable girls. Once a new age-set has been circumcised, the general focus of interest and attention will switch to the new younger *moran* and the older *moran* of the senior age-set will have a major incentive to marry and become elders.

Thus, inherent in the age-set system, the practice of polygamy, and the values attached to these, there are forces which to some extent determine the periodic length of the age-set cycle, and with time pressures build up for a new initiation. The point to stress here is that while both the Samburu and the Rendille are linked to the same periodic cycle, it is the pressures within the Samburu society alone that determines this cycle, while the age-set system of the Rendille and the associated customs is sufficiently flexible to adjust itself to this.

About one year before a new age-set is due to be initiated, a ceremony is performed by the initiates of Masula phratry at Mount Ngiro. One of the initiates' fathers (three age-sets senior to the one to be formed) provides a white ox for slaughter. This must be eaten by *every* person present and the remnants entirely burnt (or the new age-set might suffer some misfortune). Each initiate takes away a strip of its hide to wear on his arm. This ox and the ceremony are known as 'the boys' ox' (*lmongo lolayok*) and also as 'the ox which is cut with the age-set' (*lmongo odungieki laji*). Any boy circumcised after this belongs to the new age-set. Subsequently, certain other phratries (such as Nyaparai) may perform a similar ceremony.

From this point, boys may be seen gathering together, visiting the settlements of firestick elders of their clan to ask them to advance the date of circumcision, asking for livestock to kill for food, and coercing other boys of their clan dispersed throughout the district to join them. At these times, the initiates wear aprons blackened with charcoal and special ear ornaments (*lkerno*). The song they sing (*lebarta*) is held to be a particularly potent form of coercion.

Closer to the time of circumcision, another ceremony (*nangore*) is performed separately by each phratry. As with all these ceremonies, it is supervised by the new firestick elders who until now have been junior elders. Some of these elders lead their initiates to certain traditional spots as far apart as Marsabit and Baringo to collect gum (*nangore*) from certain types of tree, and sticks suitable for making bows and arrows. While the boys collect these, the elders kindle a fire using firesticks and friction, and from this point they become the official firestick elders to the new age-set: the kindling of the fire has brought a new age-set to life.

Circumcision can now take place as soon as a month is propitious and the weather is sufficiently mild to permit a gathering of each clan into larger settlements. The ceremony entails considerable demands on the small stock for food, and would normally only be held after a good wet season when this stock is in good condition. The Dorobo (because they are the circumcisers) and blacksmiths (because they have made the circumcision razors) should be circumcised first. They are succeeded by the Masula of Mount Ngiro, and then other Masula, and then other phratries. There is a diffuse tendency for the phratries of the Black Cattle moiety to circumcise before the White Cattle. Circumcisions are generally completed within several months, as occurred in 1936 and 1948. But at other times, they may cover two years, as occurred in 1893, 1912, 1921–2, or even three years, as occurred in 1960–2 due to the adverse weather conditions.

The initiations are performed in a large settlement (*lorora*) involving only those members of one clan residing in that area. Thus for any clan there are a number of circumcision centres situated at convenient spots from which any family can choose as a matter of convenience (there is a similar choice when later as *moran* they perform their *ilmugit* ceremonies). In this settlement the huts are arranged in a circle, preferably in a clockwise order of segmental seniority. There is no obligation for members of the clan not directly concerned with the circumcisions to live there or attend the ceremony.

A few days before the ceremony is to be held, the elders gather to bless various articles to be used at the circumcision, and that afternoon the mother of each initiate enlarges her hut to make room for a couch for him to lie on. Immediately before the first evening circumcisions, the initiates are called together, their hair is shaved and they are made new sandals. At this point, those few initiates whose lineages customarily circumcise in the evenings drive their family cattle into the yard and they are circumcised. Each initiate in turn is held in front of his mother's hut by one man at his back and another at his right leg: these become his ritual patrons. He should sit quite motionless throughout the operation. The skin at the end of the prepuce is cut off completely so that the penis is completely free of it, and then a small hole is cut into the top of the prepuce about a half to one inch from the end, and the penis is drawn through it. The prepuce hanging down is then trimmed. After the operation the initiate sings *lebarta* and is promised a heifer by his father. He is then carried inside his mother's hut and laid down on a couch. He drinks slightly sour milk mixed with blood (*saroi*) until he has recovered a day or so later. The circumciser is a Dorobo and he operates in order of segmental seniority.

All the children of one woman are circumcised in strict order of birth, and if among several sons to be initiated on this occasion there are any intervening daughters or girls who have twin brothers, then these must also be circumcised at the appropriate moment, but by a Dorobo woman and inside the hut.[3] All the couches in one hut are set in a line according to the order of birth.

3. It should be noted that only comparatively few girls would have to be circumcised precisely at this point in time. Even those whose circumcision

Initiates who are not full agnatic members of the clan are circumcised at the end of the segment (usually the hair sharing group) to which they have their closest relationship. The sons of Turkana immigrants to the tribe and two sub-clans of Ltoiyo are circumcised just outside the settlement by the family gateway.

Early in the following morning the remainder of the operations are performed in an identical manner. Later, the fathers (or guardians) of each initiate are blessed by other clan elders and butter is put on their heads. From this moment, the initiate is under an enhanced obligation to show respect for this person. The women of the locality then collect to sing certain jocular and even ribald circumcision songs at the entrance to each hut. In the afternoon this gives way to a general dance in which the elders may dance with the wives; and, later, the *moran* with the girls. It is at about this time that some initiates begin to emerge from their huts having partially recovered from the operation, and pay visits to one another, drinking their milk and blood beverage.

During the next day or so, those who held the initiates during their operations prepare bows and arrows from the sticks they had collected at *nangore*, and the arrows are tipped with gum previously softened in the *nangore* fire. The initiates, still in their black aprons go into the bush to shoot small birds and make head-dresses from their feathered carcasses.

For a month, the initiates shoot these birds and observe a number of ritual prohibitions: they may not touch any knife or spear, they may not sit on a stone, they may not wash, and they can only eat mutton, but not with their hands. As they enter the yard of any elder of any clan, they sing *lebarta*. He should kill a sheep, cook it and cut it up for them, otherwise his own sons or even his wives' unborn children could meet with misfortune. There is a general belief, shared by most tribes of the area (except the Turkana), that to kill a boy during this period would bring misfortune to the killer even if he is of an alien tribe.

During this period, the initiates may exchange or share certain items and adopt reciprocal terms of address which they retain throughout their lives. If one comes to the hut of another after the operation and drinks his beverage (*saroi*) then they will call each other *saroi*; if one gives another a bird (*lkweeni*) he has shot, then they will call each other *kweeni*. And if one gives another one of his arrows, then they call each other *birian*. Such terms do not entail any specific form of behaviour, but they do imply that the initiates (possibly even from different clans), were circumcised in the same

---

and marriage is held up by the delayed circumcision of an elder brother would normally wait a few months longer.

locality at about the same time and are therefore age mates *par excellence*. No initiate would want to form such a relationship with another who had flinched during the operation: the latter would be socially ostracized and would always bear a stigma. Other members of the age-set are called *murata* (*emuratare*=circumcision), and this extends not only to other Samburu clans and to those circumcised at different points in time, but also to men of other tribes who are adjudged to be of the same age-set.

The Ilmugit *Ceremonies*

In the course of a man's *moranhood* he performs in a series of *ilmugit* ceremonies with other members of his age-set and clan (referred to here as his Club). The complete cycle is outlined below.

All the *ilmugit* ceremonies have a similar basic form, although those that mark some change in status as the age-set becomes more senior have additional features. The huts of an *ilmugit* settlement are built in a circle according to a clockwise order of seniority. Each *moran* provides an ox for slaughter, or, if he is poor and the ceremony is not too important, a goat. In the centre of the settlement is an enclosure for the elders (*lkulal*) with a fire in it, and 200 yards or more from the settlement is another enclosure for the *moran* which also bears the name *ilmugit*. Prior to and during the ceremony, the elders address and harangue the *moran* with an aim of teaching them a sense of respect (*nkanyit*). In the more important *ilmugit* ceremonies, the ceremony itself begins in the evening when the *moran* are called over to the elders' enclosure for a special blessing, and on this night no outsider should be allowed to sleep in the hut of any *moran*. The stock provided by the *moran* are killed on each of the next four mornings: if there are rather few or rather many *moran*, this period may be adjusted to two or six mornings. Each segment should provide a certain number of stock on each day. When there are a number of closely related *moran* (ideally about four), they provide their oxen for slaughter on successive days according to their relative seniority. On each morning within the clan as a whole, there is a somewhat half-hearted attempt to kill the beasts in the order of segmental seniority of the providers: adherence to this principle in the first killings generally gives way later on to a more random series of killings. These killings take place in the bush and while the carcasses are being cut up and divided between the various status groups in a prescribed way on the first morning, some of the *moran* build their *ilmugit* enclosure where they eat their meat and, if they like, sleep at night. The elders take away their portions to eat elsewhere in the bush, and then the women collect the remainder and take it to the settlement.

The first *ilmugit* ceremony marks the point at which the initiates actually become junior *moran* and usually takes place one month after their circumcision. This is called the *ilmugit of the arrows* (*ilmugit lolbaa*) or the *ilmugit of the birds* (*ilmugit lenkweeni*) because the initiates take off their head-dresses (of feathered carcasses) and throw away their arrows after performing the ceremony. Two *moran*, either more senior ones of this age-set or of the preceding one, are chosen for each initiate and they help him to perform the ceremony (again, if an initiate had flinched no *moran* would agree to take on this role and two elders would be chosen). They kill his *ilmugit* ox for him, cut it up and cook it. On this occasion, the *ilmugit* enclosure is built larger than usual and all the initiates have their own fires arranged in a circle according to their relative segmental seniorities (cf. the huts in the settlement). Fat from the underside of the carcass (*nkiyu*) is used in a small but elaborate ceremony to form a relationship between the initiate and his two *moran* helpers, and from this moment they address each other as *nkiyu*, and have reciprocal powers of moral coercion similar to bond brothers. Finally, amid shouting and encouragement, the initiate breaks a hip-bone of the carcass with one blow of his knobkerrie (if possible) and takes one-half of this to his mother accompanied by both his *nkiyu*. This constitutes a vow not to eat meat seen by any married woman so long as he is a *moran*, least of all by his own mother. Such meat is known as *menong* (*a-men*=to despise). He is now a *moran* and for the first time in his life he may put red ochre on his head.

The next ceremony is the *ilmugit of the roasting sticks* (*ilmugit lowatanda*), ideally performed one month after the *ilmugit of the arrows*. During this ceremony the, *moran* are divided into two groups, left and right. Ideally brothers should belong alternately to different sides, the eldest belonging to the right. Little importance is attached to this custom other than at the time of *ilmugit* ceremonies when there are two fires in the *ilmugit* enclosure and two sets of dances, one ideally for the rights and the other for the lefts.

A more significant division in the age-set at this time is between those initiates who are fully grown (generally know as *chong' onopir*) and those who are not. These form the two senior sub-age-sets. Boys subsequently initiated in groups in this age-set form junior sub-age-sets. They perform the same series of ceremonies, although necessarily on a smaller scale as there are fewer of them: altogether these late-comers to the age-set only comprise between one-quarter and one-third of the total age-set.

For the firestick elders, the main significance of holding these two *ilmugit* ceremonies close together is that they can try to assert some control over the *moran* from the outset, especially at a time when they are likely to be somewhat high-spirited.

The *ilmugit of the name* (*ilmugit lenkarna*) follows some five years after the initiation of the age-set. It marks a point when junior *moran* are promoted to senior *moranhood*, and to emphasize its importance a further *ilmugit* ceremony is performed in the following month bearing the same name (again note the conjunction of two of these ceremonies). From this point, it is no longer unpropitious for the *moran* to beget children by circumcised women. Those whose fathers are dead can act as ceremonial guardians at the initiation of their younger brothers and sisters. But they cannot marry as yet and they have no power to influence the elders in choosing husbands for their younger sisters.

At this time, the elders of *each* phratry decide on a name for the phratry age-set of *moran* and in secret, decide to nominate a particularly mature member of it as the *ritual leader* (*launon*). During the ceremony, the elders indicate their choice to some of the more influential *moran* and, unsuspecting, the encumbent is seized, made to wear a girl's apron (common in Samburu ritual) and taken to his mother's hut. There he is held down by force until he is prepared to accept office. He is not obliged to resist, but may do so for hours or even days before he agrees. His struggle is associated with the fact that in the prime of his *moranhood* he is expected in certain respects to settle down to a premature elderhood and thereby is to some extent cut off from his age mates. He should not be involved in any affray or dispute within his phratry age-set and should generally absent himself from any conversation or behaviour that contravene the ideal norms of the society. The son of a ritual leader cannot himself become a future ritual leader.

At this time also, a deputy ritual leader (*labarnkeene*) is chosen, although he is far less important. He is generally given custody of a (lesser kudu) horn belonging to the phratry. For most phratries these two offices are linked with certain sub-clans from which they are invariably, or usually, or alternately chosen. Sometimes, the custodianship of the horn may belong to some other clan of the phratry, in which case a member of each successive age-set of *moran* is elected as its custodian. This horn is blown at times of emergency or to call the Club to a meeting.

Once the ritual leader has accepted his office, he leaves his mother's hut and leads the other *moran* in killing his *ilmugit* ox. This is a signal for his phratry age mates gathered in other parts of the district that they too can perform this ceremony now that they have a ritual leader. He subsequently tours the country accompanied by others of his Club, and uses his powers of coercion over his phratry age-set to build up at once a herd of perhaps forty female cattle. The burden of providing these animals would be divided evenly among the eldest and most senior (segmentally) *moran* of the various lineage groups of his phratry. In this way the ritual leader's herd is a combined herd of the whole phratry age-set and he is expected to apply himself to their well-being rather than dissipate his energies with the other *moran*. This collection of cattle may be repeated after subsequent *ilmugit* ceremonies and at his marriage.

The ritual leader holds a powerful curse over his phratry age-set, and his life is sacrosanct to them until his marriage. He is closely associated with the name chosen for the phratry age-set at the *ilmugit of the name*. If he wishes to curse them, then he does so with reference to this name. If he dies before his marriage, then all his phratry age mates would shave their hair, a new ritual leader and name would be chosen, and a new *ilmugit of the name* would be performed.

Perhaps six years after the *ilmugit of the name*, the *ilmugit of the bull* (*ilmugit lolaingoni*) is performed. This is the second most important ceremony and marks the point at which the ritual leader and then after him his phratry age mates may marry. No further initiations should now take place into this age-set, although it is unlikely that there will have been any for a number of years prior to it. At this ceremony, the ritual leader provides a bull from his herd which he and his Club suffocate inside the settlement.

The marriage of the ritual leader is accompanied by coercion in which he is aided by others of his phratry age-set. His relationship and that of his wife with his phratry age-set is similar to that of a senior generation in the system of alternations.

From this moment there is no precise point at which the *moran* retire to elderhood: the marriage of their ritual leader, the initiation of a new age-set and their own marriages are all stages in this process. A *moran* who wishes to marry before his ritual leader may do so by presenting him with a heifer. The final ceremony is the *ilmugit of the milk and leaves* (*ilmugit lekule e mbene*), which is only performed after the ritual leader and the majority of his phratry age-set have married. On the evening before the first oxen are killed, the elders give the *moran* a final blessing inside the elders' enclosure. Each *moran* brings some milk and a cowhide, and these hides are placed round the inside of the enclosure in order of segmental seniority. The elders bless the *moran* and they all drink milk together.

Perhaps the most decisive point when a *moran* can be said to become an elder is when he calls the elders of his clan living locally to bless him and his wife and to lift the food restrictions which he still observes as a *moran*, even with regard to his own wife (as a married woman). Once he no longer observes these restrictions, he is likely to shave off his plaited hair, if he has not already done so.

Prior to this point, the firestick elders may decide to hold other *ilmugit* ceremonies. These are calculated to instil the *moran* with a sense of respect at times when they are liable to become unruly, and to fend off misfortune which may appear to have afflicted a particular Club. These ceremonies may be called respectively, the *ilmugit of the goat-madness* (*ilmugit lenshakera*) and the *ilmugit of the smell of roasting meat* (*ilmugit lesekea*).

Once again, it becomes apparent that a particular stage in the life cycle, this time moranhood, is rich in ceremonial activity. However, one major difference as compared with ceremonies associated with birth and infancy is the extent to which those of moranhood are essentially collective ceremonies.

The Moran

These ceremonies become rather more intelligible when they are related to the social position of the *moran*. Structurally, and in certain respects socially, the *moran* are segregated from the remainder of the society. In their values and behaviour they tend towards a form of delinquency which contrasts with the ideals of peace and harmony expressed by the elders. In the mid-twentieth century, the extent to which the *moran* appear to subscribe towards warriorhood and warrior-like values must seem somewhat archaic. Indeed, it may be asked why should the institution of *moranhood* have survived when the need for a standing army is no longer present? The answer is to be found in their wider society.

Polygamy and the increasing prosperity of each family unit as it matures are two related ideals of Samburu elders: without a growing family and by implication an increasing herd, no stock owner can hope to attain the position among his clansmen where they are more dependent on him than he is on them. With a growing family and herd, an elder can hope to increase his prestige and, if he is politically minded, his general influence. However, this must depend normally on his ability to marry more than once, and as is evident from Chart 9, p. 74), polygamy among the Samburu is largely dependent on the delayed age of marriage of the men, and so the institution of *moranhood* supports and is supported by these values. It is not that the elders subscribe to the delinquency as such, but rather that in subscribing to their own ideals of polygamy and prestige they subscribe to the institution of *moranhood;* and in cutting off young men from the remainder of the society for a period of up to fifteen years, they place them in a social vacuum within which delinquency is always possible.

A recurrent feature of the *ilmugit* ceremonies in particular is that they specifically relate the *moran* to the wider society. Their mothers must build their huts in a certain order, the firestick elders lead the others in conducting the ceremony, and all persons in different categories including boys and girls have specific cuts from the *ilmugit* oxen. The *moran* are apart from the remainder of the society in their *ilmugit* enclosure, and yet they are linked to the society in a ritually defined way. The whole ceremony and its associated harangues tends to be conducted by the elders in a spirit of keeping the *moran* at a distance while not letting them get too far out of hand. This expresses the whole position of the *moran* in the wider society.

Ilmugit ceremonies are, however, only a periodic climax of the ritual position of the *moran*. They remain under ritual as well as social restrictions until the time that they marry and settle down: no *moran* should eat meat seen by a married woman, drink milk from the cattle of his mistress's hair-sharing group, drink milk when not accompanied by other *moran*, drink any form of alcohol, or associate with married women. These prohibitions are in part ritual and in part social. At one extreme, for instance, one has the belief that no *moran* should die inside a settlement: this would lead to mystical misfortune. At the other extreme, one has the highly practical and social expectation that the *moran* should generally avoid married women and so have fewer opportunities to commit adultery with them: a major concern of the elders. Between these two extremes other expectations have both social and ritual implications: the more mature the *moran* and the more serious the breach, the more expected some form of misfortune.

Clans tend to be more or less dispersed according to the season of the year. The extent to which the *moran* can free themselves of the duties of herding, especially in the wet season enables them to detach themselves from their families and join their clansmen elsewhere, especially where there is a local concentration of other *moran* or of girls. Thus during the wet season local clan clusters tend to be either denuded of their *moran* populations or to be a centre of attraction for *moran*.

A particular feature of *moranhood* is the extent to which *moran* associate with age mates of their own Club (i.e. clan), both in their performance of *ilmugit* ceremonies and at all other times. Uncircumcised girls of the clan are brought into their Club activities, especially their dances, and they jealously try to keep these girls from the advances of *moran* of other Clubs; outside seductions of these girls are a recurrent cause of affrays between Clubs.

When a *moran* wishes to form an attachment with a girl, he does so with one of his own clan and becomes her lover and protector whose honour (not to say that of the other *moran* of his lineage group or clan) is bound up with her fidelity to him. However, as they are normally of the same exogamus clan, they may not marry. The Samburu disapprove of the few instances where marriage between lovers has been permitted, since their intimate relationship would engender disrespect in a marriage where the husband should be in a more dominating position enabling him to make all final decisions from matters of migration to the alienation of stock from the wife's alloted herd. The consequences of pregnancy for lovers is not so harsh as among the Rendille; however, the *moran* would not be allowed to play a major part in any of the *ilmugit* ceremonies while the girl might not be eagerly sought after as a wife.

Warfare among the Samburu

As with the Rendille, it would be true to say that Samburu customs associated with warfare are not necessarily dead but dormant. At the same time as the Samburu retain the institution of *moranhood*, they still retain the diffuse expectation for their young men to be warriors in spirit if not in deed. Most of these young men are sufficiently well acquainted with the past customs of warfare to be able to recite them in greater detail than some of the other customs which are still very much alive in Samburu society but outside their immediate sphere of interest.

The Samburu *moran* had a rather different attitude to warfare from the Rendille. They could more easily replace lost herds, and so they tended to prize their own skins above those of their cattle. Their defensive warfare was essentially unspirited, and unlike the Rendille they did not build up a reputation as fierce defensive fighters: at the sight of an overwhelmingly superior enemy, they would leave for the hills, taking with them as many cattle as possible. They argued that if they lost their cattle in a raid but did not suffer heavy casualities, then at least they were in a position to recapture their stock in a counter-raid or to build up their own herds through careful management.

The Samburu preferred to fight on their own terms, and this implied raiding by surprise attacks or ambush: an open fight would be less certain of success. *Moran* would carry two spears and a shield, or at least one spear and a bow. (When elders accompanied them, they would often carry bows.) A man with two spears would only throw one: he would then try to retrieve it and defend himself with the other. The shields were much smaller and lighter than the better-known Masai type, and this enabled the *moran* to travel greater distances with more speed when necessary.

In general, these raids seem to have been small semi-organized skirmishes rather than highly organized attacks. Traditionally the tribe was not organized for carrying out large-scale raids. One effect of this seems to be that the Samburu did not suffer heavy casualties as a result of any specific raid, but it also meant that they were not a serious contender for power when faced with more organized tribes such as the Laikipiak at their height or the Purko Masai.

Before going on a raid, the *moran* would consult the elders and possibly a local diviner (*laibon*) and recruit others, largely from their own clans, dancing at the various settlements. Those *moran* who remained behind and girls with lovers on the raiding party would not shave their heads or put on fresh red ochre while the party was away.

On leaving their settlements and again on first sighting the enemy, a *moran* might call out the personal name of his own father: if he then showed any cowardice, the whole lineage would be dishonoured, since implicitly he had vowed to associate his deeds with their accumulated honour. A man who succeeded in killing an enemy would slit the victim's stomach on the right side, and lay him on his right side with arms and legs bent and together. He would take the ornaments of the dead man. Only if he had observed this would he perform the subsequent customs. He would mark the right-side of his forehead and his right arm and leg with chalk, he would abstain from milk, and at every Samburu settlement on his way home he would sing the Samburu version of the Rendille song, *meraat*, and the women and girls would tuck grass into the top of his loin-cloth. On reaching his home, the wives and girls, led by his own mistress, would put their beads around his neck. For one month he would 'have *meraat*', wearing these beads, abstaining from milk and singing *meraat*. During this period, it would be unpropitious for him to run away from the enemy or to be killed. If, therefore, the enemy was known to be in the vicinity, he would be encouraged to perform the final part of the ritual and to return to a normal state as soon as possible. This could be done by killing a billy-goat and returning the beads to the women. In killing the goat he would form a ritual relationship with another man and they would call each other *mugus* with reciprocal powers of moral coercion over each other. One thigh bone of the goat would be broken and the killer would carry one half of it to his mother's hut and present it to her. The remainder would be eaten by men and by boys. The skin of the goat would then be tied round the killer's own wooden milk bottle and only those who had also killed in warfare would be allowed to drink from it. The close similarities of this custom to the *ilmugit of the arrows* are quite unmistakable: both killer and initiate are under strict ritual prohibitions and it would be unpropitious for the tribe if either of them were killed; the *mugus* relationship ending the period of ritual danger and prohibition is identical in many details to the *nkiyu* relationship ending the period of initiation; in each case a broken thigh bone of a ritually slaughtered animal is presented to the mother; and both changes in status deeply involve personal and family honour, and focus on the courage of the individual.

When an enemy was attacked by several *moran*, it was the first to draw blood and not the man who actually killed him who could have *meraat*.

A principal aim of raiding besides actually killing, was the acquisition of cattle. Any herds captured jointly would be divided among the *moran* according to how each had contributed towards the success of the raid. Thus, on returning home, the spoils brought by each member of the party indicated to others how well he had performed in the raid. He would be expected to give a portion of his gains to various senior kinsmen.

The Merisho were the last age-set to go on raids following the traditional pattern. However, in a minor way, the Kiliako age-set killed a number of men in skirmishes and had *meraat*. The custom has since fallen into disuse, even among those who as a result of periodic border incidents would be entitled to perform it.

Unlike the Rendille, the Samburu did not castrate their victims, except under certain circumstances. The first was to take back the genitals as proof when an unaccompanied *moran* killed an enemy. The second was when there were Rendille present on the raid; the Samburu *moran* had no intention of allowing these Rendille to castrate corpses which they, the Samburu, had killed, or to return home with their trophies as a proof of deeds which they had never accomplished. Quite apart from the incongruity of the situation, the Samburu were apprehensive that for two men to claim and perform *meraat* for one killing would be unpropitious. They would therefore take the genitals of their own victims and hide them in some place that no Rendille was likely to discover.

Samburu Moran and Rendille Youths: a Comparison

A number of distinct differences emerge from a comparison between the Samburu *moran* and the Rendille youths. Among the
Rendille, the boundaries between boys and youths and between
youths and elders are less clear-cut than between Samburu age
grades. The youths are not regarded as rigidly separated from the
remainder of the society and no special prohibitions govern their
behaviour. They are, it is true, confined for long periods to camel
camps, but in this they are no different from uncircumcised boys.
The sanctions imposed on these youths are primarily economic as
well as social, whereas the sanctions imposed on the Samburu
moran are primarily ritual as well as social. The ceremonial activity
of the *moran* constantly emphasizes their structural relationship
to and separation from the remainder of the society, whereas apart
from the circumcision and *galgulumi* ceremonies, the ceremonial
activities of the Rendille youths are largely and often wholly confined to their age-set without entailing any form of participation
by other sectors of the society. At the same time, the Rendille youths
are not segregated from the remainder of the society by food prohibitions or any other kind of ritual constraint.

In former times of warfare, fighting among the Samburu was
primarily associated with *moranhood* and this was an important
reason for maintaining an overlap between successive age-sets
within the *moran* age grade, so that there could always be a standing army. It is true that Rendille youths were also the principal
warriors of their tribe, but there was a greater emphasis on defensive
fighting, and in this boys and young elders would participate to a
greater extent than among the Samburu. Consequently the two- or
three-year gap when there were no youths between the *naapo* of
one age-set and the circumcision of the next did not imply that the
tribe was defenceless.

The Rendille youths do not have a Club system comparable with
that of the Samburu *moran*. In so far as they have mistresses, these
belong to other Rendille clans and hence settlements. This essentially private arrangement between lovers takes second place to the
economic realities of the society. The youths spend so much of their
time either in their camps in the remoter areas or with their own
settlement and clan that they have only occasional opportunities
for meeting their mistresses. According to the Rendille, it may
only be possible for a youth to free himself from other duties to
arrange clandestine meetings with his mistress on a few occasions
in any year; and even then he will often (especially in the past)

avoid full intercourse because of the severe consequences of pregnancy.

To the Samburu *moran*, this restrained behaviour in premarital affairs seems prudish and almost sexless. The consequences of conception are serious, but not so serious as among the Rendille. In so much as they may encourage some degree of continence in their relations with girls, they also serve to encourage discreet sexual licence with the wives of elders for whom child-birth is desirable.[4] To the Rendille youths, on the other hand, such behaviour shows an immature lack of self-control, and the Samburu *moran* are seen to spend their time searching for girls, flirting with their mistresses, seducing married women, and talk-talk-talk about sex, when they could more profitably be looking after their cattle properly. It is an attitude consistent with the Rendille emphasis on the economic hazards of their camel economy, and the greater constraint to which they are subjected from an early age.

In one respect, the Rendille youths are more secure in their relationships with their mistresses than the Samburu *moran*. Each age-set marries in a body before the circumcision of the next age-set. Consequently, in the main, there are no further demands for wives until the next age-set in its turn settles down. As a result, the Rendille youths are spared the constant irritation facing the Samburu *moran* of having their mistresses taken away from them against their will by the elders. There is a custom observed by both tribes that when a mistress is married, her lover and his closer (Club) friends come to sing a song cursing the groom and the bride's family for giving her away. It may be significant that among the Samburu where such marriages are common, this amounts to little more than a show of hostility and disrespect for the elders, and a release of frustration. Among the Rendille, however, where such marriages are rare, the song is far more elaborate, each clan has its own version and there is a recognized means whereby the bride-groom should avoid the effects of this curse by offering the frustrated lover a heifer-camel (p. 56).

It is worth noting that the arguments put forward by the Samburu against marriages between lovers are not necessarily valid among the Rendille. Rendille lovers are not the same clan and hence the marriage would conform with the rules of exogamy; youths are on less intimate terms with their mistresses and hence a degree of respect could be maintained between them; and marriages are not

4. The Samburu *moran* have a sublime faith in their tenet that conception can be generally avoided by avoiding intercourse during the two or three days after menstruation. At the time of study, there was no evidence to suggest that the recent spread of venereal disease (gonorrhea) was a serious deterrent for the activities of the *moran*.

subject to the same severe strains since the Rendille do not exploit any herd allotted to their wives, and so again there can be more respect between them. Nevertheless, this is not a preferred form of marriage: as with the Samburu, the honour of the lover is closely bound to the fidelity of his mistress and there is an element of prestige and personal involvement that is somehow held to be incompatible with the ideals of marriage. In a sample of fifty-seven Rendille elders, only two had in fact married their former mistresses.

The absence of the Club system appears to be largely responsible for fewer affrays among the Rendille youths. Even so, inter-clan fights do occur between youths as was reported in 1927–8 between Lokumai (Ariaal) and Orare (Saali) when three youths were killed. At this point, the elders of both clans entered the dispute to ally themselves with their kinsmen. Inter-clan affrays are far more common among the Samburu, but it may be a significant difference between the two societies that in all the Samburu incidents I have recorded, the elders intervened to restore peace rather than to prolong the feud: the *moran* are a category apart from the remainder of the society, and their affrays tend to be regarded as something that should not extend outside their Clubs. An elder may be personally infuriated by an attack on his own son, but the other elders prevail upon him to join them in arriving at a peaceful solution. It may be that collective pressures among the Rendille under similar circumstances are less strong.

The Rendille are essentially monogamous and do not have to accommodate so large a portion of unmarried young men as the Samburu. As was noted in Chart 9, the modifications of the age-set system among the Rendille are consistent with this greater emphasis on monogamy. Their age-set system does not engender a delinquent set of young men, and the firestick relationship, though it does exist, is far less important. On the other hand, this same system among the Samburu is largely responsible for diverting certain strains which might otherwise disrupt the family, and in this respect, the Samburu have an advantage over the Rendille.

Preparations for Marriage

From the time of the *ilmugit* of the bull ceremony, the *moran* may begin to marry but there is no widespread move to settle down at once as with the Rendille. By the time the next age-set is initiated, perhaps three years later, only a small proportion of *moran* will have obtained wives, although a rather larger number will at least have made some effort to build up their herds and negotiate a marriage. Most of them act under the instructions of their fathers or guardians, who may even take a hand in negotiating for the marriage personally: the *moran* are generally felt to be too inexperienced to handle such matters.

There are two principal reasons for this delay. In the first place, there are a number of relatively young *moran* in their early twenties who, until they are replaced by the new age-set still prefer to remain as *moran* rather than face new responsibilities and (at first) a less convivial social life. Secondly, there is considerable competition for wives: the high premium on polygamy means that *moran* are not simply competing with other *moran* for their first wives, but also with elders who are looking for their second and third wives. Regardless of the ideal for any girl to be a man's first wife, her kinsmen may be more attracted to the prospect of her becoming a junior wife to a known rich and worthy man than a first wife to an unknown and possibly unworthy *moran*. So long as there are a number of suitors asking for a particular girl, her kinsmen can afford to take their time in choosing, and their choice is likely to be a compromise between a number of conflicting opinions expressed by members of the clan in different parts of the district. Inevitably with the distances involved, it must take time to arrive at a consensus. During this time, no suitor would approach any other family for an alternative bride: to do so would be taken to imply gross disrespect by both families.

Consent for the compromise suitor in any marriage must be unanimous, and this goes far beyond the immediate lineage group of the courted girl. Every elder of her father's phratry or age-set, of her mother's phratry, or any elder linked through some form of brotherhood to her family can refuse her in marriage by threatening to curse her future children. (These are, in fact, precisely the elders who cannot themselves marry her.) This is an accepted and effective hold that the elders have over *moran* (and indeed over one another). Thus, if a *moran* has incensed an elder, he may find that this man can effectively veto his marriage to possibly one-half of the girls of the tribe, and if he has incensed two or three different elders, he may find that there are very few girls that he can hope to marry. Normally, the *moran* know which elders are wanting to veto their marriages, and they will try to make peace with them by offering them gifts and admitting their wrongs in the course of trying to win over the other elders. However, no elder even with a trifling grudge is obliged to withdraw his veto, no elder need give any warning of his intention to obstruct a marriage before the day of the ceremony itself, and a man with a grudge can, if he wishes, retain it for the remainder of his life and obstruct as many attempted marriages as feasible.

A suitor whose marriage is blocked in some way may in the last resort be helped by members of his clan to obtain a wife. In *marriage by coercion (siamu)*, elders of his clan go to the settlement of the prospective bride and sit outside refusing to enter or to accept food until her father, usually under pressure from his own clansmen, allows the marriage. So long as the suitor's party observe these restrictions, this amounts to an unvoiced curse which should be heeded. In *marriage by fait accompli (nkunon)*, the suitor and some accomplices in effect perform some of the earlier features of the marriage ceremony to a point at which it is considered unpropitious not to allow them to complete it and take away the bride. They do this by forcing their way at night into a settlement where there is a circumcised girl (the bride-to-be), killing one of their own oxen (the marriage-ox), and driving a sheep into her mother's hut. The first type of forced marriage relies on a curse and is the way of the elders; the second relies on force and tends more to be the way of the *moran*. For this reason, the Samburu prefer to delay the circumcision of their daughters until the time of the wedding itself so as to avoid the second irregular form of marriage.

There are a number of occasions when a forced marriage is particularly common. The marriage of all age-set ritual leaders is by a form of coercion. Those men who have difficulty in marrying because they are physically or mentally defective or are thought by others to be unpropitious in some way may expect help from their clansmen to achieve a forced marriage if no other way is possible. If a particularly wealthy man with no close relatives dies unmarried, his clansmen may perform a forced marriage in order to marry a girl to him. The bride married on his behalf (*nkitipaashinote*) is treated like any widow: she is assigned to the care of an age-mate of the dead man's sub-clan, and her sons become members of his lineage and inherit his herds. However, they also inherit the unpropitiousness of the marriage, and may find it hard to marry except into families with a similar stigma. If, however, they manage to marry well for several successive generations then the stigma may be disregarded and possibly be eventually forgotten.

The Wedding Ceremony and Divorce

Once a particular suitor has been approved by the kinsmen of his bride-to-be, he provides some honey-beer (made by the local Dorobo) for the bride's father and his local clan group. The elders drink this and bless the engagement.

The bridewealth consists of the marriage-ox (*rukoret*), a cow and its calf (for the bride's father), a male calf, two, three, or four heifers, and a sheep (for the bride's mother). The number of heifers varies from family to family: the girl's lineage group expect a customary number and if her mother belongs to a segment of Rendille descent, then they will follow the Rendille custom of expecting a further heifer as the bride's 'mother's brothers' (q.v. p. 54).

It is the groom who decides precisely which month the marriage should take place. He indicates his intentions by asking the bride's mother to extend her hut so that the bride can be circumcised.

The circumcision itself is separate from the marriage and follows the pattern previously described except that in most marriages, the ceremony entails only this one circumcision. After it has been completed, the groom and his best man (*lchaplkera*) enter the bride's father's gate, kill the marriage-ox in front of the hut in which the bride lies (*nkaji elatim*), and tether the sheep to this hut. Her father (or guardian) then has butter put on his head and is blessed by the local clan elders. Meanwhile, the groom and his small entourage of clansmen divide up the marriage-ox. The other elders take away their portion to eat in the bush, while the party of the groom, his age mates, and all *moran* abstain. That afternoon the women hold a dance and later the *moran* also start a dance and are joined by the girls. This second set of dances is the most spectacular part of the ceremony. That evening, the groom's party and elders of the bride's local clan group meet in the circumcision hut and the bride is formally handed over. There is a prolonged discussion in which the girl is addressed and mildly harangued and the groom is reminded of his obligations to her. Next morning, he and the best man lead the bride away from her father's homestead while the other elders of all clans bless them. The party rest in a neighbouring homestead for several days until the girl is well enough to travel to her husband's settlement which may be some distance away. On arriving at his settlement, she stays for one month in the hut of his mother or senior wife, and then the other wives help her to build a hut of her own and the husband gives her her alloted herd.[5]

A modified version of the ceremony may be observed by families of Rendille descent or those who hope to avert misfortune. A 'white hut' (*nkaji naibor*) is built, collapsed, and rebuilt by women inside the settlement of the bride's father at about the time that the *moran* are holding their dance. The bride, groom, best man, and two girls sleep in it for four nights, and then wait until the new moon before leading the bride away. As soon as she arrives at the husband's settlement, she is built a hut and allotted her cattle.

*   *   *

5. For a fuller description of a Samburu marriage, see *The Samburu*, pp. 233–45.

Divorce is always possible up to the first pregnancy of the wife. From this point, however, even if it leads to a miscarriage, divorce is thought unpropitious. The remarriage of a widow would also imply a divorce from her dead husband, and for this reason would be regarded as unpropitious.

Divorce is initially a form of separation. When his wife has left him, the husband may at first demand the return of the bridewealth, but his rights over her do not end at this point. Even when she has been remarried and has borne children to her second husband, he can still assert a claim to her *and* the children. This may be done by coercion with his clansmen (again *siamu*) or simply by force. It is only when the eldest child of her second marriage has been circumcised and the father (i.e. the second husband) has been blessed by the other elders that the divorce with the first husband becomes irrevocable. During the prolonged period of separation, the outcome is indeterminate: various pressures from the clans of the first husband or of the wife may lead under different circumstances to the return of the wife or to an eventual divorce. The second husband and his clansmen have little influence in the outcome.

Samburu and Rendille Marriage: a Comparison

There are significant differences of emphasis between the Samburu and Rendille, although both subscribe to essentially the same view of marriage. As has already been noted, the implicit competition among the Rendille is not so much for wives as for suitable husbands. Elders can, and do, veto marriages of certain girls when they have a grudge against the suitor, but as a general sanction this is less likely to be effective than among the Samburu. The kinsmen of the girl have an interest in marrying her off and might try to apply pressure on a vetoer if it is not felt absolutely justified in the circumstances. Meanwhile, the suitor would find it easier to search for another bride. Altogether, as a means of social control, the practice of vetoing a man's marriage seems more aptly suited to a society in which the suitor is at an initial disadvantage. The Rendille themselves also point out that their youths tend to have more respect than the Samburu *moran*, and so it is less likely that they will have to come to terms with the elders when they wish to marry.

Be this as it may, there is another factor that could also account for the difference. This is a shift in ethos between the two societies. Both believe in the power of the curse, but the Samburu disapprove of the individual who resorts directly to it except under very dire provocation. By vetoing a marriage, a man with a grudge is simply threatening to curse, knowing fully well that proceedings will go no further. The Rendille have a more permissive attitude towards the curse, and would expect a man with a grudge to resort to it directly, the process of nurturing a grudge until such time as an adversary may choose to marry into a particular clan would seem unnecessarily devious to them in normal circumstances. This difference between the two societies is fully consistent with the general Samburu tenet that Rendille immigrants have a particularly potent curse. The Rendille are generally more tolerant of the man who openly loses his temper, and consequently more tempers appear to get lost. The Samburu are less tolerant and associate anger with an unvoiced curse. When a particular man loses his temper and will not listen to others, they may ridicule him and say: 'It was a Rendille who cut his navel!' (p. 43).

Gifts of camels between affinal kinsmen are fully prescribed by Rendille custom: the eight camels of bridewealth given by the groom are followed a generation later by two further camels from the bridewealth of each of his daughters by this marriage, while it is his affines who provide the heifer-camel given to his eldest son at circumcision. Apart from the initial bargaining at his marriage over the precise quality of these stock, there is no further question of his alienating camels to his affines. They may ceaselessly ask for small stock, but the Rendille can readily afford these. It matters less, therefore, whether or not a suitor is a particularly wealthy man in camels, and his relationship with his affines is not under constant strain.

Marriage among the Samburu is quite the contrary. The bride-wealth is small as compared with their wealth, but it is followed by ceaseless beggings for more cattle that are not prescribed by custom, and this begging is continued after the death of the husband when his affines, as mother's brothers, have predatory claims on the herds of his sons. For this reason it *does* matter to the Samburu whether the suitor is (or is likely to become) wealthy in cattle, and the relationship between affines (or with maternal kins-men) is one of mistrust and, on the whole, avoidance.

The marriage ceremony itself is notably more elaborate among the Rendille, lasting for some eight days. Whether or not this is related in some way to a greater importance of each individual marriage is hard to say. Certainly, the emphasis in the Samburu ceremony is, to a large extent, on the circumcision of the bride which could take place without her being married on this occasion. Her circumcision follows the same pattern as that of her brothers, and they should be circumcised in exact order of birth. The parallel is extended to her marriage which is sometimes compared with the boy's first *ilmugit* ceremony when he becomes a *moran*: the best man (*lchaplkera*) is her *nkiyu* (who kills the *ilmugit* ox) and has a special relationship with her; the marriage-ox that is killed is the *ilmugit* ox killed for the initiate; the new duties laid on her are the new prohibitions laid on the *moran*, and so on. The Rendille do not circumcise in strict order of birth and do not point out these parallels. They are more concerned with the marriage than with the circumcision; as an essentially monogamous society, the occasion is as unique for the husband as it is for the bride. Their principal concern is the birth and rearing of their eldest son, as compared with the Samburu who have a more diffuse ideal to raise a large family by a number of wives. The Rendille regard the Samburu attitude towards marriage as almost casual, and they have a disdain for the lack of respect shown by their wives: it is held that to marry a Samburu woman as a senior wife would bring disaster to their herds. The Samburu have consistent views: they admire the Rendille for the strength of their marriages and have a high regard for Rendille women as wives: they show respect and they do not normally run away from their husbands. On the other hand, the Samburu are also aware that the Rendille will not give away any large stock to their affines after the initial bride-wealth, and so they also are not too keen that their own daughters should be married off to Rendille husbands.

These views on the relative attributes of their womenfolk as wives are consistent also with the rather different statuses of women in the two societies. Economically, Rendille women have an easier task. With their baggage camels, they can fetch enough water in one trip to satisfy all domestic requirements for up to three weeks (e.g. possibly 30 gallons). They are not expected to milk their camels and would never herd them. The Samburu view of a Rendille wife is of a woman sitting in her hut with arms folded and refusing to do any work; but the Samburu also acknowledge that this superior status of Rendille women accompanies a greater respect between husband and wife. It does not imply a competition between them or a threat to the supremacy of the elder in his own home.

Samburu women have a much harder lot. Donkeys cannot carry great loads of water and have to be taken to the water point as often as every other day. The women milk their own cattle, and within limits may be involved in some of the herding duties, especially of small stock. Admittedly, a Samburu woman is more likely than a Rendille to have a younger co-wife to help her in these tasks, but on the other hand, her daughters are married when still comparatively young, and so she is less likely to have an adult daughter to help her. The prolonged struggle between Samburu elders and their wives, associated often with competition over the allotted herd and other strains due to polygamy, leads in general to fewer shared values and to less respect between them as the husband has constantly to assert his undeniable supremacy.

This difference between the two societies is reflected in the ornaments worn by the women. The Rendille wife is characterized by her *doko* hairstyle which signifies that she has a first-born boy: this is perhaps the most characteristic adornment of the whole tribe and is worn with pride. Samburu women, on the other hand, generally keep their heads shaved, but have thick iron wire coiled round their legs. These weigh as much as eight pounds making it altogether harder for them to move around—or run away.[6]

In so far as the Samburu have a characteristic adornment which draws attention to any sector of the society, it is the red-ochred plaited hairstyle of the *moran* who are the focus of so much interest and concern. In this respect, the most conspicuous feature of each society seems to have a deeper significance.

Death and Disposal

Death is regarded as unpropitious on all occasions. There are, however, degrees of unpropitiousness: if a man has reached old age, has several wives, a large family, and a large herd, and if he dies in his homestead with his head shaved and his sons in order of seniority holding the right-hand side of his body from his head (the senior son) to his big toe (the most junior), then his death is less unpropitious than on other occasions. After he has died, fat is put in his mouth by each son in turn and he is told to eat it. His personal ornaments are covered in fat and distributed among the sons. He is then taken into the bush by the elders with his senior son still holding his head. The body is laid on its right-hand side, with arms and legs slightly bent and together, and he is placed on a hide under a tree facing neither east nor west nor in the direction of Mount Ngiro. He wears only the apron of one of his wives and his shoes are placed at his feet. The body, the apron, the shoes, and the hide are all smeared with fat. Then everyone places a sprig of greenery over him and they tell him to lie in peace. After placing the body in the bush, all his sons, his unmarried daughters, his wives, and his age mates of his hair-sharing group have their heads shaved.

It is reasonably certain that the dead man will be mauled and eaten by some carrion animal: either birds of prey in the afternoon

6. Girls in both societies wear up to eight pounds weight of brass coiled round their arms. When they marry they begin to replace this with iron coils. And as they grow older and weaker, they discard these one by one.

or a hyena at night. Those who remember him, when they pass the spot in future, may place some tobacco or greenery on it and again tell him to lie in peace. It should be emphasized, however, that the Samburu deny a positive belief in any existence after death: they simply do not know what happens. They say, 'God knows.'

When a woman dies, her body is disposed of in essentially the same way, only it is her youngest son who holds her head and only her own children who shave their heads. A child who has died is taken to the bush with even less ceremony, and a very small infant may be buried under the sleeping hides of the hut.

If a senior son is not present at his father's death, then another son takes on the duty of holding his head and later he pays his elder brother a heifer. This custom is similar to the one of paying an elder brother a heifer if the younger is circumcised or married before him: every effort would normally be made to avoid these irregularities and the reason given for the payment is that the younger brother has acted as though the elder brother were dead: the payment saves him from dying (cf. when a father is absent at the birth of his son).

When the dead man is a *moran*, an unmarried elder or a member of certain segments (mostly of the Black Cattle moiety), a further ceremony may be held. Some months or even years after the death, an ox is killed and is eaten by the elders in the bush. They then walk together and squat down four times. They go to the hut of the dead man and drink a mixture of milk and water. Before sleeping, every participant must drink some milk elsewhere or it is said he would never wake up. The ox is referred to as a 'donkey' (a not too propitious animal that would never be eaten). When this cere- mony is being performed for a dead *moran*, other *moran* would share in eating the 'donkey'.

The death of a *moran* is also associated with other customs. He should die in the bush with an age mate holding his head. Other *moran* of his hair-sharing group should shave their hair in the bush, and should not put red ochre on their heads for a month. The mistress of the dead *moran* should also avoid putting on red ochre and should throw away some of the beads he has given her as a token of their friendship.

There is a special feature at the deaths of men who have not observed the rules of phratry exogamy (this irregularity is rather common in Masula phratry although very rare elsewhere). When he dies, his wife addresses him as 'brother' instead of 'husband', and their children address him as 'mother's-brother' instead of 'father'. They do this when they place fat in his mouth, when they lay him down in the bush, and in later years when they pass the spot. According to some, instead of saying 'Father, lie in peace' and putting a green sprig over him, they snap dry twigs over him, shout 'Mother's-brother, do not harm us' and run away. If the wife predeceases the husband, then he will address her as 'sister', but her children still call her 'mother'. A senior son could not hold his 'mother's-brother's' head: this would have to be done by the son of some other wife or by an elder. But the senior son would still have full rights in inheriting the residual herd.

Homicide

The Samburu have a rather more tolerant and institutionalized attitude towards homicide than the Rendille where traditionally a homicide is a virtual outcast from the society and might even be stoned if the killing was deliberate. Unlike the Rendille, the Samburu have a custom whereby the tension that may build up after a homicide can be resolved through forming a bond brotherhood. The mystical sanctions that support this could well be a major factor in preventing feud in the society after a killing. When several Samburu are involved in a homicide, it is the man who first draws blood and not the one who actually delivers the mortal blow, who is held solely responsible (cf. killing in war).

Following a homicide, whether deliberate or accidental, all those closely related to the killer or to the deceased are obliged to observe certain rules of behaviour to avert further misfortune, and any person who actually kills the murderer in revenge is held to have the guilt of *both* killings on his shoulders and the danger is twice as great. When there is blood between two families, they avoid drinking each other's milk and do not eat red meat or drink blood in each other's company: this is observed for as long as the homicide is remembered.

A killer has what is called *loikop*, that is, he enters into a ritually unpropitious state which may bring him severe misfortune at any time throughout his life.[7] After the killing, he does not return to his own settlement, but sleeps for four days in the bush eating only meat and wearing red beads round his neck and a woman's apron. On the fifth day, he may kill a sheep or goat and rub his entire body first with its chyme and then, after washing, with its fat. He may now enter the settlement, but he continues to wear the same clothes and to avoid milk for several months until it is felt that the immediate danger of mystical retribution is past; if he drinks milk too soon then it is said he will go mad.

7. The Samburu deny that this term has any association with their own name for themselves as a tribe: *Loikop*.

The traditional method of resolving a homicide between segments is as follows. Some time after the murder, the closer kinsmen of the deceased call together members of their own clan in secret and they set out in a body to seize by force the cattle herd of the murderer, or if he is poor they may seize the herd of a close agnatic kinsman. This would be carried out during the daytime, when the herds are out grazing. These cattle, known as *ngiroi*, are quickly driven to any deserted settlement site and a fire is lit.

When the owner of the herd and his clansmen first hear of the seizure, they may want to pursue the others to fight them for their cattle, but once they arrive on the scene and see that the cattle are inside the deserted settlement with a lighted fire, then the matter should be allowed to rest. The cattle now belong to the chief inheritant of the deceased who retains a major portion for himself and gives the remainder to his closest kinsmen and to a number of those who took part in the raid.

The timing of the seizure of stock depends apparently on the strength of feeling after the homicide. If the feeling is high and likely to lead to further bloodshed, then the elders may favour a seizure as soon as practicable after the homicide. If, on the other hand, the homicide does not appear to be unduly disruptive to the relations between the two principal groups involved, they may prefer to wait for a period of three age-sets (i.e. about forty years) before seizure.

In theory any number of seizures can be made after a single homicide. The killer can only prevent this by 'paying the head' as soon as possible after the first seizure: he and a few close friends secretly take a heifer (*kero*) one night to the settlement of the dead man or his inheritor; they open his gate and drive the beast inside, calling out the name of the dead man and shouting: 'So-and-so! Take this!' and they run away in terror of any supernatural consequences of this action. This is the only time the name of a dead man is likely to be used after his death.

A bond brotherhood has now been formed between the closest kinsman of the killer and those of the deceased. This is known as *langata*, or a crossing (*a-lang*=to cross), because a tie between them has been created which their descendants will acknowledge. In order to affirm this, men from the two groups may arrange to meet at a certain spot. Each group kills a sheep and the fat of the two animals are mixed. This fat is then rubbed all over the bodies of every man and the meat is eaten. At first they do not take advantage of the privileges that this relationship gives them in using their powers of moral coercion over each other and they continue to avoid each other's milk and avoid eating red meat together, but in the course of a generation or so, the relationship is fully established and only the avoidance on blood and red meat remains. It must be emphasized that in spite of the asymmetrical character of homicide and of the seizure of bloodwealth, the subsequent relationship is absolutely symmetrical with neither party having superior rights.

Forming a bond brotherhood after a homicide only implicates small groups of people (normally fewer than the lineage group), whereas the best known bond brotherhoods involve much larger segments and have mostly been in existence for as long as the Samburu care to remember. Some Samburu are of the opinion that all bond brotherhoods must ultimately have arisen from a homicide, even although certain myths attached to them make reference to common ancestry and not to homicide. In the general absence of an intricate mythology in this society, the stories which account for the origins of some of these intersegmentary ties are a striking exception, and they emphasize to some extent the importance that the Samburu attach to these ties.

Certain modifications in these ties occur from time to time, but again there is no concrete evidence available to show when or how they do so. In one case a whole segment (Mukutai) joined quite recently the bond brotherhood which its collateral segments observed with Parasoro clan; while in another case, the bond brotherhood between Sortoi and Mosiat clans is being ignored by an increasing number of people. All the other major ties, on the other hand, have every appearance of strength and permanence, and the cases of modification are the exceptions rather than the rule.

*   *   *

If the person killed is a woman, then traditionally this custom is modified. If it is the husband who kills her, then her agnatic kinsmen seize only his small stock as bloodwealth and there is no bond brotherhood. If it is someone else who kills her then there is not even a seizure. There is no seizure when a boy or girl is killed.

Even in pre-administration times before the police took any reported homicides into their own hands, it does not seem to have been altogether certain that a homicide would lead to the seizure of bloodwealth and to bond brotherhood. The Samburu themselves emphasize that sooner or later after a homicide, bloodwealth *must* be seized, but it seems rather likely that after a lapse of about three age-sets most, if not all, the protagonists would be dead, and the general pressure in favour of a seizure would be diminished. Certainly, I found very few memories of outstanding blood debts that dated to a period of three age-sets before my visit to the area.

Much seems to have depended on the climate of opinion: if the killing was accidental then there might be no payment, whereas if it was intentional and gave rise to a growing tension between the parties involved then the elders would approve of a quick payment. Unfortunately, there is too little case material available to reach any clear understanding. Seizures are still made from time to time when the homicide has not been in the hands of the police, and these serve to keep the tradition alive. But the intrusion of new laws and new forms of punishment coupled to an elaborate set of procedures has tended to leave the Samburu rather uncertain as to the aptness of their own customs in this matter.

When, in the past, the murder was too cold-blooded and detestable for even the clansmen of the murderer to tolerate, as for instance in a case of deliberate and cold-blooded fratricide, then the killer might be lynched by stoning. Each elder would conceal a large stone in his cloth and the murderer, unaware of their intentions, would be called to where they were debating. Then at a given signal, they would all stone him. No one would know who had actually killed him and all would share in the guilt. This was known as *lbubuu*.

IV. Samburu Religious Beliefs, and Customs Associated with Various Lineages

Religious Beliefs

The emphasis in Samburu ceremony is on the practice rather than its associated belief. To do certain things and to omit to do others, especially in a ceremonial context, are held to be unpropitious and likely to bring misfortune (*kotolo*). But this is as far as most Samburu are prepared to go: they offer no elaborate symbolic interpretation of the ceremonies. Basically, they admit to believing in one God (*Nkai*) but at other times they refer to God as a collection of guardian spirits. 'There is no one that has not got his guardian spirit (*nkai*),' they say. Men, animals, age-sets, phratries, rocks, trees, or mountains—each are an entity in themselves and have a guardian spirit. If God (or the spirit world) hates some action or some thing, then it will bring misfortune. There is a divine order of the universe of which the Samburu feel they have an incomplete knowledge. The moral order of their society, their ceremonial activities and avoidances are geared towards what they hope to be an optimum mode of existence protecting them from misfortune. The fact that other tribes have their own quite different customs is irrelevant: as tribes, they would have their own guardian spirit world/God, and hence their own divine and moral order.

Thus a misfortune is taken to follow from some unpropitious action (hated by the guardian spirit) or contact with an unpropitious object or person[8] (which may have a malicious guardian spirit). To avert further misfortune, there may be an attempt to modify custom, such as by building a 'white hut' at marriage, growing hair after a birth, or changing the time of circumcision from morning to evening. Thus the diagnosis of mystical misfortune leads to a ritual prescription to avert further misfortune; and the search towards an optimum ritual code is constantly pursued.

A central feature of the intercourse between the world of the guardian spirits and the world of human beings is the power of the blessing and of the curse. This power is accentuated in certain roles (firestick elders, bond brothers, mothers' brothers, ritual leaders, etc.), and this is seen as accentuating the divine sanction behind the moral order of Samburu society. In Samburu eyes, any man is normally under the propitious protection of his own guardian spirit. If some other Samburu blesses him, then the guardian spirit of the blesser will join to give him added protection. If, on the other hand, he is justifiably cursed, then his own guardian spirit will abandon him to his fate while the guardian spirit of the curser will try to destroy him (or his wives or children or cattle). He is now in a ritually unpropitious state and has *ng'oki*.

It is in the context of these religious beliefs that one can best appreciate the customs associated with various lineages.

Special Powers Associated with Various Samburu Lineages

(a) *Ritual Specialists* (s. *kursa*, pl. *kursai*). Ritual specialists have an accumulated knowledge which enables them to assess whether certain objects or acts are ritually propitious or unpropitious. It is a knowledge which is thought ultimately to derive from the *Boran* tribe. While it is normally handed down from father to son, it may also be acquired by any man who cares to live long enough with another ritual specialist.

Ritual specialists know how to interpret the position of the brighter planets, the shapes of clouds, the arrangement of blood vessels on the mesentery of a slaughtered animal, the bayings of a hyena, the markings on a cow, erratic behaviour in domestic or wild animals, and so on. They can assess whether a particular human action is likely to bring misfortune and how this might be ritually avoided. They are expert in ceremonial detail. Only the ritual specialists have the wisdom to discern the effects that natural phenomena will have on human destiny and fortune. Through their knowledge,

8. For unpropitiously born persons, see p. 83 above.

they perceive better than others the divine order of the universe.

Valuable as this knowledge may seem, there is no general desire to acquire the insight of ritual specialists. They have a certain diffuse prestige in the tribe, but it is said that they never build up large herds. A reason given for this is that a ritual specialist knows which of his own cattle are unpropitious from their markings, and because these cattle know that he knows, they curse him. On the whole, the Samburu prefer not to know which of their stock are unpropitious, and they may warn visiting ritual specialists not to tell them. If, on the other hand, they have been suffering misfortune, then they may ask advice from a ritual specialist who may point to an unpropitious animal, or a neglected custom, or a dangerous innovation, and suggest a remedy.

The Rendille appear to have less influential ritual specialists: those that they have are expert on relatively minor matters. This is of particular significance in the concurrence of the two age-set systems. The Rendille wait for the Samburu to initiate a new age-set, and the Samburu rely on the opinion of certain influential ritual specialists who can interpret the stars. Thus, in a sense, the fact that the Samburu take the initiative in the periodic turnover of the age-set systems of the two tribes is seen partly to hinge on the fact that they have the relevant ritual specialists for this.

(b) *Diviners* (s. *laibon* pl. *laibonok*) *and Sorcerers* (s. *lairuponi* pl. *lairupok*). Diviners have much in common with ritual specialists: they have an esoteric knowledge usually handed down to them by their fathers; they may be approached by individual Samburu who have suffered misfortune; and they may, for instance, diagnose the causes of barrenness in wives or in cattle. The differences, however, are significant. The ritual specialist relies entirely on his acquired wisdom and insight whereas there is an additional mystical aura surrounding the diviner which permits him to delve deeper into mystery. As the Samburu see it, he has a more intimate relationship with his guardian spirit that gives him a rather different type of insight. Thus, while a ritual specialist can see from the markings on a cow that it is unpropitious and will bring misfortune, a diviner can see when a man has been cursed although outwardly he looks no different from other men; a ritual specialist can interpret natural phenomena to discern the propitious and the unpropitious, whereas a diviner can go one step further and interpret the pattern of a group of objects that he has himself strewn to predict the future; or again a ritual specialist may only advise other Samburu on a propitious ritual course of action, whereas a diviner may perform the ceremony himself, and it is understood that the same ceremony performed by others would not necessarily have the desired effect. Ritual specialists are like other Samburu, and when they sleep, any dream they have does not normally have any deeper significance: it is just a dream. Diviners, on the other hand, are not quite the same, and when they dream, they may be looking into the future or into some distant part of the country. It is largely through their dreams and trances that they communicate with their guardian spirits. Ritual specialists are human; diviners are not just human.

Structurally, the significant difference between the ritual specialists and the diviners is that the former are an integral part of the tribe, and the knowledge of their wisdom gives the Samburu an added confidence in their ceremonial activities: in timing the change-over of the age-sets, they rely heavily on the opinion of the ritual specialists. The latter, on the other hand, are not in any sense an integral part of the society, and on the whole, the Samburu would prefer to be without any intruders from other tribes who claim to be diviners.

The popular faith in the insight of diviners in principle differs from the faith in the competence of individual diviners in practice. The Samburu are prepared to admit that the Masai and perhaps the Nandi tribes had powerful diviners (*laibonok*) whose ability gave them a wide political influence. Their own diviners, however, are not normally remembered for having given especially reliable advice in times of war. Those that have been trusted appear to have played down their powers as diviners and to have relied as much on their wisdom as elders.

In one respect, however, the Samburu are prepared to accept the power of diviners: this is the power shared by all sorcerers of knowing good and bad medicines or charms, and being able to cast good or bad spells. Ostensibly, diviners would only claim to work for the good of society, but they may be mistrusted when it comes to handling their own personal grievances or accepting bribes from other Samburu who wish to resort to sorcery.

In order to protect themselves from possible sorcery, the Samburu are careful in the way they preserve or dispose of certain articles. These tend to be ritually associated with the life cycle of the individual that might be harmed: the *morr* killed at a child's birth, the leather belt worn by its mother, the shoes worn by a bride at her wedding, the hide of the marriage ox, the hide of an ox killed at the *ilmugit* of the arrows, etc. Each of these are articles associated with 'life' which, the Samburu assume, a sorcerer could use. The long hair of a *moran* is an interesting example: if it is shaved off under propitious circumstances, then it should be protected from sorcery by only throwing it away in flowing water; if, on the other hand, another *moran* of the same hair-sharing group dies, then this hair is thought to be already 'dead' and is shaved and thrown away in the bush. Because it is 'dead' it could bring its owner misfortune if he continued to wear it; and also because it is 'dead', a sorcerer could not make use of it. Similarly, in cases of death, all the ritual articles that might otherwise be carefully handled would now be thrown away in the bush: they have lost their 'living' properties and are now 'dead' and in themselves unpropitious.

The Samburu are not unduly concerned with sorcery. They see these precautions as sensible, but do not pursue the matter further. Apart from certain suspect diviners, they do not believe that they have any sorcerers: the main centres of sorcery are among the Tiamus tribe of Lake Baringo and among the Dorobo tribes. When they visit these tribes, then they *are* concerned about sorcery and do not prolong their visits; but among themselves they assume that their curse is stronger than any man's sorcery. If a Samburu or a diviner was known to use malicious charms, then the elders would curse him collectively, and the curse was expected to have the more potent and immediate effect.

(c) *Laisi* (s. *lais*) *and witches* (s. *nakapelani* pl. *nkapelak*). *Laisi* is the Samburu term for the Rendille *iipire*: those families with an unusually potent curse. All Samburu *laisi* claim descent from Rendille *iipire*, and maintain their power by performing the same ceremonies each new moon and at the birth of each son (p. 62). There is, however, a shift in attitude towards *laisi*: it was noted that the Rendille have an ambivalent attitude towards *iipire*, since they enjoy a certain social immunity despite their unpropitious associations. The Samburu for their part, have a less ambivalent attitude. They regard most *laisi* as essentially unpropitious to the society although they tolerate them. As has already been noted, the ethos in the society is against the direct use of the curse, and it is significant that a considerable proportion of Rendille immigrant *iipire* cease to practise their ceremonies and so discard their powers.

The power of a *lais* is due partly to his greater influence over his guardian spirit and partly to the greater power of the spirit itself. As with the Rendille his power to bless also is less emphasized. In so much as the Samburu are prepared to tolerate *laisi*, they point out that as friends they can bless a man who is searching for a lost cow or seeking a bride, and improve his chances of success. After the death of an infant, a woman may bear her next child in the hut of a *lais* hoping to change her luck. In so far as *laisi* are expected to avoid cursing except as a last resort, the Samburu accept immigrant Rendille *iipire* into their society.

The distinction between good and bad *laisi* is also acknowledged. This is of considerable interest, in that notoriously bad *laisi* are sometimes regarded almost as witches. Many Samburu have a reluctance about visiting the Rendille because of the enhanced power of their *laisi* (i.e. *iipire*). In the case of choosing the man-of-the-fire, this is felt to be nothing less than sorcery on the part of Dibshai clan.

However, the Samburu normally distinguish between a bad *lais* and a witch: a *lais* can only have effect when he has not been respected in some way and is thus similar to a firestick elder, for instance; a witch (*nkapelani*) on the other hand, would have effect simply if he is jealous: morally, a *lais* must be in the right to have effect, whereas a witch is morally in the wrong.

The Samburu maintain that their Turkana neighbours are ridden with witchcraft. They believe that if a hungry Turkana sees a man eating, then his jealousy will be aroused, the man will become bewitched, throw a fit, and even die. If a man does behave in this way and there are Turkana in the vicinty, then the Samburu will throw a goatskin over his head and he should involuntarily call out the witch's name. Once they know who the witch is, they will force him to throw earth at his victim who should then recover. In order to protect themselves from a suspected Turkana witch, the Samburu may put their fingers into his footprint and then on their foreheads.

The Samburu do not attempt to account for the power of witchcraft in any elaborate way: in so far as the power of witches may be associated in some way with their guardian spirits, it is emphasized that they belong to other tribes (such as the Turkana) where a different moral order and a different ethos prevail. Under these circumstances the divine order itself and its form of protection over individuals may be entirely different, and witches may be the agents of malicious guardian spirits. If it came to a direct confrontation of mystical powers between the two tribes, the Samburu are rather doubtful whether their own beneficent spirit world and its divine order would necessarily prevail over the malevolent spirit world of the Turkana: their own power to curse might not be sufficient to contain the witches. For this reason, the Samburu prefer not to mix too readily with the Turkana, nor do they wish to marry Turkana women: it is thought that the power of witchcraft can be inherited by either sex from either parent, and this could be a means of introducing it into their own society.

(d) *Totemic Relationships and Blacksmiths.* The Samburu are less specific than the Rendille as regards the totemic relationships of different lineages of *laisi*. There is the general association with poisonous snakes, but this is not elaborated to any extent. There are, on the other hand, certain lineages which do claim a totemic relationship which gives them a power to curse although they do not claim to be *laisi* and do not have any associated ceremonies. These totems include fire, thorn bushes, monkeys, elephants, snakes, various kinds of infections, and madness. An animal of a man's totemic species is addressed as *karampar* and to all intents and purposes is treated as a bond brother. In a sense, his power to curse is no stronger than that of other Samburu, but the totemic relationship gives his curse or blessing a certain pointedness: a man totemically related to eye diseases, for instance, would be more likely to induce such a disease through his curse than other Samburu, and his blessing would be more likely to cure some eye soreness.

Blacksmiths (s. *lkunon* pl. *lkunono*) are a very special example of this form of totemic relationship. The Samburu attitude towards them is quite similar to that of the Rendille, though their segregation is more extreme. Samburu blacksmiths are normally expected to live in a settlement on their own, whereas Rendille blacksmiths are dispersed among the settlements of most clans. The Samburu are very careful to avoid the food of blacksmiths, whereas the Rendille are not. The Samburu avoid sexual relations with the families of blacksmiths, whereas the Rendille do not. The Samburu would abort any child begotten in their own wives by a blacksmith, whereas the Rendille would allow such a child to live. Both societies regard the blacksmith's job as a dirty and messy one, and prefer to avoid too close a contact with them, but among the Samburu, this general notion of physical contamination amounts to a diffuse belief in ritual pollution.

A blacksmith who deliberately lays aside his craft and devotes himself entirely to cattle herding may be able to break through the caste barrier after several generations. At first his sons might find wives among other families associated with blacksmiths who do not actually practise the craft (e.g. Maraato clan), and in another two generations his descendants might be able to marry with such phratries as Masula or Pisikishu who do not show quite the same aversion for blacksmiths as the others.

As among the Rendille, the blacksmiths have a potent curse associated with iron: a man who is cursed might cut himself with a knife and the wound would fester, his cattle might die after being bled with an iron-headed arrow, or his son might die after being circumcised with an iron razor. It has already been noted that blacksmiths are circumcised before other Samburu, because their ritual power over iron is associated with the circumcision razor.

The ritual association of blacksmiths with certain aspects of

Samburu life closely parallels their practical position as an integral part of the tribe, in spite of the caste barrier that separates them from others.

Two customs associated with blacksmiths may be noted. It is believed that any man who steps over a blacksmith's fire will break his legs. If he inadvertently does this, then he should cross the fire four more times and exchange a sheep for a twisted iron armlet made by the smith. From this point he forms a special friendship with the smith, calling him *sotwa*, the term used generally with his closer friends. This is the beginning of a relationship between their two families: his wife and children should also acquire similar armlets from this smith or his sons.

Secondly, women who have lost several infants may be advised to bear their next in the hut of a blacksmith or a *laisi*: in the former case, the child would be protected from any infection from the cutting (with iron) of its umbilical cord.

There is no local supply of iron in the district, and the Samburu blacksmiths have to obtain it through various forms of external trade. In the process of fashioning spears, knives, axe-heads, arrow-heads (for bleeding cattle), cow-bells, and charms, the iron is worked in a charcoal fire by the smith, while his wife maintains its heat with hand-operated bellows. The typical cost of a large spear would be a male calf or two ewes and a lamb: a small spear would cost one ewe only. This transaction is of considerable interest in that it is the only fully indigenous form of trading in the society.

*   *   *

Thus, the Samburu see different tribes that surround them as having certain specific mystical powers. Their traditional allies to the east, the Rendille, have a more developed power of the curse which does, at least, conform with the same moral order for all its unpropitious associations. Their worst enemies to the north-west, the Turkana, have a totally antisocial power of witchcraft which the Samburu are powerless to cope with (just as they found Turkana raids overbearing). The Dorobo who have never really been their allies or their enemies and whom they do not fear militarily, have a knowledge of sorcery which can be contained by their own collective power to curse individual sorcerers (although a Samburu visiting a Dorobo group elsewhere is less certain of his ground). And the Boran, who in the past have been respected enemies of the Samburu sharing many of the conventions of warfare and other customs, are respected as ritual specialists in discerning the mystical implications of natural phenomena.

In so much as the Samburu acknowledge that some of their own people have such powers, they are thought to be derived from Rendille, or Boran or Dorobo ancestry. The majority, however, claim no special powers or insights into the supernatural. When they wish to make use of the powers of others, they tend to be influenced in part by the circumstances and in part by random factors such as whether a suitable person with an apt power and a sufficient reputation happens to be in the approximate vicinity at the appropriate time. If a man suspects that a recent misfortune is due to the presence in his herd of an unpropitious ox then he can consult a ritual specialist: if he feels that it is due to his having been cursed, bewitched, or put under a sorcerer's spell then he can consult a diviner; or if he just vaguely feels that he is dogged by something unpropitious, he may summon the elders of the locality, especially of his own clan, and after killing an ox to feed them, he may be given their collective blessing. On another occasion, if a man has lost a cow, he can ask a *lais* to bless it for him so that he will find it safe, or he can ask a diviner to divine which direction it is in. He would only offer some gift for their services when the desired effect has been attained. The Samburu assert a diffuse faith in the powers of these men in general, but they are not always wholly convinced of the infallibility of any particular individual.

(e) *Lmishin*. Since their first contact with Europeans, principally through the former administration, the Samburu have looked with interest for signs of their superiority in ritual as in all other matters. Rain-gauges are thought to predict and even influence rainfall, aeroplanes and wireless may be in more direct communication with the spirit world than the diviners. Books give a greater insight than the insight of the ritual experts. But it is, of course, from the missionary societies that the Samburu expect real ritual expertise. As yet, however, no mission has really produced anything which might impress the majority of Samburu that it is in touch with a divine order of the universe that has any direct relevance for the Samburu divine order. God (or the spirit world) has given the Europeans their moral and social order and in many ways it is to be envied; but it is less certain whether he ever intended this moral and social order to extend to the Samburu.

Notes on Samburu Phratries

The Samburu sometimes assert that phratries of the Black Cattle moiety have a closer association with Dorobo (and hence sorcerers), ritual specialists (and hence paupers), and blacksmiths, while the White Cattle moiety have a larger number of Rendille immigrants (and hence *laisi*). In fact, this is only the broadest of generalizations: it is a more accurate statement of Samburu attitudes than of actual differences between the two moieties. In the notes that follow the number of tax-payers for each phratry in 1958 is given in parentheses.[9]

The Black Cattle moiety (*ngishu narok*)

(a) *Masula phratry* (2,890). This phratry alone constitutes about two-fifths of the total Samburu population, and is recognized as the most senior ritually. While the Masula pay lip-service to Samburu values and customs, in practice they often deviate from these in a number of respects: (i) the general rule that a phratry should be exogamous is not always observed, particularly in the vicinity of Mount Ngiro. (ii) Ownership of land is altogether foreign to the Samburu, but an exception is made at Mount Ngiro which is recognized as belonging to the Masula due to their close affinity to the Dorobo there. The northern third of the mountain is shared by Ltoyio and Parsipia, the southern third by Sortoi, Kwaro, and Lkerna, and the middle third belongs to Maraato. (iii) There is a localized merging of different major segments of the phratry which varies from one area to another, so that different definitions of *clan* and *sub-clan* are possible: thus the grouping of segments at Mount Ngiro (see above) is rather different from, for instance, Ngelai where Ltoiyo regard themselves as a separate clan while Soitoi tend to associate with Maraato. (iv) It is ritually the most senior phratry and is the first to perform each of the age-set ceremonies: this is based firstly on its exclusive claim to Mount Ngiro which is the most important geographic feature in Samburu ritual belief, and secondly on the presence there of a number of ritual specialists whose judgment as to when it is propitious to perform age-set ceremonies is respected among the Samburu. The Masula are dispersed throughout most of the centre of Maralal district, and in the north they comprise three-quarters of the population. Immigrants from the two sub-clans of Rongumo (Rendille) retain their bond brotherhood and their customs of intermarriage: Ungum become Kurtenkerta and retain their powers as *laisi*, while Seii become Sortoi Orok and tend normally to discard these powers on immigrating.

(b) *Nyaparai phratry* (123). Quite the smallest phratry. During the 1880's when the Samburu had lost most of their stock, Nyaparai in particular suffered heavily and many of them were killed by Boran raiders. The remnants were dispersed among many other Samburu

9. For a full chart of the Samburu segmentary system, see *The Samburu*, pp. 72–3.

phratries. No moran were circumcised inside this phratry in the Terito age-set and only one was circumcised inside it in the Merisho age-set: no ritual leaders were chosen. Before the initiation of the Kiliako age-set, however, a number of older members gathered together as many of their scattered remnants as they could to re-form the phratry as a corporate unit. Since that time, they have continued to grow, but are still somewhat scattered among other phratries. Nyaparai were once the most senior phratry and those at Mount Ngiro attached to the Masula are still circumcised before the others in acknowledgement of this. It is the Nyaparai who provide a calf for slaughter by the Rendille boys before a new age-set is initiated.

(c) *Lngwesi phratry* (317). Has a high reputation for worthiness and courage among the Samburu. It is generally assumed that, but for its size, it would perhaps be the most respected of all phratries: it is the second smallest. It is sometimes suggested that at one time the Lngwesi and the Nyaparai formed a single phratry and that this accounts for the brotherhood by descent that links them.

(d) *Pisikishu phratry* (955). Has a well-developed corporate unity for which it is highly respected. Sometimes mildly criticized for the past associations of Lanat with Dorobo. Historically, it seems to have been one of the most successful phratries in warfare. The Pisikishu are concentrated throughout the southern half of the district. In 1959 the Pisikishu *moran* were held by the administration to be the most persistent stock thieves among the Samburu.

(e) *Parasoro clan*. This is only a clan today, but it may well have been a phratry once with a very similar position and history to Nyaparai. At one time it is said to have had a ritual leader of its own, and to have been the most senior phratry: Parasoro boys at Mount Ngiro are still circumcised before other Masula (cf. Nyaparai). It is scattered among most Samburu phratries, but where it has survived in groups (e.g. at Mount Kulal and Olporoi) it is assimilated into Masula phratry. According to myth, one of its daughters cursed her phratry kinsmen for cheating her, and as a result it is doomed to remain scattered.

The White Cattle moiety (ngishu naibor)

(f) *Lorogushu phratry* (1,014). A highly respected phratry, and the main rivals to Pisikishu for prestige among the *moran*: it is generally maintained that it was the fierce rivalry that had built up between the two phratries that was primarily responsible for the series of affrays between them in the late 1920s when five *moran* were killed on each side. During the early 1930s when the administration had trouble with the Kiliako age-set, it was this phratry which were held mainly to blame, encouraged, it was thought, by their *laibon* (diviner) who was deported. It is popularly maintained that a Lorogushu (Terito) *moran* was the first Samburu to meet a European (Delamere), and as an elder this man later became the first government appointed chief for the whole tribe.

(g) *Lokumai phratry* (728). The only Samburu phratry whose name is identical to a Masai clan. Many Lokumai, however, look to the Rendille for their origins rather than to Masai-speaking tribes. This is the only phratry which does not always have just one ritual leader chosen for each age-set. The precise number varies: the Tarigirik age-set had four, the Marikon, Terito, and Merisho had one each, the Kiliako had three, and the Mekuri and Kimaniki have had two each. This fluctuation appears to be the result of different factions (clans) within the phratry rivalling one another for the stock which the ritual leader is given by his followers. In other phratries, it would be considered unpropitious to have more than one ritual leader. (It is said that Lorogushu once had two and both were killed as *moran*.)

(h) *Longeli phratry* (736). This phratry also has close connections with the Rendille and is the only Samburu segment to have a separate bond brotherhood with any Rendille clan (Uiyam and Urwen). Among the Samburu, the Longeli have a diffuse reputation imputed to all Rendille—an uncompromising implacability which encourages recurrent disputes, both internally and with other phratries.

(i) *Loimusi phratry* (360). One of the most despised of all Samburu phratries. Tales about this phratry are generally unflattering: that they are liars, that they are closely associated with the Dorobo in the north (Werkile), and with bad *laisi* who are immigrants from the Rendille (Nahagan). However, unlike far more respected phratries such as Masula, Lngwesi, Pisikishu, and Logumai they do not have any blacksmiths.

V. Customs Associated with the Samburu Ritual Calendar

The Samburu ritual calendar is generally less intricate than the Rendille. They do not have a seven-day week and they do not have a seven-year cycle. They do, however, have an annual and a lunar cycle. As in the previous chapter, the date in the annual cycle refers to the full moon in 1959.

The Annual Cycle

Soriu, 24 January. Those Samburu families who perform the *sorui* family festivals tend to be of Rendille descent. The Samburu version is much simpler although it follows the same general form. Frequently, only one member of a settlement performs it, and it becomes altogether a more intimate family affair with less emphasis on participation with the wider settlement. The method of dividing and cooking the meat also differs from the Rendille (compare pp. 58 and 129).

Soriu, 23 February. As above.

Soom, 24 March. Most men of the White Cattle moiety, and those of the Black Cattle moiety who claim Rendille descent do not marry in this month, and they avoid holding their age-set ceremonies. This does not prevent them, however, giving away their daughters in marriage. This month is sometimes associated with blacksmiths who may propitiously marry.

Kuram, 23 April. When the spring rains occur, they tend to be in this month. It is generally the most propitious month for most ceremonies.

Dipial, 22 May. Between about 28 April and 10 June, the Pleiades constellation lies beyond the sun, and during the period in which it cannot be seen no age-set ceremonies are held, but marriages may take place.

Soriu, 20 June. With the reappearance of the Pleiades in the early morning sky, this is the most propitious time to initiate a new age-set.

Soriu, 20 July. Also a propitious time for initiations. It is worth noting that the custom of circumcising at this time of the year is well adapted to the Leroghi and to parts of northern Kenya that share the Maralal pattern of rainfall with showers at this time of year (p. 5), and could be evidence to support the Samburu contention that they immigrated at one time from the west. It is not well adapted to the low country where most of the Samburu now live, as they are at the beginning of their long summer drought. The district commissioner who said ruefully in 1948 that the initiation of the Kimaniki age-set in the low country was unfortunately delayed by drought was only stating what must be a recurrent feature of Samburu circumcisions.

Rakarr, 18 August. The middle of the long dry season, and it is thought that marriage at this time would lead to great physical hardship. For this reason those who do not avoid marriage in Soom avoid it altogether in Rakarr, and those who do avoid it in Soom safeguard against this hardship by killing a sheep after returning from their marriage, and invoking a blessing on their huts.

Rakarr, 17 September. As above.

Lapa kelei, 16 October. It is thought that a man with no full brothers should not marry in this month or his wife would not bear him more than one son.

Lapa lolorok, 15 November. No recorded beliefs or customs.

Lapa lolorok, 15 December. No recorded beliefs or customs.

An annual cycle of twelve lunar months presents a mathematical problem of containing the occasional year when there are apparently thirteen months. Neither the Samburu nor the Rendille seemed to be aware that there were more than exactly twelve lunar cycles in a solar year, and would not admit that occasionally the system has to ignore an extra month in order to remain more or less synchronized. There is, however, very strong evidence that this does take place, since Marsabit administrative reports refer to the principal *soriu* festivals held in June and July 1948, and they were certainly held in the same months in 1959 and 1960. This can only mean that between 1948 and 1959, four extra lunar months have been accommodated in the annual cycles by, for instance, having three *rakarr* months or three *haiborboran / lapa lolorok* occasionally.

It could well be that both tribes accept some form of synchronization from elsewhere. Thus the Boran, who are so respected as ritual specialists, also celebrate the *soriu* festivals at the same time, and could take the lead in delaying the occasional festival by one month.

If, however, one is to look for some method of synchronizing *within* the customs observed by the two tribes considered here, the only logical clue lies with the reappearance of the Pleiades in June. Indeed, this could be a custom derived from the Boran, from whom the ritual specialists who watch the stars closely derive their knowledge. In other words, it is suggested that the annual cycle of lunar months takes its course until at the end of one particular *Dipial* month, when the Pleiades do not reappear as expected, and the *soriu* festivals and other customs associated with them are suspended for a further month. In this way, the lunar cycle would be linked to the annual cycle viewed through the procession of stars (and not to the erratic succession of dry and wet seasons).

The Lunar Cycle

1st night, ara lapa: the new moon is first seen in the late afternoon. *Laisi* perform their monthly ceremonies in the early evening. Moran who shaved off their hair in mourning during the previous month (before *neimin*) may now put on red ochre again. A settlement in which there has been a birth, an *ilmugit* ceremony, or a circumcision (either sex) in the previous month (before *neimin*) is only now permitted to migrate, and the frame of the hut in which the child was born or a person circumcised is set on fire. But this particular morning is not too propitious for migration, and to avert misfortune some ash from a fire in the settlement should be carried and put on the fire of the new settlement.

3rd night: not propitious for ceremonies.

5th night: not propitious for ceremonies. No migrations should be contemplated on this morning as this might result in attack from enemies or wild animals.

7th night: not propitious for ceremonies.

9th night: the correct night for certain families to celebrate the *soriu* family festival (ex-members of Rendille Upper Belisi).

10th night: as above for ex-members of Lower Belisi.

11th night: not propitious to begin ceremonies.

12th–15th nights, Satiman: the most propitious time for ceremonies.

13th night, Lkadet.

14th night, Lonyori (green)—full moon. The ideal night for boys' initiations and for the beginning of *ilmugit* ceremonies.

15th night, Lonyukie (red): the ideal night for girls' circumcisions, leading directly to marriage.

16th night onwards, *neimin*: (becoming late—i.e. the moon rises late).

16th night, sopiakwe: (first night of darkness).

17th night, soiaare: (second night of darkness).

18th night, dookunoto ekwe.

19th night, dookunoto esiedi.

20th night, norokutok: no further ceremonial activity should begin, but any which has previously begun (e.g. a four-day *ilmugit* ceremony or a marriage) may end during this time.

21st night, neimin ile: (the sixth night of *neimin*).

22nd night, neimin sapa: (the seventh night of *neimin*).
etc.

Appendix: The Ceremonial Division of Meat

A brief survey of the divisions of meat on different ceremonial occasions is given below. The English equivalents are only approximate as the Samburu have their particular way of cutting up the beast.

KEY to the various cuts.

a. the head (tongue and jowels)—*nkwe.*
b. the neck—*murt.*
c. ribs—*lmarein.*
d. last two ribs—*nkisen.*
e. brisket—*nkilemen.*
f. meat of the chest (excluding ribs)—*lgoo.*
g. meat around the back-bone—*nkoriong.*
h. rump—*lkurum.*
i. shin—*ltagule.*
j. meat between shin and shoulder—*ldorop.*
k. leg—*luatan.*
l. flank around the bone—*nkupes.*

m. stomach parts (including liver, kidney, tripe, etc.)—*nkoshoke.*
n. kidney alone—*lairakuj.*
o. heart—*itau.*
p. the hip (aitchbone?)—*lolua.*
q. topside—*nimpito.*
r. shoulders—*sip.*
s. meat below shoulders—*lmarai.*
t. fatty strip down the centre of the underside—*nkiyu.*
u. hump—*ruk.*
v. fat around the back—*nkdapidapata.*
w. sirloin—*murte.*

It is normally immaterial which half is given when there is a division between e.g. the two sides of the ribs. Such a division is indicated by a '$\frac{1}{2}$' sign and followed by 'rhs' or 'lhs' when the right- or left-hand side is preferred.

1. Forming a *mugus* after killing an enemy. Killer and his *mugus* first share f. and form relationship with t. Then all males present (including boys) eat the remainder.
2. At birth—the *morr.* Wives and very small girls eat everything.
3. At birth—*buutan. Women* take to their homes for their own consumption and their children and possibly even husbands: i, j, m, n, a, b, g, $\frac{1}{2}$l, p. *midwife*: d, h; *mother of infant*: r, $\frac{1}{2}$q; blacksmith: (can claim) $\frac{1}{2}$l; *elders*: (in the bush) c, f, $\frac{1}{2}$k, $\frac{1}{2}$q; c, f, (later in the homestead) $\frac{1}{2}$k; *boys*: o.
4. *Remori*, for barrenness. *Elders*: $\frac{1}{2}$l, $\frac{1}{2}$q, $\frac{1}{2}$s; *wives*: a, b, g, m, n, $\frac{1}{2}$l; *boys*: the remaining parts. The heart is boiled inside the hut of the elder and wife whom they have come to bless, and they eat it when giving the blessing.
5. Shaving the hair of mother and infant. The sheep is killed by the father, and eaten by all present and very small children. the father, and eaten by all women present and very small children.
6. Sheep killed when twins and children born by breach delivery have their incisors removed and their ear-lobes pierced. Elders: rhs. Wives lhs.
7. The 'boys' ox'. This is killed and cut up by their firestick elders. Everyone present other than *moran* should eat at least a morsel of the beast, but it is primarily killed for the boys who have the major share. The bones and other remains are put on the fire so that dogs and carnivorous animals cannot eat them.
8. *Ilmugit* oxen. *Moran*: c, f, $\frac{1}{2}$k, $\frac{1}{2}$q, $\frac{1}{2}$p. They also have i and j which they can allocate to whom they please or eat themselves —if many elders or other *moran* come to the feast then they

may be offered these parts. *Elders*: (roast in the bush) $\frac{1}{2}$k, $\frac{1}{2}$q, $\frac{1}{2}$r. *Wives*: (primarily the mother of the *moran* who takes these portions to her hut to be eaten by anyone except the *moran*) a, b, m, n. The men who held the *moran*'s back and leg as an initiate are entitled respectively to g and $\frac{1}{2}$p. The *moran*'s mistress, or wife, or, if he has neither, a sister: h. Girls come to the *ilmugit* enclosure each night and are given, amid ribald shouts and play: r, $\frac{1}{2}$l. *Boys*: $\frac{1}{2}$l, o. *Blacksmith* can also claim $\frac{1}{2}$l. *Moran* of other Clubs may be allocated *moran*'s portions of the beast and they go to eat it separately in the bush.

9. Ritual leader's ox at the *ilmugit of the name* ceremony, and his bull at the *ilmugit of the bull*. Killed and eaten at night inside settlement, but women must not see the portions allocated to the *moran*. *Moran*: $\frac{1}{2}$c, $\frac{1}{2}$i, $\frac{1}{2}$j, $\frac{1}{2}$k, $\frac{1}{2}$l (all rhs), f. *Elders*: $\frac{1}{2}$c, $\frac{1}{2}$i, $\frac{1}{2}$j, $\frac{1}{2}$k, $\frac{1}{2}$l (all lhs). The remainder is eaten as any other *ilmugit* ox. The moran sleep in the elders' enclosure (*kulal*), and do not leave until the fire there has consumed all the bones.

10. *Rukoret* at a marriage. *Wives*: (eaten at their homes) $\frac{1}{2}$p, $\frac{1}{2}$v, $\frac{1}{2}$w (all rhs), $\frac{1}{2}$k, $\frac{1}{2}$i, j, a, b, m, r. Women who hold the initiate's (i.e. the bride's) back and leg have respectively: g, u, and $\frac{1}{2}$p. Woman who sews her a new skirt: $\frac{1}{2}$l. *Her mother*: $\frac{1}{2}$n and certain portions of stomach fat. *Circumciser* (a Dorobo): $\frac{1}{2}$d, h, $\frac{1}{2}$i, $\frac{1}{2}$n, and she is given the bride's old skirt. *Elders*: (roast in the bush) $\frac{1}{2}$k, $\frac{1}{2}$q, c, s, $\frac{1}{2}$e, and remainder of f (cooked by best man at night), after blessing next day. *Blacksmith* (can claim) $\frac{1}{2}$l. *Boys*: o.

11. Sheep—pregnant ewe killed in alternative version of marriage ceremony in *kaji naibor*. Foetus is given to a dog, and other parts of womb are put on the sleeping hide of hut. Four wives of bride's father's clan who are classificatory sisters to the bridegroom cook the meat in front of the hut, and all women and girls eat it. They eat the head (a) next day.

12. The 'donkey' killed at death. There is no ritual division of the beast, which is eaten by the elders in the bush. If it is a *moran* who has died, then the *moran* also participate.

13. *Soriu. Anyone*: (roast at night in the yard) $\frac{1}{2}$c, (boiled at night inside the hut) $\frac{1}{2}$c, $\frac{1}{2}$i, $\frac{1}{2}$j, (cooked at any time) r, p, m, n, l, q, b. *Boys*: (roast at night in the yard), f, $\frac{1}{2}$i, $\frac{1}{2}$j. *Elders*: (boiled on the following morning) a, k, o. The *moran* abstain from eating as the meat is seen by women (*menong*).

4

THE ARIAAL AND THE DYNAMICS OF RENDILLE–SAMBURU RELATIONS

The Ariaal

The Rendille so far described are the Rendille proper living to the north. The political alliance between them and the Samburu is maintained by a set of processes which focuses attention on another group of Rendille to the south known among themselves as the *Ariaal* and among the Samburu as the *Masagera*. Socially, economically and geographically, the Ariaal Rendille occupy a position somewhere between the two major tribes. Altogether there are about 5,500 Ariaal Rendille as compared with about 8,000 Rendille proper and 50,000 Samburu.[1]

Many members of the Ariaal are either immigrants from the Rendille proper or first and second generation descendants of such immigrants. They retain the culture and exogamous restrictions of their former Rendille clans. At first, they continue to circumcise their sons in the bush and send them to attend the Rendille proper *galgulumi* ceremony; a few of them may even 'climb' an age-set and marry early. But sooner or later, these families join with other Ariaal in following the Samburu age-set system, circumcising their sons inside the settlements, performing *ilmugit* ceremonies, and not marrying early or 'climbing' an age-set. Each Ariaal settlement is affiliated to one of the Samburu phratries. The youths grow their hair as Samburu *moran* and form localized Clubs maintaining considerable independence of Samburu Clubs.[2]

Apart from those Ariaal who claim descent from the Rendille proper, there are a large proportion who claim Samburu descent and have cattle-owning kinsmen among the Samburu. There would never be any question of such families observing Rendille proper age-set customs. But they do observe other customs associated with the well-being of camel herds, including the *soriu* and *almhato* festivals and stock avoidances associated with the Rendille calendar.

An Ariaal settlement, then, normally consists of both ex-Rendille proper *and* ex-Samburu immigrant families. Their language and

1. This is based on the 1962 Kenya census report that there were altogether 13,724 Rendille, and the ratio of Rendille proper and Ariaal tax-payers in the Marsabit tax registers. From the census it was estimated that there were 48,750 Samburu.

2. cf. The Masula phratry among the Samburu, where Clubs tend to be localized rather than dispersed throughout the tribe (p. 121).

material culture are essentially Rendille and to a casual observer they *are* Rendille. The extent to which the putative descent of the Ariaal differs from the Rendille proper may be judged from the following table in which Nahagan and Lorogushu tax-payers at Marsabit were taken as representative of the Rendille proper and the Ariaal respectively. The significance of paying tax is that each of these men lives permanently in a Nahagan or Lorogushu settlement and if he is not actually a full member of either segment, he is very probably in the process of becoming one.

Table 5

PUTATIVE DESCENT OF NAHAGAN AND LOROGUSHU TAX-PAYERS (1958)

	I Nahagan (Rendille proper)	II Lorogushu (Ariaal)
Number of tax-payers in sample	106	201
	%	%
Undisputed members of Nahagan (I) or Lorogushu (II)	72	64
Recent immigrants from other Rendille proper clans	16	28
Recent immigrants from other Ariaal clans	6	8
Recent immigrants from Turkana tribe (impoverished herdsmen)	6	0

The table suggests that within the camel economy rather more Rendille families are in the process of immigrating than Ariaal, and that the net flow of immigration is from Rendille proper to Ariaal. Of the 64 per cent Ariaal who were undisputed members of Lorogushu phratry, about two-fifths claimed ultimate descent from some Rendille clan at a much earlier migration. A major criterion of whether or not a man was an undisputed member of a clan (or phratry) was whether or not he observed their rules of exogamy: there would be no compulsion on recent immigrants to do so.

There are a number of tribal traditions concerning the origin of the Ariaal. It is generally assumed that at one time there was a merging of Samburu who gained camels in warfare and decided to take to camel management seriously, and of poorer Rendille who decided to leave their natal clans and gained camels by raiding or by trading small stock with, for instance, the Somali. In 1960, this could still be done at Arbah Jahan and also through the traders at Marsabit.

The Ariaal Ilturia clan are regarded by many Rendille as an epitome of the Ariaal. According to their myth of descent, a group of Rendille enticed their sisters' younger sons who were still living among the Rendille proper, to come and help them manage their herds. Gradually, a tradition developed that inside the Ilturia, it was possible to build up herds of camels primarily by trading small stock with the Somali at Arbah Jahan or elsewhere. Rendille proper from many clans were tempted to join this clan: Ilturia, in fact, means literally a collection of people from all over the place (*a-turit*=to mix and grow—Samburu). Along with the other Ariaal, they live in country which is better for small stock (even if worse for camels) than the areas to the north inhabited by the Rendille proper.

These beliefs do not explain how it is that the Ariaal should find it easier to build up camel herds than the Rendille proper so that they could actually attract poorer emigrants, nor why the Rendille proper could not also augment their herds by raiding and trading. But they do at least express once again the general assumption that Rendille custom does not provide for younger sons and that this corresponds to a general shortage of camels. Accounts of immigrations of individuals in the recent and more distant past tend to reflect the same theme over and over again.

While the Ariaal do not own cattle in the strictest sense, they do have very close links with the cattle economy and live, as we have seen, in an area where they are interspersed with the Samburu. In many cases, one elder may own both camels and cattle. His first wife is often a Rendille girl who lives in one of the Ariaal settlements of his clan with his camels; and his second wife, who may be either Rendille or Samburu, lives in a Samburu settlement in the vicinity and looks after his cattle. In his Ariaal home, this man is an Ariaal, speaking Rendille and observing Ariaal Rendille customs; and in his Samburu home, when he visits it, he is a Samburu speaking Samburu and observing Samburu customs. The distinction between the two tribes is as slender as that.

In both settlements he may observe the Samburu custom of dividing his herd and allotting each wife a portion and retaining a residual portion. But a small sample of Ariaal suggested that, as with the Rendille proper, it is comparatively rare for a man to have more than one wife associated with his camels, although, like any Samburu, he may have several wives associated with his cattle.

An elder with both types of stock will generally allot his first (Ariaal) wife a portion of his cattle as well as his herd of camels. These cattle, however, will be herded separately in a Samburu settlement. The eldest son inherits the bulk, if not the whole, of his father's camel herd and builds up a herd of cattle from his mother's allotted herd (as any Samburu son). Thus, he is in a postion to follow his father in being *both* Ariaal *and* Samburu. The younger sons may try to build up herds of camels and cattle; but unlike their Rendille proper counterparts, they are well placed to turn to cattle if they find the camel economy less rewarding. In doing so they implicitly and even imperceptibly are emigrating from the Ariaal to the Samburu. The choice is an easy one and an obvious one.

The following genealogy is one of a number of recorded instances in which an Ariaal lineage progressively shed those that could not be contained within the camel economy.

Chart 10

THE PROGRESSIVE EMIGRATION OF AN ARIAAL LINEAGE TO SAMBURU

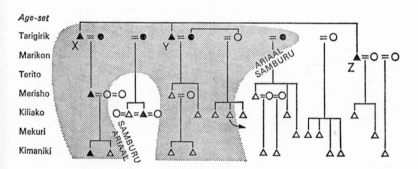

The light shading in this diagram indicates the camel-owning Ariaal members of the lineage. The others are cattle-owning Samburu. (△ & ▲ = living and dead men respectively; ○ & ● = living and dead women.)

The history of this lineage is as follows. X, Y and Z were Samburu brothers. When they were still *moran*, X and Y captured considerable herds of camels in warfare and decided to take on camel as well as cattle husbandry. Z did not gain any camels and he and his descendants have remained inside the cattle economy. X married two wives, both inside the camel economy, but he gave the second wife so few camels that her sons preferred to leave the Ariaal in order to concentrate as Samburu on cattle husbandry. X's only son by his first wife married twice: once within the camel economy and once within the cattle economy; the children of these two wives are Ariaal and Samburu respectively. Y obtained considerably more camels than his brother and was able to marry several times. His first wife died when still young and he followed the Rendille custom of marrying her younger sister: this would have been impossible among the Samburu who do not have such a custom. The youngest son of this second wife never managed to build up an adequate camel herd and he emigrated to the cattle economy to become a Samburu. Her second son was also poor and married rather late in life; his luck did not improve and in 1960 he was expected to emigrate to the cattle economy shortly. Y's third wife was married inside the camel economy also, but she was given so few camels that her sons have since emigrated to the cattle economy. Y's fourth wife was married inside the cattle economy and all her sons are Samburu. Thus in 1960, of the eighteen living adult male descendants of X and Y, seven were still camel-owning Ariaal and eleven were cattle-owning Samburu. Had X and Y been Rendille, it is unlikely that they would have married more than once and the problem of the livelihood of the junior wives and their descendants would not have arisen.

An interesting feature of this genealogy is the extent to which, taken as a whole, it is more or less typical of those collected among the Samburu with a high incidence of polygamy associated with a large age span between the sons of one man: while within the shaded area it is more typical of the Rendille proper with less polygamy, a slower rate of growth, and a smaller age span between members of the same generation.

In another recorded instance, the founder of a lineage gained camels in warfare and took up camel husbandry. In 1959, the last of his descendants returned a pauper to the Samburu cattle economy. None of the family had ever been able to make any headway with camels and the fortune won for them had dwindled over the years.

The Ariaal, then, are not merely a mixture of Rendille proper and Samburu cultures; they are also the result of successive generations of immigration from *both* Rendille *and* Samburu. Economically, the major difference between them and the Rendille proper is that many of them have cattle which provides a ready outlet for their surplus human population to become Samburu and they also have more small stock. Thus the attraction of the Ariaal for impoverished Rendille proper is that their economy offers a better selection of opportunities. As against this, it is also situated in worse country for the camels, although in practice, Ariaal with dwindling numbers of camels (if any) seem to be less concerned with this fact.

There can be little doubt that the balance of migration is from the Rendille proper to the Ariaal. This is borne out dramatically by the tax-books if one compares the Rendille proper with, for instance, the Ariaal Ilturia. For the Rendille proper the increase in tax-payers between 1945 and 1959 has been from 1,224 to 1,340: an annual average increase of 0·7 per cent. For the Ilturia the corresponding increase has been from 273 to 415: an annual average increase of 3 per cent.[3]

Chart 11 illustrates the generally accepted links between the Samburu and Rendille proper through the Ariaal. As will be seen, there are in effect five Ariaal clans, or perhaps six if one includes Lesarge. Four of these bear the identical names of the Samburu phratries with which they are associated. The fifth, Ilturia, is associated with Pisikishu phratry, although today it only consists of ex-Rendille immigrants. The sixth, Lesarge, is peripheral to the Ariaal and is associated far more closely with the Rendille proper both socially and in its seasonal migrations; but two of its sub-clans, Indi and Hlkilim, do have *moran* who grow their hair, perform *ilmugit* ceremonies and follow the Lokumai (Lewokoso) ritual leader *as well as* the Rendille ritual leader. To this extent they may be regarded as Ariaal.

It is clear from this chart that the popular assertion that the Samburu White Cattle moiety (Lorogushu, Lokumai, Longeli, and Loimusi) are more closely associated with the Rendille than the Black Cattle moiety is a very loose approximation.

To give a fuller picture, acknowledged relationships are also shown between the Samburu and the Tiamus tribe on the one hand, and between the Rendille and Odoolah on the other. The Tiamus are a Masai-speaking tribe to the south and east of Lake Baringo, from whom a number of Samburu families claim descent. The Odoolah (with only forty-one tax-payers in 1958) provide a link between the Rendille and the Boran and tend to migrate along the boundary between the two tribes (i.e. between the Rendille proper and the Gabbra Boran in the north and between the Ariaal and the Sagwiya Boran in the south). The precise tribal affiliations of this group, incidentally, is a matter of some dispute: an effort by the Odoolah to be officially accepted as Boran by the administration was strongly opposed by the Rendille who maintained that they shared close social and kinship links with the Odoolah: the chart

3. It does not seem likely that this difference is due to, for instance, a greater degree of tax evasion among the Ilturia in 1945 which could lessen their apparent size: because of the largeness of all Rendille settlements, tax evasion (as compared with the Samburu) appears to be only slight. The reason for choosing the Ilturia alone to represent the Ariaal is that there can be no question of their increase being due to any influx of Samburu from Maralal district to this clan: today, the only newcomers to Ilturia are immigrants from the Rendille.

Chart 11
INTERTRIBAL TIES AND MIGRATIONS

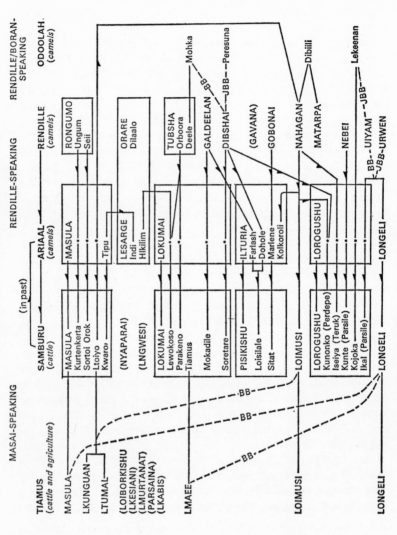

shows the nature of some of these links. In addition, the Rendille claim that they have a large number of shared camels in Odoolah herds which they might lose if they became accepted as Boran. The March moon is sometimes known as the *month of Odoolah* as no member of this group should shave his hair or cut any wood at this time. Altogether their customs are reported to be rather different from the remainder of the Rendille and they do not participate in the same tribal ceremonies. They tend to be regarded by Rendille almost as vagrants.[4]

Intertribal Migration and Marriage

A major problem facing the Rendille is that any increase in their human population is unlikely to be matched by a corresponding increase in their stock. An immediate solution is for any surplus population that cannot be contained within the camel economy to migrate to the Samburu cattle economy where it can be contained. Quite apart from the relatively undramatic transfer of some Ariaal from the Rendille camel economy to the Samburu cattle economy described in the previous section, migration can and does take place directly from the Rendille proper to the Samburu. Perhaps one-third of the Samburu claim ultimate Rendille descent and they assume that their immigrating ancestors were those that could not be contained within the camel economy. It is a logical inference, for this is precisely what is happening today. With every generation there are new arrivals from the Rendille seeking out their close and distant agnatic kinsmen who migrated in previous generations and settled down among the Samburu. Chart 11 indicates the most popular channels of migration: there is no mythical fiction in the 'brotherhoods by descent' that link segments of the two tribes, for the intermittent flow of immigration is a present reality.

Thus, an emigrating Rendille may go either to a linked Ariaal clan and continue living inside the camel economy or he may be tempted to consider a complete change and take up cattle-rearing among the Samburu. If he immigrates to the Ariaal, then he remains in the familiar cultural setting of his former life and finds many personal links with others who have close Rendille connections. If he goes to the Samburu, then he may at first find himself an out-

---

4. Unfortunately, during my period of field work I did not examine the extent to which the Odoolah served as blacksmiths to the Rendille, although indirect evidence suggested that this might be so (as for instance in the associations of the month of March—pp. 69 and 124). In this case, individual Odoolah families might well be interspersed among the Rendille, entering their economy, fulfilling the role of blacksmiths in certain of their ceremonies and paying tax as members of other clans.

sider to all save his closest friends and kinsmen, but at least by changing from the camel to the cattle economy he has the prospect of being able to build up a herd of his own which was virtually denied him among the Rendille.

The extensive immigration of Rendille men to the cattle economy is matched by an extensive marriage of Rendille girls to the Samburu, so that the Rendille are in a sense losing women as well. The extent to which this is not counteracted by an equivalent degree of marriage of Samburu girls to Rendille may be judged from Table 6. This is quite consistent with the fact that the Rendille customs of delayed marriage for men and monogamy creates a surplus of marriageable women, while the Samburu custom of insatiable polygamy creates a shortage of marriageable women.

Table 6
INTERMARRIAGE BETWEEN SAMBURU, ARIAAL AND RENDILLE PROPER (percentage)[5]

Tribe of husband	Tribe of wife				Sample size
	Samburu	Ariaal	Rendille	Others	
A. Samburu (past generation)	78	5	16	1	110
B. Samburu (present generation)	83	8	7	2	149
C. Samburu (ex-Rendille families)	72	11	13	4	75
D. Well established Ariaal	9	16	74	1	70
E. New Ariaal (ex. Rendille)	3	47	43	7	30
F. Rendille proper	1·5	15	82·5	1	121

This general transfer of human population from the Rendille to the Samburu through migration is accompanied by the transfer of certain rights in ownership over large stock. Since the camels and cattle remain in the separate economies this successive transfer of rights is somewhat complex: unlike the unilateral almost irreversible transfer of the human population, there is an element of reciprocity between the two tribes leading to circulation of rights of ownership between them.

5. The hyphenated lines on this chart are intended to emphasize the distinct change in pattern between the two economies, the majority of marriages remaining within each one. The chart does not suggest that ex-Rendille families marry Rendille wives significantly more often than other Samburu. However, new Ariaal (E) appear to marry into the Ariaal more often and into the Rendille proper less often than other Ariaal (D) or Rendille (F): in some cases this may have been a result of their migration and in others a contributory cause. It can also be seen from the chart that a very high proportion of Rendille women are married to Ariaal men (in fact, the proportion is so high that the randomness of the Ariaal sample is perhaps suspect), and it should be remembered that the Ariaal are basically polygamous and so they are in a strong position to absorb the surplus Rendille women.

This circular process is as follows. When a Rendille decides to leave the camel economy, it is probable that he still has at least a few camels of his own. When they hear that he intends to leave, other elders may come to beg these remaining animals from him. But he only gives them away as shared beasts, and in future years he and his sons and grandsons who have settled among the Samburu may claim that they still have herds of camels of their own among the Rendille. Yet it is essentially an unrealistic claim, for, as they themselves admit, no one will return their camels to them except for an occasional heifer. There is, however, one occasion above all when they can justifiably claim a heifer-camel, and this is when they come to marry a Rendille girl. On these occasions, the bride-wealth is one heifer-camel (for the bride's father), one ox-camel (the *birnan*), and six cattle. In other words, by leaving behind a few shared camels, each Rendille emigrant adds to the shared herds which he, his descendants and their newly formed Samburu friends can exploit when they wish to marry Rendille girls. (The problem of obtaining an ox-camel is less intractable as it has no lasting value for the Rendille.) Thus the circulation of rights in camels concerns those left behind by emigrants (which then become shared by 'Samburu'). At a later stage when animals from these herds are begged back at a marriage, they revert to full ownership, at first of the bridegroom, and then of his Rendille father-in-law.

There is a similar circulation of rights in cattle. The Rendille do not traditionally have cattle, and consequently they have no use for the six cattle of bridewealth. These are therefore loaned out among the Samburu.

It is when close Rendille kinsmen of the bride decide to immigrate to the Samburu and take up cattle husbandry that they have most use of these cattle, and as noted in Chapter 3, loaned cattle can be demanded unconditionally. In addition, immigrating Rendille can follow the Samburu custom of asking their sisters' husbands for gifts of cattle from the allotted herds and can augment their own herds in this way. Once again there is a circulation of rights over large stock (this time cattle), from full ownership by the Samburu bridegroom to a loan by the Rendille father-in-law, to full ownership again by an emigrant kinsman.

One might almost say that when a Rendille girl is married to a Rendille, it tends to be the elder brother who gains, for it is he (or his father) who has the major claim to the bridewealth; and when she is married to a Samburu, it tends to be the younger brothers who gain, for they are more likely to migrate to the cattle economy and claim their rights over stock through her. The following diagram shows the circulation of rights of ownership in stock between the two tribes. It should be noted that the number of stock in circulation is small among the Rendille where animals shared out and bridewealth is limited to the odd heifer-camel, and large among the Samburu where considerable numbers of cattle may be involved. It is also worth noting that in earlier times of warfare, each tribe could adopt the same custom for disposing of their unwanted gains: the Samburu who had gained camels could 'share' them out to the Rendille, and Rendille who had gained cattle could 'loan' them to the Samburu. Each was a form of investment.

Chart 12
CIRCULATION OF RIGHTS OF OWNERSHIP IN STOCK
BETWEEN TRIBES DUE TO:
A INTERMARRIAGE, AND B EMIGRATION

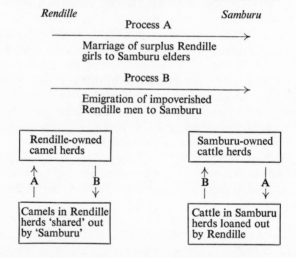

The Ecological Balance between the Two Economies

In previous chapters, the ecology of the two tribes was treated largely as a matter of comparing and contrasting their problems. Each was seen to have diverging economic and social solutions to these problems. At a more inclusive level, we can consider the ecological balance of both societies taken together as one system. The cultural barrier between them cannot be overemphasized. Their languages are mutually incomprehensible and their customs are quite dissimilar in a number of ways. The friendship between them is not due to any great love or admiration: each can be sharply critical of the other. In certain respects their economies may not overlap or compete, but still there is considerable room for dispute, especially at and around the water points. The relationship between them is not protected by some overriding belief that a dispute would result in mystical misfortune for both sides (as exists between the Samburu and Suk for instance).

This raises the question as to what factors prevent the two tribes from either merging into one or separating altogether. What forces have been and are in play that have kept them at a cool distance but at peace, apparently for countless generations? First let us consider the forces that have prevented a coalescence of the two societies into one with a joint economy of camels, cattle, and small stock.

Some of the reasons have already been noted. Cattle and camels prefer rather different types of country. In fact what is generally acknowledged as the very best camel country in the district is the area in the north around Lamagaati where the Rendille proper are concentrated, and this is altogether too harsh for cattle. Further south where the Samburu are interspersed with the Ariaal, it is necessary for the cattle camps and settlements to be closer to the water points than the camel camps and settlements. It would be quite uneconomic (though not perhaps impossible) to herd and water the different types of stock together; and to keep them together in the same settlement could mean that certain diseases to which the cattle have a higher resistance would be transmitted unnecessarily to the camels.

Historically, a further reason that has been given is the vulnerability of cattle to ambush. In earlier times, the Rendille with their camels could exploit different tracts of land every day and could avoid the water points for long periods. Cattle, on the other hand, normally had to be watered every two or three days, and were prone to ambush on the paths leading to the water points.

Above and beyond this, there is little doubt that purely practical considerations are reinforced by values that tend to exclude the possibility of merging from the outset. The Rendille assume that if they were to keep both forms of stock, the cattle herds would inevitably expand and begin to replace the camel herds which would eventually disappear. Rendille custom and ideology is geared to preserving their camel herds intact at all costs, and there is a constant horror at the thought of any change that might threaten their herds or customs associated with these herds. As they see it, to take on cattle would be to acquire Samburu customs and norms of behaviour. In time this could only lead to the ultimate extermination of the Rendille as a separate tribe, as they imperceptibly become like Samburu.

The Samburu, for their part, feel that they have less to gain from keeping camels. Several elders have one or two camels in their herds which they graze alongside their cattle in the more suitable parts of the country. But their economy, their society, and their future hopes are pinned on the prosperity of their cattle herds.

What, then, prevents the two societies from dissociating altogether? What benefits accrue to each through this close association of such different cultures? The answer is that the two tribes are inextricably linked by economic and structural ties that virtually preclude any radical separation between them. For countless generations, Samburu have claimed certain rights in Rendille camels and Rendille have claimed certain rights in Samburu cattle. With every marriage and every individual migration, these rights are fully exercised and the claims are made good.

Certain early reports from the area noted that while each tribe had its different stock economy, the Samburu would look after the Rendille cattle and the Rendille would look after the Samburu camels. While the writers did not amplify these arrangements, they seem to have been referring to precisely the processes that have been described in this chapter. Even the Ariaal, some of whom have a foot in each camp, prefer to keep the two economies quite separate.

Social Change among the Rendille

In comparing the Rendille and the Samburu, again and again one finds that contrasts between the two social systems can be correlated with differences in their economics. This is not to assert that the social differences are economically determined, however. On the contrary, both tribes have some degree of choice in the type of stock they breed, and there is every reason to suppose that to some extent their economies are actually *socially* determined. In other words, the investment that each tribe has in its mode of social life may limit the freedom of choice in its economic organization. There is every reason to suppose, for instance, that if the Rendille were prepared to live in smaller settlements, their herds would be less vulnerable to contagious diseases and would increase. Equally, there is every reason to suppose that if the Samburu accepted a discipline which limited the freedom of individual stock owners to exploit *any* piece of land in the district, then they could also have an altogether richer economy. Conceivably, either tribe might be quite different if a greater social value were placed on the economically valuable small stock.

Certain recent changes, especially among the Rendille, are of considerable interest when examining the extent to which their customs and practices are in the last resort ecologically influenced (if not exactly determined). Thus living in large settlements for safety from raiders, refusing to take on cattle because of their proneness to ambush, marrying only one wife to keep the camel herd intact, killing certain boys at birth because they are unpropitious, or delaying the marriage of certain girls (*sapade*) for similar reasons, have each been related directly or indirectly with the viability of Rendille society and their economy. Even when the principal reasons given are mystical rather than practical, the people themselves recognize the practical consequences of these customs.

And yet, each of these practices has been modified in some way in response to circumstance. In the 1950s, because of the greater safety in the area, the Rendille clans were more prepared to disperse into smaller settlements during the dry season, and their economy could be expected to have benefited from this even if the magnitude of their social life suffered. Again, there was an increasing number of Rendille proper who, instead of returning any acquired cattle to the Samburu as a loan, were keeping them in order to build up herds of their own in a separate cattle settlement and polygamy was increasing. The extent to which this trend may continue is strictly limited by the future stability of this area and its suitability for cattle: apart from the vicinity of Mount Kulal and Ldoinyo Mara (where Samburu already live), the opportunities for expansion are limited. It is altogether too early to assert that a new trend has begun which could conceivably affect the relationship between the two tribes. But at least in a number of families the younger sons may choose to turn to cattle *and* remain in the area rather than emigrate to the Ariaal or the Samburu. Unlike the Ariaal, they may even remain in close association with the customs of the Rendille proper.

The custom of killing certain boys at birth also seems to be modifying as more and more Rendille are sending them to be brought up elsewhere, especially by their maternal kinsmen and by the Ariaal. The custom of delaying the marriage of certain girls has not been modified recently, but it is claimed that in the past when this custom nearly led to the extinction of the tribe, it was relaxed for one of the two *teeria* age-set lines that practised it (p. 35). Thus once again, one has a change in custom influenced by a highly practical problem.

Again, another change that occurred prior to European intervention in the area has been the development of the Ariaal as a compromise between Samburu and Rendille ways of life. While this has not been a very recent development, the depths of various Ariaal genealogies suggest that it may not be a very ancient one. As a compromise, the Ariaal arrangement seems highly practical, and the readiness with which new immigrants are prepared to abandon customs which are sacrosanct among the Rendille proper is evidence of a certain flexibility: in the course of one or two generations, a new set of beliefs and practices is accepted.

Finally, there is a new trend which for the Rendille is perhaps the most ominous of all. During the 1940s, some youths of the Lipaale age-set began to follow their Samburu coevals of the Mekuri age-set and grew and plaited their hair. At first this was done rather crudely, but with the succeeding Irpaandif age-set their plaiting techniques became more refined and a large number adopted it. The Rendille see this as a sign of restlessness among their youths as they begin to acquire some of the accoutrements and even social characteristics of the Samburu moran. Only a minority of youths were affected by 1960, but some Rendille saw the trend as a sign of things to come and even felt that they were losing a degree of control over their young men. There was even a tendency to refer to this age-set by its Samburu equivalent name of Kimaniki rather than by the Rendille name of Irpaandif.

It may be that the clear majority of Rendille society today is as close to its traditional form as it was in the past. Or it may be that the tribe is changing as men begin to take on further wives, to keep cattle, and (in the case of the younger men) to adopt Samburu custom. In so far as these signs of change are products of a period of peace and stability in the area, further development in this direction will depend entirely on whether the current political uncertainty in northern Kenya is resolved.

Conclusion

The human ecology of the area in which one tribe remains at a fairly constant size, while the other is growing relatively quickly, is a reflection of their two economies. Under Rendille management, camel herds increase slowly, if at all; while under Samburu management, cattle herds appear to grow quickly up to a point where the availability of sufficient labour is the limiting factor. The human population is growing at a rate between these two extremes, and the surplus population of the camel economy is absorbed into the cattle economy.

It should now become clear why this study is of necessity of the Rendille *and* Samburu. In spite of considerable cultural differences, in spite of the often critical attitudes they have for one another, and in spite of the official administrative attitude that they are distinct tribes living in different Provinces of Kenya, they are, nevertheless, bound by ties which transcend cultural and political barriers. Table

6 speaks for itself. Marriage with girls outside the Samburu–Rendille cluster accounted for only eleven of all the 555 marriages recorded in the total sample. Moreover, since the official Maralal–Marsabit provincial boundary was drawn between the two tribes, there appears to have been no significant change in the number of new marriage ties that have been formed between them.

In considering the relationship between the two tribes, the Ariaal (or southern Rendille) are of particular importance. The Ariaal do not observe customs associated with the limitations of the Rendille economy. They do not have a delayed circumcision for girls or an early marriage for youths. Instead, they circumcise all children as they mature in strict order of birth without regard for their sex, and after this the girls are married at once while the young men remain unmarried for a considerable period as *moran*. These are essentially Samburu customs and they are well adapted to polygamy where there is inevitably a shortage of marriageable girls. This apparent contrast to the Rendille proper in the north is readily explained by the easy access that the Ariaal have to cattle: many of them own both camels in an Ariaal settlement and cattle in a Samburu settlement with a wife in each. Junior sons and poorer men can enter the cattle economy as Samburu without real difficulty. For the Rendille proper, who are not familiar with cattle management and have only distant ties with the Samburu, it is not so easy a decision to make. Even so, there is a persistent trickle of Rendille, often middle-aged men, into the Samburu economy where they take up cattle husbandry in preference for camels and in time become fully absorbed as Samburu.

5

THE RECENT HISTORY OF THE SAMBURU AND RENDILLE

A major hazard in trying to piece together a history of the area is the extent to which available evidence, both through earlier writings and through current memories, is vague and often quite contradictory. As we saw in the last chapter, there is a certain awareness of change, even in the days before the advent of British administration, but there is also a prevalent tendency to deny that these are in any sense changing societies. The changes are regarded as anomalies rather than norms, even though a certain degree of change in an area of political instability might be expected. One is led to suspect, therefore, that generalized assertions by the Samburu and Rendille as regards the stability of their societies in the past may reflect their faith in the security offered by this traditional form, and exaggerate the degree to which there has been no change.

In this chapter, available evidence is considered in order to assess the extent to which a historical reconstruction of events is possible. As an initial step towards this reconstruction, consider the following table.

This table shows some of the tribes of East Africa grouped to-

Table 7
COMPARISON OF ELEVEN EAST AFRICAN LANGUAGES

	Reshiat	Elmolo	Boran	Somali	Rendille	Samburu	Masai	Turkana	Bari	Suk	Mukogodo	Tribal group
Reshiat	—	28	15	14	20	6	5	2	1	3	7	
Elmolo	28	—	20	14	25	4	3	2	1	2	7	
Boran	15	20	—	18	19	3	2	4	2	0	6	Cushitic
Somali	14	14	18	—	38	5	4	6	1	2	5	
Rendille	20	25	19	38	—	5	4	4	2	2	7	
Samburu	6	4	3	5	5	—	95	25	19	13	8	
Masai	5	3	2	4	4	95	—	23	21	11	9	Nilo-Hamitic
Turkana	2	2	4	6	4	25	23	—	20	8	5	
Bari	1	1	2	1	2	19	21	20	—	10	6	
Suk	3	2	0	2	2	13	11	8	10	—	6	
Mukogodo	7	7	6	5	7	8	9	5	6	6	—	
Tribal group	Cushitic					Nilo-Hamitic						

gether according to superficial similarities in their vocabularies. The figures are based on the number of similarities in a sample of 100 commonly used words.[1] As a rough and ready yardstick for comparison, the table shows two very distinct groupings of tribes. The figures essentially confirm the linguistic division of the area into Nilo-Hamitic and Cushitic. The figures are generally well above 10 (words in common out of 100) within each group and well below 10 between the groups. Only Mukogodo does not fall clearly into either group, while Suk is rather less close to the other Nilo-Hamitic languages than they are to each other. Two features in the table should be noted in particular: the first is that Samburu, with 95 words out of 100 in common with Masai, is essentially a Masai dialect; and the second is that Somali and Rendille, with a figure of 38, are more alike than any other languages in their group.

The Samburu and Rendille are well aware of these similarities and differences, and account for them in terms of their origins as tribes. The Samburu, for instance, see the close similarity of their language to Masai as evidence supporting the belief that they were at one time a branch of the Laikipiak Masai. Similarly, the Rendille see the rather more remote similarity of their language to Somali as evidence supporting their belief that they were, in fact, once Muslems and of Somali origin.[2]

Such an approach to historical analysis is not confined to the people themselves. For some time, linguistic evidence has been taken to ascertain the histories of various tribes by scholars. Thus Johnston noted the similarity between the languages of the Masai and the Bari–Lotuko group and suggested that this indicated that the former home of the Masai was in the Bari–Lotuko area of the Southern Sudan.[3] Later Seligman elaborated this view to suggest that the Masai (of which the Samburu could be regarded as a splinter group) were originally a mixture of the Nilotic and Hamitic (Cushitic) races following the influx of the latter into East Africa: whence he suggested the term Nilo-Hamitic.[4]

1. Where the words were virtually identical, one mark was ascribed, and where they were only comparatively similar, a half-mark was ascribed. This method of course, ignored the more sophisticated points relating to similarities in verb construction or other aspects of grammatical structure.
2. Individual Rendille clans claim descent from the following groups. *Somali:* Saali (Fakhashiini), Dibshai (Rakhwen-Dafara), Matarpa (Ugaden), Nahagan (Ugaden), Nebei Lekila (Saakh), Odoolah (Garri), *Boran:* Dibshai (Furr), Tubsha (Deele). *Reshiat:* Rongumo, Galdeelan. Note also those Rendille customs which suggest *the east* as a more propitious direction than *the west* (*orelogoraha* p. 49; *almhato* p. 59; and Sunday p. 66).
3. Johnston, 1902, p. 796 and pp. 885 ff. Because this view has gained some acceptance, I have included the Bari language in the table on the previous page: it seems to be no closer to Masai than to Turkana, for instance.
4. Seligman, 1930, pp. 155 ff.

Supporting Seligman's argument, it is, perhaps, worth noting that so far as two tribes of East Africa are concerned, the Samburu (Nilo-Hamitic) are still interacting and mixing with a 'Hamitic' tribe (the Rendille) as was seen in the last chapter. The weakness of such an approach, however, is that it is essentially speculative and in any case does not throw any useful light on the processes which may have been involved in such diffusion. There are, for instance, at least two tribes in the area (the Elmolo and the Mukogodo)[5] that have adopted a form of Masai during the present century and so have jumped from one linguistic group to another. In the case of the Elmolo this was done without any significant degree of intermarriage or intermigration. Or again, despite the fact that one-third of the Samburu claim Rendille descent and many marry Rendille women, the two languages are noticeably dissimilar. The evidence, then, points to the conclusion that there are other forces involved in linguistic change and assimilation besides simple intermarriage and intermigration, and that language taken alone may suggest a rather misguided and inconclusive approach to the study of the history. Where tribes have similar languages, at the most one may posit some form of cultural contact at some time, and the presence of forces which encouraged a degree of assimilation.

*   *   *

In trying to piece together a history of the era, it is difficult to delve into events that took place only 100 years ago, let alone several centuries when some of the major processes of migration and diffusion may have taken place. The chapter examines the unfolding of Samburu and Rendille history from the vaguest and most contradictory statements about earlier times by the oldest living men to the fuller (and sometimes equally contradictory) contemporary writings.

The account falls conveniently into four sections. The first covers the prehistoric era before the earliest European explorers traversed the area in 1888. The second covers the early history before a permanent administration was set up in 1921; during this period, reminiscences of the early lives of the oldest living men in 1960 are supplemented spasmodically by the accounts of travellers. The third and fourth cover the more recent histories of the two tribes after they had been officially confined to separate administrative districts. Because most of my evidence was collected from Samburu and not Rendille, I have slanted this account more towards the former. A further reason for this is that change, initially in terms of establishing peace in the area and more recently in terms of imposing some form

5. See the Appendix on *The Dorobo and Elmolo of Northern Kenya*.

of grazing control, has affected the Samburu to a far greater extent than the Rendille.

The Prehistoric Era

The Samburu believe that they are derived culturally and to a large extent biologically from the Laikipiak Masai of whom they were once a branch. Similarly, the Rendille believe that they had earlier connections with the Somali. But there is no stress on pure descent: clans are largely composite in character and the various segments frequently suggest that they originally became members of the Samburu or Rendille through migrating from some other tribe. The principal beliefs as regards the migrations are consistent with the inter-tribal links shown in Chart 11, although there is often contradiction as to the nature of the original link.

Amid all the contradictions and general disinterest as regards their ultimate descents or their places of origin, one fact is firmly maintained by both tribes. This is that the alliance between the Samburu and the Rendille goes back much further than any vaguely remembered history. It is vigorously claimed that for many centuries, the two fought against their common enemies together, migrated to new tracts of land together, and lived interspersed with the Samburu herding their cattle and the Rendille herding their camels together.

For the purposes of trying to reconstruct a more recent history it is fortuitous that the two tribes should have an age-set system. This provides a useful tool for dating certain events, since they tend to link these events with specific age-sets. Thus the *moran* of the Samburu Kipeko age-set were remembered as having captured Mount Ngiro from the Boran. If we accept this piece of information at its face value, it is only necessary to estimate when the Kipeko age-set were initiated in order to put a date to the capture of Mount Ngiro.

So far as dating is concerned, one can be reasonably confident of the more recent initiations since the time of regular European contact, but earlier dates must necessarily be guesses. I have therefore assumed that in prehistoric times as at present, initiations were on average spaced out by periods of fourteen years. At first sight, this may seem in rather dangerous assumption; but it would imply, quite reasonably, that when my oldest Samburu informants (in their eighties) were young boys, the oldest men they saw were themselves in their eighties (as assessed from their age-sets). It would also be consistent with my own impression that measures taken by the administration to control the age-set system have not fundamentally affected its periodic intervals. Nevertheless, it must be emphasized that the earlier dates that I put forward are essentially speculative.[6]

Had I been undertaking my field work fifty years earlier, then I should, no doubt, have been able to trace the history of the area further back by fifty years. There is, however, every reason to suppose that there would have been a similar cumulative elaboration of detail about each successive age-set, as each one was remembered more clearly than the last, and the basic pattern would have been much the same without necessarily revealing any further depth. In other words, there is no reason to assume that the people of the area are losing their tribal memories now more rapidly than in the past.

The following outline shows how events are associated with each successive age-set of Samburu *moran* (and Rendille youths), and how they began to unfold themselves to me in 1960 when my informants were among the oldest living men of the two tribes.

1. *Salkanya* (age-set). Among the half-dozen or so age-sets that are remembered to have preceded the Meishopo age-set, only the Salkanya age-set is consistently referred to by the older informants, but little is known about it. It possibly was the immediate predecessor of the Meishopo or perhaps it was an unusually notable age-set of its time.

2. *Meishopo* (initiated *c.* 1781). This is the earliest age-set whose exact position in relation to subsequent age-sets was consistently remembered by the oldest and best informants in 1960. It was also the earliest age-set to which any known genealogy could be traced, members of it being the grandfathers and the great-grandfathers of some of the oldest living men.

3. *Kurukua* (initiated *c.* 1795).

4. *Lpetaa* (initiated *c.* 1809). My oldest reliable informant claimed to have seen a man of this age-set when he was a small boy (i.e. in about 1885).

5. *Kipayang* (initiated *c.* 1823). This is the earliest age-set to which the (jural) father of any living man is known to have belonged. At this point the Samburu are depicted as living on the Leroghi Plateau and in the area to the north of Lake Baringo, while the Rendille tended to be concentrated further north on the Lbarta Plains and in the Suguta valley. The Masai-speaking Tiamus (Njemps) tribe lived and cultivated around Lake Baringo itself and

6. This reasoning lies behind the dates estimated in Chart 7. The period of fourteen years was arrived at altogether independently of the fact that Rendille age-sets are spaced apart by exact multiples of seven years.

Map 3
TRIBAL MIGRATIONS DURING THE MID-NINETEENTH CENTURY
(and the disposition of Dorobo groups (numbered) in 1900).

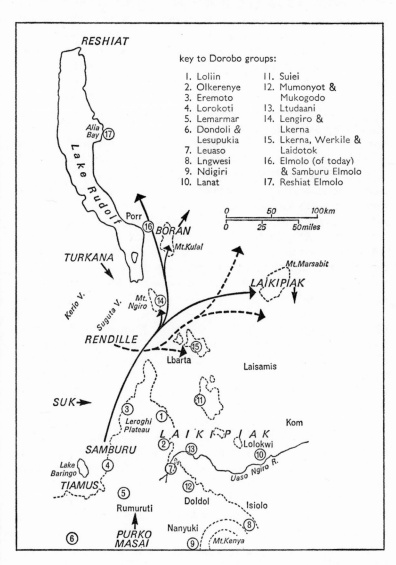

key to Dorobo groups:

1. Loliin	11. Suiei
2. Olkerenye	12. Mumonyot &
3. Eremoto	Mukogodo
4. Lorokoti	13. Ltudaani
5. Lemarmar	14. Lengiro &
6. Dondoli &	Lkerna
Lesupukia	15. Lkerna, Werkile &
7. Leuaso	Laidotok
8. Lngwesi	16. Elmolo (of today)
9. Ndigiri	& Samburu Elmolo
10. Lanat	17. Reshiat Elmolo

were regarded as friends and allies by the Samburu (cf. the links between the two tribes shown in Chart 11). There is no precise idea of how long these tribes had been in these areas.

It appears to have been during this period that the Samburu first came into contact with the Turkana who were pushing south-eastwards from the area west of Lake Rudolf. The Turkana were fierce fighters who did not acknowledge the conventions of warfare shared by most of the other tribes in the area. Those in the van-guard of this movement were for the most part stockless and greedy for cattle and camels. Altogether they were too poor to offer any tempting prize for such tribes as the Samburu and Rendille who would only attack them in retaliation if at all. At first, the initial contact appears to have been slight; this age-set of Samburu *moran* is more vividly remembered for having adopted the Turkana blue coiffure instead of their own red-ochred braided hairstyle, than for having actually fought the Turkana. Apart from the fact that fashions tend to vary among the Samburu *moran* from one age-set to the next (in dress, hairstyle, songs, and slang) and that the new cultural contact with the Turkana introduced the Samburu to a new set of ideas for fashions, no explanations have been offered for this abrupt change. There is no suggestion of any close contact with the Turkana at this stage, but only of a new awareness of their exist-ence to the north.

6. *Kipeko* (initiated *c.* 1837). This age-set reverted to the normal Samburu hairstyle using red-ochre. Epics and tribal migrations associated with various age-sets when they were *moran* only begin to emerge clearly at this point. Most old men remember having known elders of this age-set, and this gives a certain testimony for the truth of their tales.

From, say, 1840 the Samburu migrated from the Baringo area in a north-easterly direction. The period has almost become a tribal legend. Glowing accounts today make no mention of defeat or explanation of *why* migration was necessary; they focus more on the capturing of Mounts Ngiro and Kulal from the Boran and Mount Marsabit from the Laikipiak Masai.[7] Meanwhile the Rendille are thought to have migrated eastwards from the Kerio valley to the land they occupy today, driving the Laikipiak southwards.

7. Much of this information is confirmed by Samburu witnesses before the Kenya Land Commission (Evidence to the Kenya Land Commission, 1933, pp. 1604–5, 1613–14). Two witnesses state that the Samburu left Leroghi because the Laikipaik drove them out, and a third states that they migrated north because they had lost some of their stock and were starving—a state-ment echoed by several informants of my own. Witnesses also told the Commission that Mount Kulal had previously belonged to the Gabbra Boran and Mount Marsabit to the Laikipiak before the Samburu drove them out.

No mention is made anywhere of the Suk who later took possession of the land vacated by the Samburu, although according to at least two writers, they claim to have ousted the Samburu.[8] There is a Samburu belief that fighting between themselves and the Suk would bring mystical misfortune for either tribe and under all circumstances should be avoided. It is said that in the remote past the elders of both tribes jointly pronounced a curse on anyone who violated the truce between them (cf. a bond brotherhood). Apart from this isolated belief, the Suk play curiously little part in this history: they are neither traditional friends nor enemies of the Samburu and the Rendille.

7. *Kiteku* (initiated *c.* 1851). This age-set of Samburu *moran* continued to lead the migration northwards along the eastern shore of Lake Rudolf and established a friendly contact with the Reshiat (Merille) tribe at the northern end of the lake. However, by this time, the northerly movement had weakened contact with the Tiamus of Lake Baringo and the former link of friendship was broken. By now the Turkana had reached the northern end of the Kerio valley and were to become an increasing menace for the Samburu and Rendille on the Lbarta Plains during the next half-century. As respect for the tribe's fighting prowess and fear of their witchcraft increased, so the Samburu preferred to keep their distance from them.

8. *Tarigirik* (initiated *c.* 1865). With the initiation of this age-set, relations between the Samburu and Laikipiak became once again strained and a series of incidents led, according to one informant, to a major battle. This led to a truce between the Tarigirik and the corresponding age-set of Laikipiak *moran*. The Samburu and Rendille then turned their attention to their more traditional enemies (the Boran) and coped with the Turkana as best they could. The Laikipiak, for their part, appear to have consolidated their position by relinquishing their more northerly territories in order to be better able to face the Purko Masai in the south who were becoming their most dangerous enemies.

At this time there was a small off-shoot of the Rendille tribe called the Kirimani. The close relationship between the camel-owning Rendille-speaking Kirimani and the cattle-owning Masai-speaking Laikipiak is thought to have been very similar to that between the Rendille and the Samburu today. Hostility between the Rendille and the Kirimani increased to a point where the Ariaal Rendille attacked and utterly routed them, augmenting their own

8. Beech 1911, pp. 3–4; Macdonald, J. R. L. 1899, p. 240.

herds considerably. The Rendille proper preferred not to associate themselves with this rout of their Kirimani kinsmen and took no part in it. A number of collected genealogies suggest that this may well have been a specific opportunity for expansion by the Ariaal. Today, there are many descendants of the Kirimani among the Rendille, and they have been absorbed into various clans.

Christie reported in 1876 that a cholera epidemic swept through the area in 1869 and depleted the Samburu (his *Soma-Gurra*) severely.[9] My informants had no information on this or on any other malignant epidemic at about this time.

9. *Marikon* (initiated *c.* 1879). This was the age-set of the oldest men alive in 1960, although at that time those that I met were too old to be particularly reliable informants.

Two events are of importance during this period. The first was a cattle plague which affected all pastoral tribes of the area, but was particularly devastating among Samburu cattle. They refer to it as *emutai*, a term which can best be translated as *The Disaster* (*a-mut* =to finish off). Many of them had to disperse in order to survive, and they settled down among the Rendille, Reshiat, Elmolo, Dorobo, and possibly among other tribes such as the Turkana. However, a reasonable number—even the majority—appear to have subsisted with their small stock in the Marsabit area and they gradually built up herds of cattle again by rearing what few they had left, by raiding, and by trading with the more fortunate tribes who would take their small stock.

The other event of importance was the utter defeat of the Laikipiak Masai by the Purko Masai. The Laikipiak followed their defeat with an attack on their northern neighbours (the Samburu, Rendille and Boran) in at attempt to recover some of their former territory, but were ruthlessly hounded down by these tribes and were finally routed. Today, there are comparatively few families in the area that claim descent from the survivors of this rout, and there is virtually no memory of the Laikipiak customs or social organization.

Early History: 1888–1921

Up to this point European writers had obtained their knowledge of the area and its inhabitants from second- and third-hand tales

9. Christie J., 1876, p. 211. *Soma-Gurra*, which Christie equates with Samburu may be a corruption of the same name (cf. Boyes, 1911 p. 163, who refers to them as *Sambura*); it could equally well refer to the *Somali Gerra*. It seems remotely possible even that it was an inadvertent spoonerism for *Masagera*—the Samburu term for the Ariaal.

brought back by non-European ivory hunters and traders. Only one of these writers, Leon des Avanchers who wrote in 1859, appears to have shown any degree of consistency with later known facts. He rightly places the Rendille at the south-eastern corner of Lake Rudolf,[10] but his description of them as being red with long hair and large numbers of cattle suggests the Samburu rather than the Rendille. No other early writer appears to have been at all meticulous in collecting and arranging his information and this results in considerable confusion and contradiction.

In 1888, Teleki and von Höhnel were the first European explorers to traverse the area and it now becomes possible to be more definite about events and migrations occurring at the time. But it must be emphasized that the writings of all the early explorers are to be treated with considerable reserve. Even von Höhnel, who in many ways was one of the most graphic and concise of all these writers and who wrote many things that have been confirmed by my own informants, was capable of colouring his descriptions without apparent justification, of confusing tribal identities, and of over-simplifying what must have been a rather complicated history of the area. He and other explorers were frequently misled by previous writers, and working through interpreters via the Swahili language must have led to many misunderstandings and misinterpretations. The period is still one in which the statements of the oldest Samburu and Rendille who were alive in 1960 (and who were incidentally coevals of many of these explorers) are the basic source of information; but it is now possible to check their statements and to put certain dates to certain events. Before trying to put together this jig-saw puzzle, it is worth noting the usefulness and the accuracy of some of the writers. They were as follows:

1883—Thomson: travelled to the south of the Samburu and Rendille, but gives useful and unique information on the Laikipiak Masai.

1888—von Höhnel: discovered Lake Rudolf with Teleki and made some contact with the Samburu and Rendille. A very useful account in many ways.

1889–90—Peters: shot his way through the Masai, but again travelled to the south of the Samburu and Rendille. A useless account.

1892–3—Chanler: met the Samburu and Rendille in the south at Kom. Gave the first clear account of the Rendille, but a careless ethnographer.

10. This is referred to as *Lac Boo* (cf. *Mbaso* in Samburu). However, des Avanchers' astonishing consistency in describing the landmarks and tribes to the north and east of the lake as they appeared thirty years later to von Höhnel makes it almost certain that it must have been Lake Rudolf.

1894–6—Neumann: had unusually close contact with the Dorobo and Reshiat, and his account consequently is a good one. However, he had little contact with the Samburu or Rendille.

1895—Donaldson Smith: hurried through the area from north to south with camels, and his ethnography is poor.

1896—Bottego: I have been unable to trace his work on the area. However, von Höhnel is an admirable summary of the early explorations of the Lake Rudolf region (1938) summarizes his findings, and only one point seems relevant to the present history.

1897—Cavendish: skirted the area inhabited by the Samburu and Rendille. His article (if it can be relied on) reveals some interesting points.

1897—Delamere: his meeting with the Samburu at Marsabit is referred to by Huxley (1935). This is of considerable interest as the Samburu like to believe that it was the first important meeting that they had with Europeans and created a bond of friendship between them and the British.

1899—Wellby: his journey round Lake Rudolf with an armed Ethiopian entourage made it impossible for him to collect any useful information from local tribesmen, who tended to run away as he approached.

1900—Donaldson Smith: conducted an even more hurried visit.

1900—Arkell-Hardwick: an interesting supplement to Chanler's account of the Samburu and Rendille in the south.

1901—Wickenburg: little information of value on the tribes, but later travellers collected interesting information on Wickenburg.

1902—Tate: a very brief journey to Marsabit led to two uninteresting articles.

1903—Maud: his journey down the east side of Lake Rudolf led to an article with a useful description of the Elmolo.

1906—Boyes: travelled through the area from north to south. Has very little to say on the Samburu and Rendille.

1908—Patterson: in a whole book written about a visit to Marsabit, he has surprisingly little of interest to say on the tribes.

1909—Stigand: a very full account of a journey through Samburu and Rendille country with useful information.

After Stigand had completed his journey, regular books and articles on the area ceased to appear, possibly because it had been adequately discovered and they were beginning to lose their market value.

*   *   *

Joseph Thomson was the only European explorer who actually saw and wrote of the Laikipiak Masai, and he describes the battles which took place in 1883 between them and the Purko Masai in suspiciously melodramatic terms.[11] However, with regard to the Samburu and Rendille, history may be said to date from 1888 with the discovery of Lake Rudolf by Teleki and von Höhnel; and by this time the Laikipiak had been routed.[12]

The smallpox epidemic which von Höhnel noted was breaking out among the Reshiat in 1888[13] became epidemic shortly after his departure, and the tribes to the north of Lake Rudolf, including the Reshiat, Samburu and Rendille, were either dispersed or sadly reduced in size by raids from the Boran.[14] Today, there is only a lingering memory among the Samburu and Rendille of their earlier ties with the Reshiat, and the fates of those that remained in the area are unknown.

10. *Terito* (initiated 1893?). There is more certainty about this date as the Samburu circumcised at this time remember seeing or hearing about Chanler's visit to Kom.[15] The Samburu were still an impoverished tribe trying to rebuild their lost herds of cattle by raiding and by exchanging donkeys or small stock for cattle.[16] This was the last age-set to take part in any serious inter-tribal fighting along traditional lines. Owing to a scarcity of boys to form a new age-set and the general desire of the Terito to build up their own herds before marrying, they remained unmarried *moran* for an unusually long period. To add to their difficulties, smallpox spread among them (probably from the north) in the 1890s and reduced their numbers considerably. Young men in the Rendille camel camps suffered very badly from this epidemic,[17] and the Rendille lost many of their camels, partly because there were too few men to defend them from raiders but mainly because there were too few to manage them adequately. A number of survivors

11. Thomson, 1885, p. 348.
12. von Höhnel, 1894, ii, pp. 2–3, and also i, p. 398.
13. von Höhnel, 1894, ii, p. 207.
14. Donaldson Smith, 1897, pp. 295–6, Cavendish, 1898, p. 382, Huxley, 1935, p. 43. Botego (von Höhnel, 1938, p. 32) found an isolated Rendille village to the north-west of the Lake in 1896, and Cavendish (1898, p. 384) reports a Masai-speaking Dorobo group known as *Legumi* who were allied to the Turkana in this area in 1897. (The Samburu *Lokumai* phratry claim to have a lost section among the Turkana.) Shackleton, writing in 1932, notes the *Irantale* and *Nkor* sections of the Reshiat. His description hardly tallies with the Rendille or Samburu of today, but there is an unmistakable similarity to their names for one another (*Rentile* and *Kooro*).
15. Chanler, 1896, p. 306.
16. Chanler, 1896, p. 306, Boyes, 1928, p. 312. Boyes records that the Samburu offered him thirty-five sheep for each cow: this expensive figure is fully consistent with the accounts of older men today. They did most of their trading for cattle with the Somali. Elsewhere Boyes (1911, p. 163) reports this as sixty sheep for each cow.
17. Arkell-Hardwick, 1903, pp. 214, 220, 238.

inherited the vast herds of their dead kinsmen and yet were reduced to poverty again within a few years because of this.

Thus, while in 1890 the Samburu had been scattered and reduced to poverty, many of them depending on the Rendille in order to survive, by 1900 the fortunes of the two tribes had been reversed, and the Samburu now emerged as the more powerful tribe. This is essentially consistent with the differences between Chanler's and Arkell-Hardwick's accounts based on visits in 1892–3 and 1900 respectively.[18]

A number of later reports on this period state that the Samburu were generally afraid of the Purko Masai who had drifted on to the Leroghi Plateau after the collapse of the Laikipiak. But there is no evidence that severe fighting ever occurred between them, and the very fact that during the first decade of the century the Samburu occupied the land immediately below Leroghi and were actually found on the plateau itself close to the Purko in 1911 indicates that they had considerable confidence in the goodwill of the Maisai, who were undoubtedly the stronger tribe.[19] Indeed, the Purko might almost be described as indirect benefactors of the Samburu since in about 1900 they dealt a crushing blow to the Turkana on the Lbarta Plains in a single raid as a reprisal for isolated Turkana raids on them. The immediate effect was to check the south-easterly drift of the Turkana for a time.

During the latter part of this period, the British were establishing administrative stations in the area and imposing an uneasy peace as their influence spread northwards. Stations were set up at Rumuruti and Archer's Post, and later at Marsabit.

11. *Merisho* (initiated 1912). The date of initiation is fairly certain as it preceded the final eviction of the Purko Masai from Leroghi to the Masai reserve further south in 1913.

Surprisingly little seems to have occurred among the Rendille during the time that the Merisho were *moran*. There are records in 1919 of a raid by the Reshiat and a counter-raid in which heavy casualties were suffered by both sides. But on the whole the Rendille, always known as ferocious defensive fighters, appear to have been unaffected by new changes. This is a pattern which is to be seen in the years which follow: while most other tribes of the area, including the Samburu, have been affected by political and economic changes introduced by the new administration, the Rendille have remained more or less as they were.

18. Chanler, 1896, p. 316; Arkell-Hardwick, 1903, p. 241. See p. 1 above.
19. *Kenya Land Commission, Evidence,* 1933, pp. 1541 and 1488. Also see Stigand (1910, p. 55), who notes the Samburu immediately below Leroghi.

The Samburu were steadily rebuilding their cattle herds at an impressive rate, as can be judged from the fact that in 1922, perhaps thirty-five years after The Disaster, a census was carried out on Leroghi and they were found to have fifteen head of cattle and ten head of small stock per person: a higher proportion than in 1958. But they were still depleted in numbers and they found the repeated incursions of the Turkana a serious menace to their security,[20] while to the east around Marsabit they were harassed by Boran raiders from the north: these tribes were now obtaining guns from Ethiopia against which the Samburu had little protection. They therefore asked the British Administration for military help. Kittermaster at Marsabit was in no position to offer them protection from the north, and in 1914 he ordered them to leave the area for their own good and to make use of pastures further south. But the British did at least help the Samburu settle an old score with the Turkana; they had a score of their own to settle. A punitive expedition was organized in 1914 by the King's African Rifles (K.A.R.) which *moran* of the Merisho and Terito age-set were allowed to join. These returned with large numbers of stock that helped to compensate their losses.

During the years of the 1914–18 War, administration in the area was inevitably curtailed, and the Samburu, evicted from Marsabit, crept onto Leroghi in the wake of the Purko Masai, while others crossed the Uaso Ngiro river in search of pastures to the south. It was not until 1919 that a further attempt was made to administer the area, and when in 1921 the army (King's African Rifles) took over control of the Northern Frontier District from the civil authorities, the area was policed for the first time on a permanent basis. From this point there are regular administrative reports and it is useful to consider the history of the two tribes separately.

Recent Samburu History: 1921–62

In 1921, the military administration first set out to demarcate the official limits of Samburu District. The north-eastern Rendille boundary was formed by drawing on the map a series of lines between water points shared by both tribes. A southern boundary was established on the Leroghi Plateau and the Samburu living to the south of this and of the Uaso Ngiro river were returned north. The Turkana were still in possession of the Lbarta Plains and land to the south, and they had infiltrated as far as Isiolo. In 1921–2

20. There are repeated references to these incursions in the literature: von Höhnel 1894, ii, pp. 101 and 112; Chanler, 1896, p. 314; Donaldson Smith, 1897, p. 351; and Stigand, 1910, p. 86.

they were moved to their own district which had been established in the north-west. It was during this move that the Samburu first experienced the full implications of the new rule they were to submit to during the next forty years. Some *moran* of the Merisho age-set attacked and killed several Turkana on the convoy moving north. The principal offenders were seized by the army escort and were publicly executed before other Samburu.

The Samburu did not immediately occupy the land vacated in the north or curb subsequent Turkana incursions: their respect for them as fighters was increased by the general fear of their witchcraft. The Turkana were subsequently allowed to return to the area to the west of Baragoi where Stigand had found them in 1909. Today there is relatively little social contact between the Samburu and Turkana or intermarriage: the general mistrust tainted with fear that the Samburu have for the Turkana has remained.

12. *Kiliako* (initiated 1921–2). The date of these initiations are reasonably certain as they occurred shortly after the government station was built at Barsaloi. This was in 1921. In contrast to the Merisho who had been a small age-set settling down quickly to elderhood, the Kiliako were unusually large and showed considerable truculence towards attempts by the British administration to impose peace on the area. Their whole period of *moranhood* was marked by a general unrest, including widespread stock theft, and sporadic murders of neighbouring tribesmen and herdboys on European ranches to the south. Two incidents that were regarded very seriously by the administration were the presumed murder of a missing European government officer and a serious affray between Lorogushu and Pisikishu *moran* in 1929 that led to ten deaths. Fighting on this scale within the tribe is held to be without precedent.

There were two principal causes of the Kiliako unrest. The first was due to the fact that they were the first age-set whose traditional role as true warriors and defenders was substantially undermined by the protection offered by the British. This placed the *moran* in a limbo, which as a problem has never been wholly resolved by either tribe or administration. For the Kiliako age-set who as boys had been brought up to expect warriorhood in the fullest sense, the conflict in expectations was particularly acute.

The second cause was the uncertainty that hung for years over the tribe's very best grazing land on the Leroghi Plateau. The Samburu had constantly been warned by the administration that this land was intended for European settlers, but no real attempt had been made to evict them. Eventually this became one of the key issues before the Kenya Land Commission of 1933.

Briefly, the case was as follows. The Masai had been evicted from Leroghi in 1913 and during the unadministered 1914–18 period, a large number of Samburu had migrated on to it. By the early 1920s one-half of the tribe was thought to be living on the plateau. The European settlers now claimed that the land had originally been cleared of Masai for their own use, although no official records substantiated this claim. At first the argument was conducted as a historical issue hinging on the claims of the Samburu to Leroghi both before and after it was occupied by the Masai, and the claims of Europeans as to the reasons for evicting the Masai. The difficulties of delving into a tentative Samburu history even before 1920 soon became apparent. Eventually the case was seen to hinge more realistically on what alternative land could be found for the Samburu to compensate them for Leroghi, especially as they had been removed from good grazing areas on Marsabit in 1914 and from the area to the south of the Uaso Ngiro river in 1921. No other land equivalent to Leroghi could be found and it was awarded to the Samburu.

The troubles did not end in 1933. In awarding Leroghi to the Samburu, the commission considered that measures to reduce the numbers of uneconomic Samburu stock (i.e. oxen and older cattle) were necessary. It was felt that the Samburu would have more nourishment from their stock if 30–40 per cent were immediately culled, leaving the remainder better fed and tended. After the years of uncertainty, the Samburu would not easily accept that the land had finally been awarded them. Their suspicions were aroused by the new official attempts at stock control, and by the knowledge that their European neighbours to the south were still a powerful pressure group in government circles. Largely as a result of this pressure, control over the Samburu was transferred from the Northern Frontier Province (where the Rendille remained) to the Rift Valley Province (where the settlers lived) in 1934, and then a year later, their district was amalgamated with Laikipia to the south which largely comprised the European farmed area. At the same time, the administrative H.Q. moved at first to Maralal on top of the Leroghi Plateau, and then to Rumuruti in the heart of the European settled area. From this point until administration was returned to Maralal as a separate district again in 1944, the settlers appear to have had a strong voice in the determination of Samburu policies, although the Samburu still retained Leroghi.

In 1934 the Samburu were still uncertain of their future, murders continued and a levy force was called in during the year and again in 1936 to disarm the *moran* of their spears and shields. The administration then demanded that the Kiliako *moran* should marry and settle down, and that a new age-set should be initiated.

Reports over the next few years were unduly optimistic. Different observers noted that Samburu *moranhood* was an anachronism and would die a natural death; that the whole organization of the tribe had been destroyed and simply required reshaping into and acceptable form; and that the Kiliako age-set were marrying and settling down quickly.

Nothing could have been further from the truth. The Kiliako had been disarmed and made to discard their *moran* apparel, it is true, but they had not yet built up adequate herds of cattle with which to compete with older and richer men in marriage, and there was nothing that the administration could do to force such a large age-set to marry especially when only a limited number of Samburu were prepared to give them their daughters and kinswomen in marriage.

As the administration gained confidence in its ability to control, so the Samburu became more of a governed and less of a self-governing tribe. Their uncertainty in the future of Leroghi did not abate, and matters came to a head in 1939 when it was proposed to cull their stock in a final effort to curb over-grazing. This led to a minor uprising in which the two notable features were the revival of the Kiliako age-set who wore their former *moran* ornaments and carried spears, and the threats levelled against the government-appointed headmen who retired for safety to Maralal. The trouble started in January, became serious in March, and was over by June after another levy force had been called in. The plan to make a census of all stock and to cull them was then abandoned.

It is now clear, of course, that the Kiliako had not settled down, that the indigenous social system of the tribe had not been destroyed, and that proposals for de-stocking the district were premature. The assumption that the Kiliako age-set could settle down to elderhood at once (rather as the Rendille might) was quite unjustified as events of 1939 showed only too clearly.

It should be noted that during this troubled period, the elders did wish to co-operate with the administration in maintaining peace in the area and appear to have controlled the activities of the *moran* to a far greater extent than was officially acknowledged. The principal criticism was that they did not actively help the British to bring murderers to (British) justice; a justice that was as cold-blooded and inhuman in Samburu eyes as inter-tribal murders were to the British.[21] In fairness to the administration, they did acknow-

21. The Samburu custom of lynching certain offenders (*lbubuu*, p. 112), might be regarded as a tribal precedent for capital punishment, although the

ledge the essential loyalty of the Samburu tribe. When the future of Leroghi was being debated before the Land Commission, it was a number of ex-administrators of this period, notably Bader and Glenday, who came to support the Samburu case and in effect won it on their behalf.

13. *Mekuri* (initiated 1936). This age-set was the first to be brought directly under administrative control. It was at first planned that its members should only remain *moran* for two or three years, after which time they would marry and a new age-set would be formed. In this way, it was hoped that there would be fewer *moran* to give any trouble and that their truculent spirit would be broken. In order to hasten the progress of the age-set through *moranhood*, the Mekuri were made to perform their total series of *ilmugit* ceremonies in a matter of months where they would normally have taken as many years. By the end of 1937 most phratries had been made to perform all the ceremonies up to the *ilmugit* of the bull ceremony, ignoring and apparently ignorant of the fact that only a portion of the Kiliako age-set had as yet succeeded in marrying.

There is no doubt that the administration had a firm hold over the Samburu at this time, and that the Mekuri have since been regarded with some contempt by other Samburu for the weak position in which they were placed. It was significant that the Mekuri did not play a leading part in the uprising of 1939: it was still the Kiliako who came to the forefront at a time of unrest. Nevertheless, in the light of later known facts, government reports concerning the complete lack of spirit among the Mekuri were exaggerated. The Mekuri seem to have paid little attention to official restrictions not to sing certain provocative songs, not to eat meat in the bush, and not to have mistresses of their own. In so much as they took heed, it was to avoid widespread stock theft and murder. In spite of official reports that most of the Mekuri had settled down and married by 1942, only a handful are known to have done so before 1948 when the next age-set was eventually initiated.

The Second World War provided an opportune interruption to government measures which seemed to have reached an impasse with the uprising of 1939. An attempt to initiate the next age-set in 1940 was successfully opposed by the Samburu elders. With the war no new measures could effectively be introduced. But the Samburu could, if they wanted to, become *askaris* (soldiers) in the King's African Rifles, and this provided the Mekuri age-set with an outlet

---

Samburu would not admit this: it is regarded as an anomalous, unpropitious, and rare practice of the past.

they badly needed: a chance to opt out of their humiliating position at home with an occupation abroad worthy of a warrior and fully connived at by both elders and administration. During the war years, 348 volunteers were accepted by the K.A.R. and many others rejected. Assuming that these were mostly from the Mekuri age-set (a few Kiliako are known to have volunteered), this would have been between 17 per cent and 20 per cent of the total age-set at that time.[22] This is an impressively high proportion and it is the foundation of a tradition that has grown up among the Samburu in recent years for military service at first in the army and later extended also to the police.

The first reports of the Samburu as good fighters ever to be recorded came from their officers during the war. Up to this point it had always been assumed that they were a cowardly tribe, but now they were praised in glowing terms, and according to one report they were 'second to no other East African tribesmen as askaris on active service'. From this point the Samburu were regarded benevolently as a loyal and progressive tribe, and administrating them took on a new look. The difficulties of the Kiliako era had been surmounted by the chance of a war.

14. *Kimaniki* (initiated 1948).[23] The proposal to initiate the successors to the Mekuri in 1940 never came to fruition, and it was not until 1948 that this occurred; not, it is true, without some prodding, but at least without any direct orders from the administration or levy forces. It seems likely that a new age-set was due to be initiated at this time just as one had previously been due in 1936 (or very soon after). It was becoming clear that the administration now intended to allow the Samburu to run their age-set system as they wished. The tractable Mekuri had obliterated the memory of the past, and almost every other year a new district commissioner took charge of the district without, perhaps, realizing how rapidly relations between the Samburu and administration were improving.

The Kimaniki were an unusually large age-set, and without actually being truculent as the Kiliako had been, they did show considerable spirit. The former practice of blooding their spears as a mark of prestige had by this time been abandoned, but the desire to gain prestige by stealing at least one cow was still a major incentive to stock theft. Although this led to occasional fines imposed

22. According to another (later) estimate, there were 401 askaris in the K.A.R. during the war and this would represent between 20 per cent and 23 per cent. Possibly fifty-three had been serving before large-scale recruitment started.

23. My field work was carried out during the period that the Kimaniki were *moran*. Chapter 6 of *The Samburu* is essentially about this age-set.

on the tribe as a whole, the stock theft was unofficially regarded as an undesirable by-product of Samburu society rather than as something that called for radically new policies. The administration's concern over the excesses of the Kimaniki age-set was tempered by the extent to which they followed the Mekuri age-set in enlisting for military service, at first in Malaya (in 1952) and later against the Mau Mau. While figures for recruitment during the post-war years are not available, they must have been considerable.

Another reason which served to moderate the administration's attitude towards the Kimaniki as *moran* was the changing nature of the problems facing them. Progressively during the 1950s, official concern focused attention on grazing control and the eroded state of the land. In this matter, the government were confronted by the elders who controlled the adherence to traditional methods of grazing, and the *moran* were essentially onlookers with little or no influence. Until the policy was abandoned in 1961, grazing control and grazing trespass became the principal matter of contention between the Samburu and the British administration, overshadowing the stock theft that was constantly taking place.

15. *Kishili* (initiated 1960–2). Under pressure from the administration, the Masula phratry agreed to initiate their boys in 1960. It had been hoped in official circles that this would encourage the high-spirited Kimaniki age-set to settle down to elderhood, and so reduce the amount of stock theft in the area. However, a combination of passive resistance to this policy and a severe drought led to further delays, and the remainder of the tribe did not follow with their initiations until 1962.

Recent Rendille History: 1921–62

Since 1921, when the Samburu and Rendille were officially confined to separate districts, the traditional links have been maintained. Indeed, as Table 6 (p. 138) shows, there appears to have been no significant decrease in the degree of intermarriage between them.[24] The traditional linking of age-sets has also continued (Chart 7, p. 33); but unlike the Samburu, the periodic division of time by age-sets is not particularly useful when studying Rendille history. They did not have a comparable institution of *moranhood*, and important events would not focus attention on their young men.

24. The present generation of Samburu (149+75 marriages in the table) have an estimated 18 per cent of wives from the Rendille proper and the Ariaal, while the fathers of these same men (the 110 marriages of the past generation, which would all have occurred before 1921) had an estimated 21 per cent. The differences between these estimates is not significant.

As a corollary to this, the administration did not face the problems of coping with their young men who, in any case, tended to accept the arrival of elderhood with a greater willingness. In fact, the Rendille conformed well with the type of society that the administration would have liked the Samburu to adopt in 1936.

Grazing control also caused less of a problem. The only rudimentary form that was at all practicable with the widely dispersed camel economy was to define territorial limits for the tribe as a whole, and to attempt somewhat spasmodically to curb trespass beyond these.

At first during the 1920s, there was some attempt by the administration to encourage the Rendille to develop so as to bring them more into line with the other tribes of Kenya: otherwise, it was felt, they would be relegated to a second class tribe. However, the response from the Rendille to each new attempt varied from complete disinterest to considerable hostility. Two principal causes of Rendille resentment were the imposition of taxes and attempts at using their labour compulsorily to build roads. By the 1930s, the Northern Frontier Province generally was recognized as posing different types of problems from the tribal reserves further south and a more *laissez-faire* policy was adopted towards their development. This led to a considerable improvement in the relations between the Rendille and the administration based primarily on a mutual unconcern.

A particular hazard with which the Rendille have had to contend in the more recent years has been their closeness to the Ethiopian frontier. The Reshiat and Boran tribes both straddled this frontier, and could obtain firearms in Ethiopia. This has led to a succession of armed raids and counter-raids from the north on unarmed settlements in the south, many of the raiders being Kenyans who have crossed the frontier to collect arms. Warfare of this kind has principally been between the Reshiat and the Boran, but the Rendille have suffered at intervals from these raids. By tradition, the Boran are their enemies and the Reshiat their distant allies. In practice, however, quite the worst Rendille casualties appear to have been suffered at the hands of armed Reshiat raiders (who mistook them on at least one occasion for Boran): 57 Rendille were killed in one raid in 1919, 16 in another in 1932, and 76 in another in 1952. All raids at the hands of the Boran have led to only a few deaths: usually one or two. Official reports on these raids have paid tribute to the spirit with which the Rendille have defended themselves and have counter-attacked, but with only spears they have always been at a disadvantage. The government view has confirmed the tribal belief that the Rendille immunity to many more raids was largely due to the widespread respect for their fighting prowess.

Faced with this uneasy and extensive frontier situation, the administration at Marsabit have admitted that the Rendille are the least administered tribe in the area, and this has been a major factor encouraging their *laissez-faire* policy.

The Second World War did not affect the Rendille unduly. They have since been criticized by some for not volunteering for service in the K.A.R. at this time (according to one report less than five Rendille were serving compared with the official figure of 348 Samburu). But it is perhaps less well known except among the Rendille that when a contingent of the South African army was passing through their country to fight in the Abyssinian Campaign, elders of Galdeelan clan at the personal request of the Governor of Kenya gave them their blessing, an unusually potent one. The Italians were defeated shortly after this.

During the 1950s, some attempt has been made to develop the water resources of the District and to impose grazing restrictions on Mount Kulal. But this has affected the cattle owners rather than the camel owners. The diffuse tendency for certain Rendille to keep cattle and to acquire certain Samburu characteristics related to polygamy and *moranhood* was noted in the previous chapter.

Conclusion

The Samburu and Rendille do not have what might be described as a developed sense of history. Trible myths are few, memories are conflicting and the apparent inconsistencies for the inquiring ethnographer are not regarded as particularly significant by the people themselves. In so far as they look for some charter expressing their social relations, it is not so much to a putative past as to their traditions of ceremonial practice. These, at least, have been described in some detail in Chapters 2 and 3.

It would be wrong, therefore, to approach the problems encountered by the administration in this area wholly in terms of a historical framework. Nevertheless, the difficulties experienced by the British administration during its forty years in the area provide a basis from which to analyse certain critical problems. This is the topic of the next chapter.

6

THE SAMBURU AND RENDILLE UNDER BRITISH ADMINISTRATION

The outline of recent history, considered in the previous chapter, serves as an introduction to the problems facing the former British administration from the times that they were primarily concerned with maintaining peace in the area to the more recent times when they were more concerned with such domestic problems as grazing control.

It is useful to contrast these two fundamentally different types of problem. The policy of maintaining peace between warring tribes was essentially one in which there was little option except to impose a solution by force, and as a solution it was generally popular among weaker tribes such as the Samburu. The later policy of introducing grazing control, on the other hand, was one that depended for its success on the willing co-operation of the people themselves and on making full use of their indigenous system of tribal control to supplement the limited resources of the administration.

The aim of this chapter is to examine the extent to which the British administration succeeded in harnessing this indigenous system, and the nature of the forces that were opposing them. In order to do this, four broad areas that have concerned the administration are examined in detail. The first concerns the imposed and the indigenous systems of control and the appointment of chiefs. The second concerns the problem of coping with the Samburu *moran*. The third concerns the imposition of grazing control and the implications that this has for the total Samburu (and Rendille) economy. And the fourth concerns the nature of the Samburu–Rendille boundary and the problems created largely by the administration themselves rather than by the two tribes. These topics tend to involve the Samburu rather than the Rendille, largely because they have presented more problems for administration in addition to having closer contact with the forces of change elsewhere in Kenya.

Administration of the area has since been handed over to the Kenya Government, and the details of this analysis are in effect matters of history. However, in so much as the problems facing the British administration earlier in the century are still very real problems today and likely to remain so for some time, the lessons to be learnt from earlier mistakes as well as successes have a current and future value. Here, then, we are more concerned with assessing these problems in the light of experience than with positing any novel solutions for the area.

Imposed and Indigenous Systems of Control

Just how affected have the Rendille and Samburu been by the changes that East Africa has undergone during the present century? Taking the Samburu as the more affected of the two, limited statistics are available which presented in a certain way imply considerable progress, and dependence on recent innovations. Thus, as a measure of progress, there were between five and six times as many children at school in Maralal (Samburu) District in 1961 as there had been in 1952; and as a measure of dependence, hospitals in the district were so popular that during 1961 there were almost half as many out-patient visits for treatment as people in the district: an average of one visit per person every other year. Presented in another way, however, these statistics do not necessarily suggest a society in the throes of a social and cultural upheaval. Hospital treatment is free and demonstrably more effective than Samburu medical treatment: it therefore offers something valuable to the people without demanding anything in return. School education can hardly be said to be a major facet of Samburu life: the actual number of children attending school in 1961 still only represented about 1·2 per cent of those in the district who were eligible. Moreover, figures for hospitals and schools are deceptive in that they were established at each of the three administrative centres where there was a considerable cosmopolitan detribalized fringe who found hospitals more convenient and schools more promising than the vast majority of Samburu. The Turkana at Baragoi, the Dorobo at Wamba, and the members of a number of tribes at Maralal benefited from these to a very marked extent; and to this extent, the Samburu elsewhere did not benefit as much as the figures might suggest.

Regardless of the future implications of modern medicines and education, these are not direct measures of social change. Indeed, in so far as the Samburu tended to hoard their prescribed medicines for use in *any* illness and to withdraw their sons from school as soon as they were of an age to herd cattle, one wonders how deeply even these innovations would be felt in the last analysis.

A far more critical measure of the extent to which modern innovations affected the Samburu way of life was to be seen in the use that was made of the civil courts set up by the administration. While these courts had no traditional precedent whatsoever, they were administered by some of the most respected Samburu elders. One can assume quite reasonably, therefore, that the extent to which other Samburu resorted to these courts to settle their grievances was a measure of the extent to which the tribal system of control was being superseded by the imposed system, and a fundamental measure of tribal disintegration.

The following table shows the number of cases of civil litigation officially recorded over the years:

Table 8
CIVIL LITIGATION BETWEEN 1931 AND 1961

Period	Total number of cases heard	Average number of cases for each year
1931–36	151	25·1
1937–42	117	19·5
(1943–44	no figures available)	(?)
1945–50	223	37·2
1951–56	126	21·0
1957–61	159	31·8

A detailed examination of all the cases occurring in one specific year showed that more than 60 per cent involved at least one litigant (and often both) from another tribe. In other words, this implies that in solving their own internal disputes, the Samburu as a whole resorted to the courts about ten times a year, and that this figure remained relatively constant for a period of thirty years. When one considers that there were partially detribalized Samburu living in the three administrative centres, this figure is astonishly low, and suggests that the principal role of the courts was to settle intertribal grievances.

The manner whereby the Samburu settle their scores has already been outlined in Chapter 3. By resorting to tribal means of obtaining satisfaction in some dispute, a man may have to wait months or even years, and eventually he may have to accept some compromise. By resorting to a civil court, he may hope for a definite judgment and prompt satisfaction. The principal cause for adherence to tribal methods and compromise solutions is that a litigant must continue to live among his fellows and he does not strengthen his position by turning his back on tribal methods. By accepting the compromise judgment of his local clansmen, his reputation as a worthy man is upheld, and his adversary remains morally indebted to him. In so far as there is compromise rather than a clear-cut solution, it is because the pros and cons of the case, and the context of the relationships involved, are not simple. The debated compromise solution is a part of continuing relationship. The court decision is arrived at outside the context in which the dispute arose and is less likely to give a permanent satisfaction. Several instances have been recorded in which Samburu elders, dissatisfied with the justice delivered by the court, either because they were unable to prove their case or because the judgment delivered was considered too harsh or too lenient, have resorted to customary ways of obtaining satisfaction. In other cases, local custom has been turned against certain court elders who were felt to have given unfair judgments by Samburu standards. Having been involved in domestic disputes at an official level, they have found themselves involved at a popular level.

Thus, while the first half of the twentieth century had an undeniable impact on life in the area and alternative forms of control were often preferred by the administration, all available evidence suggests that the Samburu were in full control of their indigenous system of internal control. That this was equally true of the Rendille can hardly be doubted when one considers the extent to which they were less in touch with new ideas and new pressures.

It is to this extent that the customs outlined in Chapters 3 and 4 relating to social control in the two tribes have more than a merely historical relevance. Such apparently irrelevant aspects of their lives as the control over their marriage suits and disputes play a critical part in their system of control (p. 104). So long as they are allowed a free rein in handling their affairs and individuals are not encouraged to use the new courts as a means of exploiting the traditional system, they can largely resolve any issues to their own satisfaction which the official courts through lack of resources or evidence may have to leave unresolved.

Government Appointed Elders

The Rendille chiefs and headmen 'are consistently inferior. ... One does not expect much one gets less but they are wild people and they have been taught little of the world and its ways.'

'The Samburu Chiefs and Headmen are a collection of the most useless and boneless and effete tribal rulers I have ever had to do with in my experience of fifteen years of Native tribes.'

Two administrators in the 1920s

In their efforts to establish firm control over the Rendille and Samburu, the early administrators naturally searched for some indigenous system of authority which might help them in their task. But they did not always make allowance for the fact that in these societies, prominent elders had a certain influence over one another rather than a well defined power, and that this was due primarily to their status in a rather broad sense and not to any offices they held. These were not societies in which there was concentration of power in the hands of a chosen elite, and the above quotations express some of the early frustration of these administrators when faced with this type of situation. It was not simply that the men appointed as chiefs and headmen did not have the necessary qualities to fulfil these roles adequately, but that local values were not geared towards this form of authority.

Reports on headmen (and chiefs)[1] over the years reveal certain characteristic patterns. Thus, in the first place criticisms tend to be strongest when and where official policies most intruded on the lives of the two tribes. Among the Rendille, it was during the 1920s that attempts were made to introduce new and progressive measures, and criticisms of their headmen were common. These attempts were relaxed during the 1930s and since then the official records have regularly paid a brief tribute to the effectiveness of these men in maintaining peace within the tribe. Among the Samburu, there were also early criticisms of the headmen during periods when the government was trying to extend its powers or maintain a firmer control over the tribe. More recently, these criticisms have very generally spread down from the headmen on Leroghi to those in the low country as grazing schemes have been extended in this direction.

The dilemma of these men has been essentially their conflict in loyalties. The Rendille and Samburu generally have not readily appreciated the official point of view that although there might be prior local consultation, the headmen were government appointments (and hence accountable primarily to the administration) and not some kind of elected representatives (accountable to the people). In so far as headmen have had any influence prior to their appointment, it has been because their wisdom and powers of persuasion have been linked to a sensitivity to subtle changes in public opinion, a preparedness to back down when they have found themselves in a clear minority, and in the last resort an accountability to the consensus of tribal opinion. With each appointment, however, the administrations unwittingly wanted to reverse this accountability. From this point, the incumbents were deprived of one of the basic conditions on which much of their influence had previously relied: their unquestioning allegiance to their fellow tribesmen. Without this basic condition, the new and alien powers with which they were endowed had a hollow significance.[2]

1. Government *Chiefs* are senior to *Headmen*. This section is relevant to both, and for convenience, they are referred to here collectively as *headmen*.
2. For a fuller discussion on the nature of pressures which govern the freedom and the influence of informal leaders, see Homans, G. C., *The Human Group*, especially Chapter VIII.

A second characteristic pattern to be inferred from these official reports over the years is in the careers of some of these men, appointed first as headmen and then, sometimes, promoted to become chiefs. There is no doubt that a few outstanding men have succeeded for a time not only in influencing their fellows on some major issues, but also in modifying certain government policies; these have tended to be in areas where the government has impinged only partially on the lives of the people without having introduced radically new and unpopular policies. With changes in policies and district commissioners, however, these men have tended to lose their influence in current problems and have faced the unenviable choice either of sheltering behind government policies (and losing their traditional influence), or of openly defying government policies (and being removed from office), or of doing nothing. The majority of headmen throughout their careers have preferred to do nothing, but have succeeded in retaining their official position by virtue of minimum co-operation, or by occasionally surpassing themselves in a way which has persuaded a reluctant administration that they are still probably the best men available for the job.

A third characteristic pattern is the contrast between the general praise that successive administrators have had for each tribe (putting to one side certain differences over policy) on the one hand, and the recurrent criticism, especially among the Samburu, that there has been for the headmen. It is as if the problem of communicating with the tribe through these men has never been more than partially resolved.

In so far as there has been any attempt at encouraging self-government on minor issues by the administration of either tribe, it has been in setting up local African District Councils (A.D.C.s) which would meet several times a year. Potentially, the A.D.C. was an embryonic form of local government for each district, very much intended to represent a consensus of local views. In theory, at least, as the area developed, so direct government rule in domestic matters (through the appointed headmen) could give way to indirect rule through the A.D.C.s. For a number of reasons, however, the A.D.C.s never really looked as though they might shoulder an increasing responsibility. One reason for this was that the indigenous systems of control continued to cope quite adequately with new domestic problems without having to resort to any official body (cf. the popular disinterest in the courts). Secondly, the majority of elders serving on the A.D.C. were chiefs, headmen, court elders, or some other government-appointed men, and the district commissioner was the *ex-officio* chairman. Thus, what might in time conceivably have developed into a new form of administration, involved very much the same people as the existing form, and its meetings would reflect the existing structure rather than some new departure. The district commissioner (and other European officers) would address the assembly to expound some new aspect of policy (e.g. on grazing, on game, on roads, etc.) and the assembly would on the whole listen. Generally speaking there would be little playback from the floor, and virtually none from those elders who did not hold some official post. Where the official policies were unpopular, there would not normally be any practical alternative proposed. Where there was any organized opposition, it was often quite evident that the issue had been decided by the elders beforehand. Under these circumstances, the administration was not encouraged to relinquish a major degree of control over policies to the A.D.C. Indeed, as recently as the mid-1950s, the official reports were still advocating that the Samburu administration should show no sign of weakness in controlling unpopular policies. By implication, both tribes were to be treated very much as governed tribes almost until the time that Kenya became independent.

The consequences of this situation were almost inevitable. There were two sets of values with little in common (save mutual goodwill on both sides) and two worlds of reality coexisting in one district. Communication from the top of the grass roots was frequently misunderstood and misinterpreted. Effective communication from the grass roots was virtually absent, except through a group of headmen who had the future of their appointments to consider.

Ironically, among the Samburu where this process was more pronounced, the Samburu term which the administration had coined for their headmen, *laiguenak* (s. *laiguenani*), acquired a new nuance.[3] Previously, it had referred to influential men who in debate could act as spokesmen for public opinion in an issue, summarizing the popular feeling and giving wise counsel. Now, in so far as the government headmen had a role to play, it was frequently that of appearing to act as spokesmen for the administration, implicitly accepting their policies rather than voicing the popular reaction against these policies. These men came to be known as *laiguenak lolsirkali*, or spokesmen of the government, as opposed to *laiguenak loongishu*, or spokesmen of the people: the latter included those elders who retained an influence among their fellows following the traditional pattern whether or not they held some government appointment. According to the popular image, the *laiguenak lolsirkali* were constantly loitering in the vicinity of the government stations, in touch with the government affairs of the district but out of touch with the affairs of their own home and clans; while the *laiguenak loongishu* in

3. For a fuller discussion of this, see *The Samburu*, p. 181.

turning their backs on the glamour of station life retained their popularity and the confidence of their fellows. Thus, corresponding to the
two worlds of reality, there were seen to be two types of *laiguenak*.
This state of affairs gave rise to a series of incongruous situations
described in subsequent sections of this chapter.

Control over the Samburu Moran

'The existing *moran* system is now an anachronism which in these days
can only lead to trouble, as it creates an idle class of irresponsible youths,
who, deprived of their former work of defending the tribe are bound to
get into mischief.'

An administrator in 1930s

The historical background to the governmental policy towards
the Samburu *moran* was outlined in Chapter 5. While the administration in the 1930s apparently achieved its primary aim of bringing
the *moran* under control, it misjudged their position in the contemporary society and its claims to have destroyed the institution of
moranhood were premature and were later shown to be unfounded.
The government officers clearly recognized that the *moran* were still
warrior-oriented and that it was their desire to gain prestige within
their Clubs which led them to commit wanton murders. But they
looked no further than this. They assumed that by bringing the
offenders to justice, by degrading the *moran* and by forcing them
to retire to an early elderhood, they could change their attitudes.
With this in view, they disarmed the senior *moran* of the Kiliako
age-set, they brought in a levy force whenever there was serious
trouble, they made the succeeding Mekuri age-set perform all their
ilmugit ceremonies in a short space of time and forbade them to
observe certain other customs traditionally associated with *moranhood*. As one administrator put it, 'We have now forced them (the
Samburu) to accept males who have no tribal claim to manhood, a
very drastic step, and, while no one can possibly criticize the Government for its action, clearly the Samburu cannot be left without any
social organization or they will develop some new, and probably
undesirable, system of their own.'

Why has this 'anachronism', then, persisted for another thirty
years? What false assumptions did the administrators of the 1930s
make? The answer to these questions are to be found in Chapter 3.
The essential point that they failed to grasp was that the age-set of
unmarried *moran* was not simply linked to a warrior-oriented
society; it was also a vital part of the wider social organization
related to highly polygamous families and a concentration of power
and wives among the older men. To this extent at least, the society

was not an anachronism, and only a major social upheaval of the economic organization and of the distribution of power could have led to the abandonment of the *moran* system.

Thus, when the administration proposed to force the initiation of a new age-set every third year or so, they saw only one aspect of the total problem and argued that each age-set would be small and would marry and settle down to elderhood quietly as soon as it was replaced by a new age-set. Seen in a broader context, it is at once evident that had this policy been carried out, instead of one small age-set of unmarried men to cope with at a time and two during the period of change over, there would have been three, four, or even five small age-sets of unmarried men; but the rate of polygamy need not have been affected, for the fathers and kinsmen of marriageable girls would still have been unprepared to allow their daughters to be married to young men who had not yet learned to show respect and had not yet built up adequate herds of their own.

This misjudgement of the *moran* and of the place they occupied in the society at any time is a recurrent feature of the official records. Thus, the rate at which the Kiliako age-set were settling down to elderhood was completely over-estimated in 1936 so that when this age-set emerged once again as *moran* and played a prominent part in the insurrection of 1939, the authorities appear to have been totally unprepared and baffled. Again, the extent to which the subsequent Mekuri age-set were still in many ways *moran* in the traditional sense appears to have been misrepresented: it was not simply that surreptitiously they continued with their customs of eating meat in the bush and having mistresses (both forbidden by the authorities), but that they were constantly reported to be ostentatiously singing forbidden songs and dancing forbidden dances. While it was officially claimed in 1942 that most of them had married, a more recent census has indicated that the clear majority did not have a chance to settle down until the change-over of age-sets six years later. A similar claim was made with regard to the Kimaniki age-set in 1956 when it was officially reported that they were all either married or marriageable: this was two years before they were marriageable (through the performance of the *ilmugit* of the bull ceremonies) and at least six years before the majority of them began to marry.

These inaccurate reports are an indication of the extent to which the authorities over the years appear to have been essentially out of touch with the *moran* and their activities and more closely in touch with elders who preferred to give the impression that each successive age-set of *moran* was very much under control, not to say on the verge of elderhood. The authorities for their part wanted no better news than this.

Another misinterpretation of the *moran* system and source of government confusion was the position of the leading *moran* in each phratry. They too were called *laiguenak* by the Samburu, and were expected to have some influence among the other *moran* in managing their own affairs, in making representations to the elders, and in initiating raids. In a sense the *moran laiguenak* were expected to embody the warrior ideal of *moranhood* just as the elder *laiguenak* were expected to embody the worthy ideals of elderhood. While they had the capacity to influence and even to lead *moran*, it did not follow that they would in time become influential *laiguenak* of the elders: they often had the wrong qualities for this.

Faced with the problem of coping with the *moran*, the government hoped to be able to gain a direct access to them through their *moran laiguenak*. This once again attached too great an importance to the term *laiguenak* and tended to assume a type of authority that did not exist in the tribal system. It led to a similar situation as with the elder *laiguenak*: those *moran* with the qualities best suited to the government's purpose either did not get appointed as official *laiguenak*, or refused to be appointed, or never built up a rapport with the administration; while those that tried to cultivate a rapport with the administration rapidly lost influence over some of their more truculent age mates.

But there was a further incongruity in recognizing the *moran laiguenak* as being in a position of authority over the *moran*. The policy ignored and was apparently ignorant of the very real control that the elders, notably the firestick elders, could have over the *moran*. To regard the *moran* at any time as delinquents and hooligans was to ignore the fact that they unquestioningly accepted indigenous tribal conventions and tribal control: their worst excesses were essentially in defiance of newly imposed restrictions. Many of the most effective government headmen were in fact firestick elders, and used their powers as such to control the *moran* to a greater extent than perhaps the administration realized. The incongruity to the Samburu was that while the government seemed often to expect too much from the headmen in matters over which they had no traditional control, they did not encourage them enough to assert their traditional powers in controlling the *moran*. Instead, they would invite the *moran laiguenak* to attend the A.D.C. meetings and in a number of ways cultivate them when in Samburu eyes, they were still little more than children.

*   *   *

In 1962 there was every sign that the new age-set of *moran* would continue to be *moran* in as full a sense as their two predecessors: there was, for instance, no indication that they were being circumcised at an altogether younger age than in the past nor that they would retire to elderhood any sooner. But the problem of how the *moran* might be managed remained, especially in a Kenya that was fast developing.

It seems likely that they will welcome opportunities for congenial outside employment if these are offered. Two immediately beneficial effects that one can foresee are that to the extent that they are given this employment, the problems of control over them will be less; and secondly, as a future generation of elders, they will have an altogether more accurate appreciation of the transformation of Kenya to the south under modern conditions. As against this, it could be argued that exposure to other more westernized forms of society could lead to a challenge to the traditional authority of the elders and to a breakdown of social control and custom.

In answer to the last point, up to 1960 it could be claimed that *moran* from the Mekuri and Kimaniki age-sets when they returned from services in the forces have shown themselves only too willing to settle down to the traditional way of life. The strong hold that this system has over them that it can draw young men back after years spent elsewhere has perhaps three principal causes. In the first place, apart from the handful that had been kept at school, they had been exposed to the traditional society until they were mature enough to be accepted into one or other of the services at the age of at least 17, and it had ingrained itself as a form of life worth having. Secondly, by the time that these young men returned to their homes, they were on the verge of elderhood; and with everything to gain from becoming elders they had had a clear stake in preserving the traditional system. And thirdly, so long as the society at large had control over who should marry whom, it could bring to heel even young men who rejected the traditional authority: short of abducting young women or of successfully appealing above the heads of the elders to the higher courts, young rebels to the system would find themselves powerless to re-enter the society on their own terms.

From the administration's point of view also, there appears to be a very good reason for allowing those *moran* who choose to remain in their traditional society to occupy their traditional position. In spite of the bad reputation that the Samburu *moran* of the Kimaniki age-set had for stock theft, there is good reason to assume that in other ways they caused less trouble to the authorities than many other young men elsewhere. Thus, to quote one instance: as against the popular belief that they would hunt lions and other wild animals, there were only twenty known offences against protected game in the district in 1955, and seven of these were committed by Europeans who had been granted permission to visit the district. To quote another instance: a European police officer once remarked to me that from his own experience in Kenya, the Samburu were one of the easiest tribes to handle: they were capable of managing their own internal affairs, and because they were not in the habit of drinking, there were fewer cases of homicide arising out of drunken brawls. This was, he suggested, a tribute to the extent to which the *moran* were still essentially under tribal control.

Land Development and Stock Control among the Samburu

In 1934, as a result of the Kenya Land Commission, the right of the Samburu to live on the Leroghi Plateau was confirmed, and it was awarded to them on condition that the number of stock on it should be limited. New positive policies seemed to be called for and administrative activity entered a new phase in which emphasis was placed on the need for stock control. Officially, the prolonged period of uncertainty over Leroghi was at an end; but for the Samburu themselves, the decision did not appear to resolve their land problems finally. It was seen as just one more tactical move in the battle for Leroghi, and their suspicions were confirmed by the new proposals for stock restrictions. The further troubles of the 1930s that largely derived from this did not, however, divert the administration from pursuing their new and ostensibly progressive policies.

Initially, the neighbouring European settlers had considerable influence in the area and indirectly affected the policies adopted towards the Samburu on Leroghi. Later, however, it developed into a political issue between the administration and the Samburu themselves, so that by the 1950s, when the European settlers had no direct influence over administrative policies, it became the most important issue in the general policy towards the Samburu and the most salient cause of Samburu mistrust.

The recent history of the development of stock control has already been outlined in Chapter 5, and the general form of the grazing schemes in Chapter 1. The two principal arguments that were put forward in favour of grazing schemes were that they provided the only way to prevent the Samburu from suffering chronic starvation as their numbers increased and their land deteriorated, and that once Kenya gained its independence, a tribe that did not effectively conserve its land would be treated as a second-class tribe and would be less likely to qualify for grants for further development;

indeed it might even be legally deprived of some of its best land on these grounds. The critical issue was whether the Samburu would respond to progress with progress or, like the Rendille in the 1920s, would virtually force the administration to revert to a more *laissez-faire* policy. Unlike the Rendille, however, the Samburu had more to lose; and until they accepted grazing control and recognized its advantages, the administration had to be prepared to face an unpleasant period of friction between those supporting traditional values and those favouring progress. In the event, it was the traditional values that survived and the grazing schemes that were abandoned. Was the attempt at imposing these schemes contending with impossible odds? In the remainder of this section, a further examination is made of the two sides of the controversy.

*   *   *

The conflict between the two points of view is expressed very well in the published evidence to the Kenya Land Commission when a Samburu elder was asked at an inquiry for his views:

'*Capt. Wilson:* If your cattle go on increasing and the grass gets finished, what will you do?'

'*Nibilei s/o Olkopen:* I would still keep my cattle. I do not want them to die. I want to look after them. They are our life. As the Government likes shillings, so we Samburu like cattle.'

'*Capt. Wilson:* Would you rather have three hundred cattle or five hundred starving ones?'

'*Nibilei:* I would rather have a thousand starving ones until God gives us grass, because if a man has a lot of cattle, and some die, he still has some left, but if a man has a few cattle and they die, he has none left.'[4]

Although this conversation dates from the 1930s, there has been so little change in attitudes that it could almost have taken place in 1960. It reflects on the one hand a view of calculated stock breeding in which the optimum size of a herd has been worked out and the hazards minimized; and on the other hand a view in which the hazards are so great that the optimum size is seen as the largest herd possible.

While the administrative policy under the British was fully supported by expert opinion on the state of the soil and the degree of

4. *Kenya Land Commission, Evidence*, 1933, p. 1602.

over-grazing, it should be noted that historical evidence that was cited in support of grazing control appears to have been slender to say the least. On balance, historical evidence supports, if anything, the Samburu contention that there has been no further soil erosion in recent times.

Thus, in support of stock control one older man has been officially quoted who remembers the long grass that once grew in the now barren Barsaloi area, and at least one earlier traveller has been misquoted. And yet Stigand who travelled through the Barsaloi area in 1909 describes it as barren and on his map he marks it as thorn desert.[5] The depressing accounts of grazing in the area in 1933 could generally have been applied to the situation in 1960.[6] One witness who had visited the country in 1905 and 1911 described the whole area as being grazed down: 'It never looked like a country that would carry a lot of cattle.' And of the land to the east of the Matthews Range, he said that it was 'perfectly terrible country. No water, and it just slopes down to desert.'[7] More recent forecasts predicted that by 1956 this eastern area would be utterly uninhabitable at the present rate of soil erosion; and yet immigration continued to the area until in 1959, it carried perhaps one-sixth of the Samburu cattle and up to two-fifths of their small stock.

The consensus of expert opinion is impressively weighted towards the view that there has been soil erosion and that this is constantly taking place, but one still has the impression that the case has been overstated from time to time and that expert opinion may have underrated the recuperative powers of some of the vegetation. In 1962, after a prolonged drought had severely depleted Samburu herds, fresh rains brought a completely new look to the countryside and long grass was to be seen almost everywhere—including Barsaloi.

A further argument in favour of stock control has been the putative increase in Samburu stock. Official estimates throughout the 1950s ranged from 10 per cent to 16 per cent a year. Once again, this seems to be an overstatement of the case. Table 2 on page 10 suggests that regardless of veterinary medicines and the development of water resources, the ratio of stock to the human population has

5. Stigand, 1910, p. 80. Perhaps it is worth noting that in the early literature generally, one has the impression that in the no-man's-lands between the tribes and in the areas infested with tsetse fly, grazing was often good precisely because no pastoralists cared to stay in these parts, while elsewhere it was bad or non-existent. Under these circumstances, the Barsaloi area could well have recovered and flourished during the 1920s since during this time the Samburu are reported to have kept well south of the district in order to avoid the Turkana further north.
6. *Kenya Land Commission, Evidence*, pp. 1562–9, 1713–15.
7. ibid., pp. 1550–1.

tended to remain comparatively stable, and it is very unlikely that the human population will have increased as fast as even 2 per cent a year. (Moreover, it is noticeable that in spite of the 10–16 per cent claims, official estimates for Samburu cattle set at 300–350,000 head normally did not vary from one year to the next.)

This is not to suggest that the arguments which concluded that few cattle in the area would give the Samburu more milk and meat were necessarily wrong, or that the large numbers of cattle were altogether beneficial for the land, but simply that the situation has possibly been closer to some kind of an ecological balance than has officially been acknowledged and that the Samburu case against grazing control has been stronger than has been conceded.

*   *   *

More can be said of the grazing schemes themselves. In the 1950s, it tended to be the best grazing areas that were first developed as schemes partly because they were more easily accessible for general development and partly because there was a lingering doubt in the minds of government officers as to whether anything could be done about the more eroded and drier areas, or whether any scheme could be effectively enforced. The contrast between the state of the land inside and outside the schemes can best be appreciated when one considers that 73 per cent of the area covered by these schemes in 1959 included the whole of Leroghi, Seiya-Barsalinga, Wamba, and Lbarta; and yet in 1933 it was claimed that apart from these four areas, 'the remaining areas [of the whole district] are not considered capable of supporting cattle'.[8] Much of the remaining 27 per cent of the land inside the schemes and the land subsequently incorporated in 1960 and 1961 was altogether superior to most of the uncontrolled areas.

The effects on the total district of progressively imposing grazing schemes in this way are best appreciated with reference to the densities of livestock which may be taken as a measure of the pressure on the land. At first, the scheme on Leroghi (1952) could accommodate a comparatively high density because of the reliable rainfall. But as new schemes were opened up in increasingly arid parts of the district, so the densities had to be reduced in order to comply with the standards prescribed by soil conservation experts. This meant that more and more cattle had to be squeezed out of the new scheme areas at the expense of the still uncontrolled areas where increasing numbers of stock had to be accommodated in a decreasing reserve. This was particularly exaggerated with sheep and

8. *Kenya Land Commission, Evidence*, 1933, p. 1624.

Table 9

THE CUMULATIVE EFFECT OF GRAZING SCHEMES ON DENSITIES OF LIVESTOCK IN UNCONTROLLED AREAS

| Year | Area of total district inside schemes | Aggregate densities of stock (per 100 acres) | | | | | |
| | | A. In schemes | | B. In uncontrolled areas, assuming no growth of herds | | C. In uncontrolled areas, assuming growth of herds | |
		Cattle	Sheep & goats	Cattle	Sheep & goats	Cattle	Sheep & goats
1952	7·8%	10·2	0·0	8·6	9·7	7·8	6·3
1957	8·4%	10·2	0·0	8·6	9·8	7·9	8·5
1958	12·7%	9·0	0·2	8·7	10·4	8·4	9·7
1959	22·6%	6·9	0·5	9·4	12·0	9·4	12·0
1960	25·8%	(6·8)	(0·4)	(9·7)	(12·8)	(10·0)	(13·6)
1961	31·5%	(7·0)	(0·4)	(9·8)	(14·6)	(10·7)	(17·6)

goats since on principle, these were normally excluded from the schemes because of the destructiveness of the goats.

Table 9 shows the effects of this trend. The true number of stock in the uncontrolled areas and their rates of growth were not actually known, but whatever this number and whether it remained constant (B) or increased (C), there was still the same pattern of increase in densities outside the schemes and decrease inside the schemes (A).[9]

This table has been compiled to demonstrate the trend that was taking place during the 1950s. In so far as it takes no account of differences in quality of land between controlled and uncontrolled areas, it understates the total problem: up to ten cattle per 100 acres in the wetter scheme areas was a relative luxury, whereas the same density in the more arid uncontrolled areas was a considerable overcrowding.

As new schemes devoured the land to the east and north of Leroghi, so the Samburu living in these areas were faced with the choice of joining them or of migrating to the still uncontrolled areas. The relationship between these two types of area was closer than perhaps many officials realized. It was not simply that members of schemes had close kinsmen living in the uncontrolled areas, but

9. In order to calculate the densities for constant size in the uncontrolled areas (B), the official broad estimate for 1959 of 350,000 cattle and 350,000 sheep and goats has been accepted here. In order to calculate for a constant rate of growth, this 1959 estimate has been compared with an earlier one of 300,000 cattle and 250,000 sheep and goats suggested in 1954. The point here is that whatever assumptions one might make concerning the size of herds and their rate of growth, there would still be a similar contrast between A on the one hand and B and C on the other. The figures for 1960 and 1961 are in parentheses since the long drought from 1959 to 1961 would have effectively diminished all densities both inside and outside the schemes and no allowances have been made for this.

also that they positively needed these kinsmen to look after their surplus stock that could not be kept inside the schemes. This surplus stock included all (or nearly all) their small stock, any cattle above and beyond their initially agreed quota, and any increase from their scheme cattle. Officially this increase was to be sold at the local stock sales, but in practice the Samburu preferred to keep their investments in the form of cattle. Thus, in addition to the high pressure of grazing on land in the uncontrolled areas, these were expected by the Samburu to absorb the increase in stock for the district as a whole.

Once again, the Samburu made a distinction between their way of doing things and the administration's. The controlled areas were referred to as *sikim*—a corruption of (grazing) *scheme*—and the uncontrolled areas were referred to as *risaab*—a corruption of (tribal) *reserve*. Those in the *risaab* followed their traditional pattern of life, anxiously watching at the same time the ominous creep of schemes that were devouring more and more of their free land; and those in the *sikim* followed their way of life as well as they could within the imposed limits.

There is little doubt that the more recently imposed schemes made every effort to adapt themselves to the harsher climate of the low country. In the first place, the rigid standards suggested by soil experts were often relaxed so as to include a larger number of Samburu. Secondly, in spite of a technical preference for smaller scheme areas, it was recognized that in these areas where rain was unpredictable and often localized, only the largest schemes with wide expanses for grazing could hope to include at least one area where there would be an adequate rainfall. In the event, when there was the prolonged drought from 1959 to 1961, even these larger schemes proved too small and restrictions had to be relaxed prior to complete abandonment in 1961. However, the larger schemes did at least promise the Samburu greater ease, not only of movement but also of intermigration between settlements.

The one area where there was least freedom of movement and for the Samburu the greatest threat to their traditional mode of existence was on Leroghi. Here the excessive zeal among government officers had led to a gigantic chess-board in which the plateau was divided during 1956 into 244 blocks of about 1,600 acres each. Registered stock owners were forced not only to live in the area allocated to their phratry, but also to remain living in the same block. This contrasted with life in the uncontrolled areas where there was a constant migration between settlements of one phratry and at any one time up to 25 per cent of the stock owners would be living in some settlement associated with some phratry other than their own.

For the officers controlling the Leroghi scheme, proof of its success was seen in the fact that cattle did not erode the land by travelling long distances to grazing and water, kicking up the turf and leaving bare tracks. Further confirmation was seen in the fact that they received relatively few complaints from the Samburu. For the Samburu, there was nothing to be gained from complaining, and those who felt strongly enough had long since left for the uncontrolled areas of the low country. The popular feeling was that any complaint would only lead to more restrictive measures. The Samburu strongly disapproved of schemes elsewhere, but on Leroghi, prior to a loosening of restrictions in 1959, their social life suffered considerably. Even requests to move to another block in order to live with another group would normally be met with a blank refusal. The government officers, in their efforts to control the movements of cattle, had an unduly restrictive effect on the free movement and social life of the people.

While it became apparent to the administration that the zeal of the officers on Leroghi had led to a general worsening of relations with the Samburu, it was still thought that the less restrictive low country schemes could and should be made to work. The policy was known to be unpopular, but felt to be in the very best interests of the Samburu. When new schemes were mooted, a considerable number of Samburu felt free at least to voice their hostility towards them, but official doubts were dispelled by the extent to which many other Samburu appeared ready to comply and one or two were even reported to have asked for further new schemes.

These were not, however, true signs of the popularity of low country schemes. Each new scheme tended to envelop the best remaining grazing land of the uncontrolled areas. For the Samburu, accepting a new scheme in an area to which they were attached was often preferable to moving to an unfamiliar and harsher area. Moreover, they would argue that if the administration intended to cover the whole district with schemes, it was perhaps better to stake a claim at an early stage and make certain of having at least one foot inside a relatively good scheme. If there had to be schemes, then possibly more might be lost by opting out of them at once than by opting in at once and reserving the right to opt out at a later stage (which many of them did).

The Samburu almost universally disapproved of their fellows who made it easier for the administration to impose new schemes (including those chiefs and headmen who actively collaborated in these schemes), but when it came to making a decision for themselves they often preferred to err on the side of caution.

As the administration saw it, the schemes attracted the more progressive Samburu, while as the Samburu saw it, the uncontrolled areas attracted those who were prepared to live a harsher life in order to maintain their traditional form of existence. *Sikim* and *Risaab* were not just different economic responses to a technical problem: they were also different patterns of social existence.

Paradoxically, the Samburu inside schemes were in a rather similar position to the Ariaal Rendille. Their herds could not multiply and as families grew in size, the new junior wives and the growing adult sons could no longer be contained inside the schemes. Thus, the uncontrolled area collected both surplus Samburu from the schemes (with their surplus stock) as well as impoverished Rendille. So long as the uncontrolled area still contained adequate grazing, the system could continue. But inevitably there was a limit; and as the uncontrolled areas were robbed of some of their best grazing land in the later 1950s, this limit was rapidly approaching.

* * *

The success of these schemes depended largely upon the extent to which the underlying principles were adhered to. And when so many Samburu would accept neither the logic of these principles nor the right of the administration to impose them, the problem of control became a crucial one. According to the formula of these schemes, only one block of land should be used at any one time while the grass in the other blocks was allowed to recuperate: but inevitably this grass, once it had started to grow, was a temptation to would-be trespassers with their cattle. Altogether in the schemes that had actually been opened by 1960, there were 1,500 square miles of land officially closed to grazing at any one time because of the schemes. Much of this land was in the low country where it was broken up and covered with large patches of bush that made it easy for a trespasser to drive his cattle undetected. In addition, there were 1,700 square miles of forested reserve in the mountainous areas where trespass was also possible.

In order to enforce the grazing restrictions, a number of grazing guards and forest guards were employed, but even with the help of other men in government employment, the task of preventing trespass effectively was altogether too large for them to cope with.

The extent to which trespass passed unreported was noted by the administration with concern. It was not simply that the grazing guards reported comparatively few cases of trespass, but also that any government officer passing through the district by Land-Rover was quite likely to see for himself a number of cases.

Grazing trespass was a major issue throughout the 1950s and feelings ran high on both sides. When it became apparent that present measures were not going to curb stock trespass, fines were doubled, threats were made to expel offenders from the grazing schemes and even to confiscate their entire herds.

There is no doubt that these serious warnings had the effect of curbing trespass at certain times and in certain areas, just as the presence of grazing guards served to curtail open defiance of the regulations. But the whole system was inadequately controlled and prone to abuse and even bribery. In so far as a number of the grazing guards were poorer Samburu, they were in a virtually impossible position: they could not both carry out their job and acknowledge their traditional obligations to other Samburu. Others were Dorobo and Turkana, and they too found themselves sooner rather than later having to come to terms with the members of the schemes: they had to be prepared to face an angry mob of elders (and possibly *moran*) whenever they threatened to report an offence, and at night they had to rely on the local Samburu for hospitality so long as they remained in the areas remote from the three principal government stations. Inevitably, a local compromise had to be reached in which the trespass was partially restricted and the task of the grazing guards was not made altogether impossible. To this extent, the grazing guards fulfilled their task, and a certain degree of bribery became locally accepted as a part of the local bargaining, even if it would have been condemned outright by the administration.

When making more severe threats, the administration had perhaps forgotten that in 1949, two *moran* had been killed by police when trying to spear a European officer who had confiscated their cattle for trespass. The grazing guards, at least, were well aware of the potential danger of imposing too harsh a control when feelings ran so high, and were more prepared to compromise.

*   *   *

Grazing schemes brought the Samburu one step closer to the monetary economy that governed Kenya to the south. Any man living inside a scheme was expected to maintain the size of his herd within a fixed quota and to sell off the increase at cattle sales held periodically in the district for the meat market. For a man with, say, fifty head of cattle in a scheme, he could in theory make between £20 and £50 a year simply from the sale of his surplus stock, and after paying his scheme fees and tax, he could regard the balance as sheer profit. In practice, however, the Samburu elder who had told a European that: 'As the Government likes shillings, so we Samburu like cattle' had very aptly summarized the general attitude of the whole tribe. The Samburu would only sell as many stock as they had to in order to pay these fees in addition to any fines and minor purchases, and they would send the remaining surplus stock to the uncontrolled areas.[10]

Altogether, the wrong conditions existed to build up Samburu confidence in the monetary economy. There were at least four major deterrents. In the first place, the prices offered at stock sales seemed to be erratic. The average prices from one year to the next might vary anywhere between 10 per cent and 40 per cent and variations between successive sales were sometimes even higher. The broad increase of about 8 per cent per annum offered during the 1950s seemed to indicate that they had been offered unduly low prices earlier on rather than that their cattle were improving in condition, or that these prices were subject to market pressures. They were well aware that higher prices would be offered for the same cattle at stock sales held in other districts further south, and the more enterprising Samburu would smuggle their market stock to these sales, and return to confirm this popular impression. Moreover, in so much as the need for money to buy supplementary food was felt more acutely in the dry season, this tended to encourage the Samburu to sell their stock at a time when their cattle were in poor condition and prices generally low: the very stock that would fetch the best prices in the height of the wet season—their fattest oxen— also happened to be the ones most prized inside their herds. Above and beyond this, the periodic outbreak of epidemics led to quarantine restrictions and the frequent suspension of stock sales. For the Samburu stock sales were neither a regular nor a reliable outlet for their surplus stock.

Secondly, the fines imposed for offences were to Samburu ways of thinking quite erratic. They could accept the imposition of a £10 fine and a twelve-month imprisonment on a *moran* for stock theft as a form of justice, but they could not reconcile this easily with a £25 fine and a six-month imprisonment for a game offence or with a £50 fine for a stock trespass. This was one more erratic feature which indicated to the Samburu that control over money and money values was outside their grasp. In the last resort, therefore, money was not to be trusted, especially during a severe drought when the tribe was on the verge of starvation.

Thirdly, the Samburu were vulnerable to each other's predatory habits. With cattle, and even with small stock, they could refuse requests from their kinsmen and affines, or at least bargain with them. But money provided an altogether smaller unit of currency which could more easily be frittered away as different men came to beg small amounts. It was largely because of this vulnerability that

10. A typical annual monetary budget for a Samburu has been estimated in Table 3.

servicemen returning home with their savings would prefer to spend them buying cattle from those who needed the money to pay taxes, fees, and so on. They knew only too well that if, for instance, they used them to set up a small store, then their age mates, their clansmen, their maternal kin, their wives' kin, and others would eventually ruin them by an insatiable demand for credit.

And fourthly, so long as the bulk of the tribe remained nomadic, there was no particular desire to encumber themselves with an accumulation of inessential goods that their money might be used to buy.

These were the principal disincentives to entering the monetary economy. On the other side of the coin, there was the positive incentive to foster their stock, and in particular their cattle. Their whole economy was essentially geared towards the expansion of the herd as a means of insuring themselves against disaster. Between the periodic misfortunes, it was quite usual for a diligent man's herd to double in five years. This would be equivalent to an annual increase of nearly 15 per cent and would have belittled any other form of short-term investment, even had the Samburu known about it.

*　　*　　*

By 1961, grazing schemes covered nearly one-third of the whole district, and while there had been temporary relaxation to alleviate the immediate hardships of the drought, it was still suggested that the policy should be extended to yet new areas. At this point, the hostility towards the schemes came to a head and the elders from all phratries gathered together to curse all those who had in any way collaborated in imposing the schemes. (The effect of the curse was demonstrated for the Samburu at least when shortly after this, an avalanche killed some of the wives, family, and stock of one of the chiefs who had taken a major part in trying to initiate a new scheme, largely, it was thought, to protect his own interests.)

When almost the whole tribe was hostile to the introduction of these schemes, their control posed a considerable problem. Ultimately, it proved too big for the administration to handle, and in order to allow the Samburu some responsibility for their future in what was to be an independent Kenya, the A.D.C. elders were asked in 1961 to choose between retaining the schemes or abolishing them. They chose to abolish them, and the whole district outside the protected forest areas became once again uncontrolled.

At this time, some of the more cynical European observers were led to suggest that the severe drought between 1959 and 1961 had done more to restore a balance of nature than nine years of grazing schemes.

And yet, the problem cannot simply be dismissed. It may well be that the resilience of the stock to survive is matched by the resilience of the land to recover partially, and it may well be that soil erosion has not been as rapid as experts have supposed and that veterinary medicines and developed water resources have not led to so sharp an increase in Samburu cattle as is often assumed. The evidence supporting this view has been put forward in the preceding pages. But still, the balance of nature in this area (if one can ever speak of such a thing) has shown that it can be ruthless and indiscriminate to the human population. Disasters to the herds have been sudden and harsh. Years when the rainfall has been adequate and when both the stock and the human population have grown, have been interspersed with sudden periods of drought, bringing with it hunger, disease, and death. Grazing control may have had serious shortcomings; but as a serious attempt at helping the Samburu conquer their environment, the sincerity of its objectives cannot be doubted.

The shortcomings of these policies were both ideological and technological. On an ideological level, they did not make allowances for a people who felt that a partially monetary economy offered no ready alternative to a wholly stock economy: the true value of money was outside their control and in the final resort it could not be trusted to help a man faced with the realities of drought and starvation. And secondly, the administration had to contend with a people who regarded their rights to graze their own land in their own way as inviolable: their position was not altogether different from planners elsewhere who face a general long-term problem caused by the excessive demands of individual 'rights': this type of situation is by no means confined to more primitive societies. Britain in the 1970s faces it in terms of car-ownership and the use of urban roads, or of prices and incomes.

On the technological level, as the experiences of the 1950s showed, grazing control policies were concerned with less than the total problem, and to this extent they were bound sooner or later to encounter serious difficulties. To begin with, they were concerned only with the part of the district that contained the schemes. Had they accepted that each new scheme affected the Samburu excluded from the schemes as much as those included, then a policy for the whole district would have been necessary and this would have called for a revised strategy. In the event, one is justified in asking whether the good that schemes did for the areas they protected was greater than the harm that they did for the uncontrolled areas where the pressure on the land steadily increased as a result. Secondly, schemes were only approached from the point of view of the cattle economy with virtually no allowance for the small stock. Quite apart from the fact that this led to an even sharper overcrowding in the uncontrolled areas, it also completely ignored the role that small stock might play in the domestic economy of the Samburu. This has been outlined in Chapter 1. And thirdly, the success of the schemes depended largely on the ability of the stock sales to take away surplus stock. So long as the administration found itself unable to hold these regularly it lost control over the total problem.

Any future attempts at grazing control in the area, then, must surely depend for their success on the extent to which both the ideological and the technological problems can be surmounted. It seems rather unlikely that any new grazing policies, however technically sound, can hope to succeed without the ready collaboration of the people themselves. It seems equally unlikely that any concerted move in this direction by the tribe as a whole can hope to succeed if it is based on an imperfect appreciation of the total problem.

The Rendille–Samburu Boundary

'There are frequent disputes caused by Rendille claiming Samburu grazing but there is seldom any serious quarrelling between the two tribes.'
'... the relations between the Samburu and Rendille are excellent. Their respective elders ... always happily settle any minor disputes that may arise on the border.'

Marsabit District records in the 1930s

'It would be to their advantage probably if these two tribes were administered in one district ...'

Marsabit District records in the 1940s

In a book whose principal theme is the inseparability of the Rendille and Samburu tribes, there is perhaps a danger of understating the very real pressures that led to imposing a boundary between them, at first in 1921 as separate districts within one province of Kenya, and later in 1934 as districts within two separate provinces.

The relationship between the two tribes has been discussed in a number of contexts. Politically and economically they have been shown to rely heavily on one another over the years with the Ariaal Rendille overlapping the fringes of both societies. Possibly for centuries, there has been an intermittent trickle of refugees from the Rendille economy into the more tolerant Samburu economy. The extent to which the Rendille and Samburu form an interdependent self-contained group is vividly illustrated by Table 6 (p. 138): of the 555 marriages considered in this table, 208 are between Rendille, 264 are between Samburu, 72 (13 per cent) are between Rendille and Samburu, and only 11 (2 per cent) are with other tribes. The table also suggests that the degree of intermarriage has not significantly decreased since the official separation in 1921 (p. 165).

But the fact remains that the two tribes have very different languages and somewhat ambivalent attitudes towards one another. In spite of their political and economic interdependence—which they are very ready to stress—each tribe has been essentially self-contained socially and has had very little interest in affairs that have not directly affected it. When provoked, either can be very critical of the other: the Rendille are critical of the unruliness and nefariousness of Samburu *moran*, and the Samburu are critical of the liberal use of cursing among the Rendille. This has been illustrated to Europeans on a number of occasions from the time of 1900 when Arkell-Hardwick reported that the Rendille had complained of the Samburu 'looting' both their small stock and their women[11] to an incident in 1959 which led the Samburu elders to demand that their administration in Maralal should enforce the official boundary and confiscate the stock of any trespassing Rendille.

On individual issues, considerable heatedness may be aroused, although this stops short of open aggression and is normally quickly resolved. The important clue in the administrative records is not that disputes never arose between the tribes, but rather that such disputes were settled peacefully without administrative interference. It is worth noting that a number of minor disputes have involved Rendille immigrants to the Samburu cattle economy and their kinsmen still living in the camel economy; and the only serious fighting recorded in the area was between two clans of the Rendille proper and of the Ariaal Rendille. In other words, a number of incidents do not entail the relationship between the Rendille and Samburu as separate tribes.

The 1959 demand for enforcing the boundary, however, clearly was an intertribal issue. Before examining this in greater detail, it is worth recalling the history of the boundary between the two tribes.

In the earliest days of administration in the area, there was a reasonable case to be made in favour of dividing the two tribes between separate districts: they were obviously different tribal groups largely scattered, it seemed, over separate areas in the wastes of northern Kenya. In an immense area through which travel was slow and government resources limited, such an obvious division was more to be regarded as fortuitous than to be questioned. Marsabit provided an ideal site for a government station and was strategically placed for administration over the Rendille and the Boran

11. In the case of the 'women', this is almost certain to have been seduction rather than abduction: the vernacular for seduce, steal, and loot are the same.

tribes to the north. The concentration of Samburu, however, was altogether too far south-west for them to be administered from Marsabit.

Until 1934, the Samburu and Rendille were officially confined to separate districts of the same province: the Northern Frontier Province (N.F.P.). The circumstances which brought the Samburu out of the N.F.P. into the more progressive Rift Valley Province (R.V.P.) concerned principally the award of the Leroghi Plateau by the Kenya Land Commission and the unsettled relationship between the Samburu and a handful of influential European settlers who owned largely unfarmed land to the south. To all governmental intents and purposes, however, the Samburu remained in the Northern Frontier area: by the 1950s, the Game Department, the Forestry Department, the Veterinary Department, the African Land Development officers, and the administration were facing problems that had far more in common with the N.F.P. than with the R.V.P., and the policies adopted were broadly those of the Northern Frontier generally. Even grazing control was now being imposed in parts of the N.F.P. and hence was not a policy or problem wholly confined to the more southerly provinces.

To some extent, wherever a provincial boundary was drawn, there were bound to be certain administrative anomalies. In the case of the Samburu, however, this anomaly was perhaps greater than elsewhere. It was not simply that the state of advancement of the Samburu as a tribe, their dispersal, their nomadic life, their climate, or their rough arid countryside were essentially similar to those of the N.F.P.; it was also that their boundary with the N.F.P. extended for 370 ill-defined miles that could never be policed effectively, while their boundary with the remainder of the R.V.P. to the south extended for only 50 miles, and the length adjoining settlers' ranches was shorter still. The decision to transfer the Samburu to the R.V.P. was largely due to their 900 square miles of land on Leroghi, and had little to do with their 7,000 square miles of lowland country to the north and east in which more than three-quarters of the population lived, and which, incidentally, lay fairly and squarely between the Rendille administration at Marsabit and their provincial H.Q. at Isiolo.

Along this somewhat anomalous boundary with the N.F.P. was 150 miles dividing the Samburu from the Rendille. The close affinity between the two tribes had long been recognized, and it had been agreed by past administrations to adopt an essentially permissive policy towards the boundary which consisted of a series of lines on the map joining water points which both tribes shared. Members of either tribe were officially allowed to take their stock to graze across this line, but were not permitted to build settlements on the wrong side. In the early records at Marsabit, it was recognized that the cattle owners who paid tax as Rendille were in fact Samburu who, it was thought, had never left the area to settle in Maralal District and so had acquired a certain right to remain inside Marsabit District. One or two later Marsabit administrators regarded these as cattle-owning Rendille rather than as Samburu, but all agreed that the cattle owners and the camel owners lived side by side and across the boundary very amicably, while the borders that separated these people from such tribes as the Turkana and the Boran were constant sources of trouble and dispute.

As a border, then, so long as a permissive policy was carried out to the point of complete non-interference, the provincial boundary between the Rendille and the Samburu was of little concern to anyone, least of all to the tribesmen themselves. Indeed, one might even argue that so long as it gave so little administrative trouble, there was a strong case for maintaining the boundary here rather than elsewhere—so long, that is, as a blind eye was turned to the administrative anomaly and to tribal transgressions. To the extent that the relations between the Samburu and Rendille were peaceful, the problems of policing the northern two-thirds of Kenya were simplified by 150 miles of rough, arid, ill-defined, and inessential border.

The incident in 1959, when the Samburu elders demanded a stricter enforcement of their boundary with the Rendille, would seem at first sight to contradict this broad analysis of the situation and to have defied all conventions that had existed between the two tribes. These demands were provoked by a government employed Rendille who had reported some Samburu trespassers to the Marsabit authorities. This had led to a confiscation of the trespassers' cattle. It was in retaliation for this that the Samburu elders asked their administration in Maralal to withdraw all grazing concessions to the Rendille and to confiscate any trespassing camels. Again, the significant feature of this incident was not just that it occurred, but that once the Samburu had expressed their outrage at this unnecessary betrayal of confidence by a Rendille and generalized their feelings to the whole Rendille tribe and its administration, they quickly returned to a normal relationship with the Rendille in the border area. This was no doubt made more easy by the Rendille, who carefully took no part in trying to provoke the situation any further. On the contrary, at a local level they conferred with the Samburu to restore harmony, and among themselves they took action against the government employee by persuading his Rendille wife to run away to her parents. This was noted with approval by the Samburu.

All evidence seems to suggest that the Rendille–Samburu boundary is largely a problem created for itself by the administration, and
is likely to remain so, as long as the two tribes are separately administered. The above incident is one in which administrative policy
had a secondary effect on the relationship between the two tribes.
Other incidents in the official records give a distinct impression that
the two tribes found it easier to resolve their difference than the
two administrations.

The conclusion of the last section—that any future grazing policies
should be adapted to the *whole* problem—is relevant here. Any
policy affecting the economy of either tribe will ultimately affect the
other. In terms of grazing control, the whole problem is not simply
grazing in Maralal District: it extends to the whole area occupied
by the Samburu and Rendille.

Conclusions

In this chapter, the extent to which two very different types of life
impinge on one another has been examined. The most immediate
and in many ways the most far-reaching effect has been the establishment of intertribal peace in the area: the British administration
insisted on it and the tribesmen have welcomed it—not perhaps
without sporadic outbursts, but at least with an overwhelming consensus of approval. The influence that the administration and its
associated government departments have had in the area is out of
all proportion to its numerical strength: in Maralal district in 1960,
there were 10 European officers assisted by 3 clerks and 21 chiefs
and headmen who had charge over what was thought to be 30,000
persons. The fact that this figure was revised after a census in 1962
to nearly 50,000 is a measure of the extent to which the administration had to cope with a problem whose magnitude could only be
guessed. There were also four mission stations running most of the
schools in the district and the hospital at Baragoi. In Marsabit
district, there were even fewer officers and government personnel,
and their attention was divided between all the tribal groups of the
district, among whom the Rendille and Samburu were regarded as
causing least trouble and requiring least administration.

Above and beyond the maintenance of peace in the area, the
administration could choose between on the one hand a *laissez-faire*
policy which would maintain some form of *status quo* and would
largely allow the tribesmen to be masters of their own fates for
better or for worse, and on the other hand, a progressive policy in
the sincere belief that the twentieth century in Kenya would relegate
backward and unprogressive tribes to a position where they might

be in very real danger of moral disintegration and even extinction. Certain decisions, such as the inclusion of the Samburu in the Rift Valley Province or the deportation of a locally popular *laibon* in 1934 were made largely at the instigation of self-interested European settlers, but there is no doubt that for the most part the major policies and decisions have been made with the ultimate welfare and best interests of the tribesmen in mind. Whether these could best be served through a progressive or a permissive policy has largely been a matter of personal opinion and choice among successive administrators. With the Rendille, they chose a more progressive policy during the 1920s until it was recognized that there was neither response from the people nor resources from the government to enforce this. The very nature of their problems elsewhere diverted the attention of the Marsabit administration from the Rendille to the tribes bordering on Ethiopia and a permissive policy then prevailed.

With the Samburu, the administration were facing a rather different problem. In the first place, maintaining peace in the area entailed more than establishing control on the frontiers with other tribes: it also entailed quelling the excesses of the *moran* whose position in the tribal system caused a recurrent problem of restlessness not present among the Rendille. In so far as the administration found itself impelled to interfere in one aspect of tribal life, it could quite reasonably ask itself what it was destroying and what it should put in its place: a more progressive and less permissive policy was to some extent forced on it. Secondly, from 1944 when the administration over the Samburu was transferred from Rumuruti to Maralal, the Samburu in effect comprised a district to themselves, and the attention of the local administration was focused almost entirely upon them: unlike the Rendille, it was not a question of permissiveness by force of circumstance. And thirdly, the whole of the Leroghi Plateau provided very easy means of communication which again suggested that progressive policies could be effectively carried out from Maralal which was strategically placed on it. Thus it was that grazing control was introduced as a major scheme on Leroghi in the early 1950s and was later extended to those lowland areas that were comparatively accessible.

Broadly speaking, there have been two phases of applying progressive policies to the Samburu. The first in the 1930s was concerned with controlling the *moran* system to a point of suppression and with culling the stock on Leroghi. After what appeared to be a highly successful start to this policy, it had to be abandoned in 1939 when an uprising of the *moran* against the culling demonstrated to the administration the forces with which they had to contend. The Second World War precluded any further immediate attempts by the administration to introduce ambitious new measures. The second phase was introduced in an altogether different climate. The worst excesses of the *moran* appeared to have been quelled, although the system remained intact. The focus of administrative attention shifted to the growing pressure on the land and the soil erosion that this was causing. A policy for stock control was introduced on Leroghi in 1952 and spread to the low country in 1957. By 1961, over 30 per cent of the area of the district was under some form of grazing control. But this rapid increase was only achieved at the expense of increasing congestion in the uncontrolled areas, increasing disregard for the regulations, and increasing hostility towards the schemes. Faced with increasing lack of collaboration in running the schemes, the administration was obliged at some point to modify or abandon them. In the event they were abandoned in 1961 after a severe drought.

Thus, in 1962 when the British administration were on the point of handing over control to the newly independent Kenya Government, two initially successful attempts at progressive policies among the Samburu and one totally unsuccessful attempt at progressive policies among the Rendille had led to a re-establishment of *laissez faire*. As the earlier sections of this chapter imply, there is no real evidence that over these periods of 'progress' either tribe has come to rely on new modes of social control or that the administrations have succeeded in harnessing to their own ends the very effective powers of indigenous control outlined in Chapters 2 and 3.

With the limited resources available for development, it is difficult to visualize how any progressive policy can be successfully imposed without the wholehearted support of the tribes themselves. The policy of curbing the *moran* in the 1930s had this support from the elders, although the policy of destroying the *moran* system did not: as a result, the *moran* were curbed but the system remains.

The problem surely of the future of the Rendille and the Samburu cannot be solved by any administration which aims at imposing progressive policies which are not seen by the people themselves as a form of progress. It can only be solved once the Rendille and the Samburu are fully aware of their problems. Their future is primarily in their own hands, and it is to be hoped that their land will not have eroded away before they come to terms with the new ecological and political balance of their country in the twentieth century—or the twenty-first. Certainly, until that point and so long as there is an uncertainty of the future hanging over northern Kenya, their own indigenous organization, intact as it is, is an asset which simplifies the problems of administration and maintains their feeling of control over their destiny. Moreover, once that point is reached, the indigenous organization of the tribes could prove one of their most valuable assets during the period of transition.

APPENDIX

THE DOROBO AND ELMOLO OF NORTHERN KENYA

'... I would claim that it is largely an academic fiction to suppose that in a "normal" ethnographic situation one ordinarily finds distinct "tribes" distributed about the map in orderly fashion with clear-cut boundaries between them.... My own view is that the ethnographer has often only managed to discern the existence of "a tribe" because he took it as axiomaic that this kind of cultural entity must exist. Many such tribes are, in a sense, ethnographic fictions.'[1]   *E. R. Leach*

A survey of the area, its history and relationships between tribes would not be complete without at least some account of the Dorobo, the small tribes of Masai-speaking people who until recently subsisted by hunting, fishing, and gathering. The Elmolo are discussed later as a particular type of Dorobo.

From the time that the first Europeans visited the area to the present, observers have noted that the Dorobo tribes, or groups as I shall call them, have social relations with certain neighbouring pastoral and agricultural tribes. Thomson (visiting the area in 1883) writes that the Dorobo are 'a small race of people scattered over Masailand' who 'always find neighbouring tribes less skilful in hunting, eager to exchange vegetable food for game.... They enjoy considerable immunity from attack by the Masai.... They also act as go-betweens or middlemen in getting the married people the vegetable food they require' (by buying it from the Kikuyu and selling it again to the Masai—probably for small stock).[2] There is also evidence in the early literature of a certain degree of inter-migration between tribes, especially between the Dorobo and others.[3] This literature and my own field material suggests that this state of affairs has continued for an indefinite period. It is a familiar topic both in tribal myth and in current events.

Without stock or agriculture the Dorobo had virtually no material possessions and were driven to take whatever chances presented themselves for subsistence: a fact which perhaps accounts for the extent to which they readily made friends with the early travellers and later volunteered their services to the newly formed British administration.[4] Von Höhnel writes: 'The word Ndorobbo means in

1. Leach, 1954, pp. 290–1.
2. Thomson, 1885, p. 447.
3. e.g. Chanler, 1896, pp. 281–2, 374–5; Neumann, 1898, pp. 246, 267, 291; and Stigand, 1910, p. 78.
4. cf. Maguire's comments on the Dorobo of Tanganyika (Maguire, 1948), p. 2.

Masai language poor folk without cattle or other possessions.'[5] And Donaldson Smith writes: 'I use the Masai term "wandorobbo" to designate the poor of any tribe, who live by hunting and fishing.'[6]

Since the time of these earliest visitors it has often been assumed and implied in the writings of such men as K. R. Dundas and Sir Harry Johnston that the Dorobo are the remnants of an aboriginal race, and that only recently have they begun to intermarry with the other tribes who are immigrants to the area.[7] I do not wish to deny that there are among the Dorobo occasional physical characteristics that differ from those of their neighbours, or that certain groups, such as the Mukogodo and until recently the Elmolo, have languages of their own. It does, however, seem unnecessary to assume that the term Dorobo refers essentially to a racial stock rather than to the status of the hunting groups in the area with respect to other tribes. In point of fact, the extent of the intermarriage and intermigration in the area, and the constant interchange of cultural and even institutional features between groups makes any search for racial origins futile. Indeed, as I have shown in the earlier chapters, there is little in Samburu and Rendille beliefs and values which supports any myth of racial purity and this may be equally true of other Kenya tribes.

So often has this essentially straightforward state of affairs been overlooked that it is refreshing to find the following statement in an official handbook: 'At present all these tribes [the various Dorobo groups] more or less share the characteristics of the people to whom they are attached, a fact which is partly explained by their having incorporated outcasts and remnants of broken tribes, especially in times of famine, when pastoral or agricultural natives are driven to live with hunting tribes.'[8] One has only to accept that this state of affairs has probably been in existence for an indefinite period and analysis is enormously simplified.

Notes on the Dorobo Groups

While it is necessary to avoid a false prehistorical perspective, it is still useful to examine the former position of the Dorobo in historical times in order to appreciate more fully their position today. The map on page 151 shows the approximate disposition of the major tribes and Dorobo groups in 1900. Just before this time two events are important. The first was the utter defeat of the Laikipiak Masai

5. von Höhnel, 1894, vol. i, p. 260.
6. Donaldson Smith, 1897, p. 303.
7. Dundas, 1908, pp. 136–9; Johnston, 1902, p. 857.
8. *Handbook of Kenya Colony and Protectorate*, app. 1920, pp. 233–4.

and the second was the cattle plague that affected all the cattle-owning tribes in the area, and in particular the Samburu. Both of these events probably occurred during the 1880s.

In the notes that follow, certain groups are referred to as Laikipiak Dorobo, Samburu Dorobo, etc. This is their own description of themselves and refers to the tribe (e.g. the Laikipiak, the Samburu, etc.) that they had been on friendly terms with, exchanging skins, honey beer, and ivory for small stock, and occasionally absorbing immigrants from each other. Such ties would be useful to the pastoralists if epidemic or defeat resulted in the total loss of their stock and the survivors had to turn to some other means of liveli-hood. They were also useful to the Dorobo as a means of obtaining small stock and of becoming pastoralists themselves if any of them wished to abandon their present mode of living and the opportunity presented itself.[9]

(a) *Laikipiak Dorobo*

Loliin: Also known as Coliin. Had bee-hives at Olporoi and Ilbukoi. Probably the Dorobo that Neumann and Chanler met in that area in the 1890s.[10]

Olkerenye: Also known as Lekerisia as they had bee-hives in the Karissia Hills. Closely associated with the Loliin and sometimes loosely referred to as Loliin.

Eremoto: Had bee-hives on the Tinga river and were mainly found to the west of Leroghi.

Lorokoti: Did not cultivate bees to any extent. Hunted in the Ngelesha and Amaya areas, which they regarded as their territory.

Lemarmar: Lived at Marmanet and Siron. Had no bees. Were badly defeated by the Purko Masai.

Dondoli: Lived to the south of Solai. Had no bees. Associated closely with the Purko Masai after the defeat of the Laikipiak.

Lesupukia: Lived close to the Dondoli and associated with them; also had no bees and associated with the Purko after the defeat of the Laikipiak. Informants are generally vague as to the exact hunting territories of the Dondoli and Lesupukia in these earlier times.

9 e.g. as recorded by Stigand, 1910, p. 78.
10. Neumann, 1898, pp. 94 f; Chanler, pp. 355 f.

Leuaso: Had bee-hives along the Uaso Ngiro river between Kirimun and Lase Rumuru. The centre of their territory was the fork of the Uaso Ngiro and the Uaso Narok rivers. Lived mainly on the east bank.

Lngwesi: After the defeat of the Laikipiak, they associated closely with the Meru and were probably the Dorobo that Neumann refers to at Katheri.[11] Had no bees. Since 1900 they have twice been removed from Meru locations by the administration. There is no substantial evidence to confirm the opinions of some informants that the Lngwesi Dorobo and the Lngwesi phratry of Samburu were once related. The view seems to rest entirely on the common name they share which in Masai also means 'wild beasts'.

Ndigiri: Mixed Kikuyu, Masai, and Laikipiak Dorobo. Spoke Masai and associated with the Kikuyu at Nyeri and later with the Purko Masai. A part of them may have been the middlemen to which Thomson refers at Mianzini,[12] and they seem also to have been the Dorobo referred to by Boyes.[13] Had no bees, and when removed from their original territory by Europeans had to hunt far and wide for game. Seem to have formed links with the Purko Masai during this period.

Lanat: Had no bees except possibly on Lolokwi where Chanler met them and Laishamunye.[14] Also hunted over a wide area— probably the Dorobo met by Donaldson Smith at Laisamis.[15] After the defeat of the Laikipiak in the 1880s they associated closely with the Samburu and became fully incorporated as a clan of Pisikishu phratry.[16]

Suiei:[17] Have bees on the Matthews Range. Possibly because of their inaccessibility, they did not at first associate with the Samburu after the defeat of the Laikipiak and have only recently adopted such items of Samburu culture as their age-set system (about 1920).

Mumonyot: A defeated Laikipiak remnant who settled down as

11. Neumann, 1898, pp. 128 and 246 (also see Chanler, 1896, p. 375).
12. Thomson, 1885, p. 448; also referred to by von Höhnel (1894, vol. i, pp. 286–7)—unless he is merely quoting Thomson.
13. Boyes, 1911, Chapter VIII. Boyes, however, reports that these Dorobo gave him some honey, which suggests at first sight that they may well have been some other group.
14. Chanler, 1896, pp. 275 f.
15. Donaldson Smith, 1897, p. 354.
16. Thus Hobley (1910, pp. 159–60) mentions only *three* Pisikishu clans (Sitat, 01 Lesilali, Maletis) and then refers to Lanat separately as Dorobo. Today there are generally acknowledged to be *four* clans including Lanat.
17. For a more detailed account of the Suiei, see *The Samburu*, pp. 282–5.

Dorobo in close association with the Mukogodo (see below). They were previously reported to be living near the Lorian swamp.[18]

Mukogodo: A Dorobo group who inhabit the Mukogodo mountains where they cultivate bees, and where some of them are said to have lived in caves. They have a language of their own. Since the end of the last century the Mukogodo have associated closely with the Mumonyot, and when the latter began to rebuild their cattle herds, they married a number of Mukogodo girls in return for cattle, and taught the Mukogodo cattle husbandry. Today, the Mukodo are bilingual in their own language and Masai.

Ltudaani: Reputed to have been a Laikipiak Dorobo group who were utterly routed by the Purko Masai at the time of the defeat of the Laikipiak. It is thought that a large number of them are now in the Masai reserve. They lived and kept bees at one time between Seiya (Swiyeni) and Barsalinga.

Of these original Laikipiak Dorobo, the Dondoli and Lesupukia subsequently associated with the Purko; the Lngwesi with the Meru; the Ndigiri with the Kikuyu and Purko; and the Lanat and ultimately Suiei with the Samburu. Certain segments such as Loibor-sikireshi of the Suiei and certain groups such as the Mumonyot claim to have been Laikipiak in the fullest sense before their rout as a tribe. But all the other groups maintain they were Dorobo even in these earlier times.

(b) *Samburu Dorobo*

Lengiro: According to tribal legend, the core of these were originally Boran Dorobo living on Mount Ngiro and having bee-hives there. When the Samburu invaded the area from the south in about 1840, the pastoral Boran fled and the Dorobo remained. They were joined by segments of Masula phratry and are now living interspersed with members of this phratry. Mount Ngiro has become (if it was not before) a centre of ceremonial interest and social aloofness from the remainder of the society. On the one hand, it has its Dorobo associations coupled with a certain disregard for Samburu ideals and to this extent its people are despised. On the other hand, the insight of its ritual specialists, the ceremonial seniority of the Masula, and the ritual primacy of the mountain itself combine to give the Masula of this area an unquestionable ceremonial superiority over all Samburu: this is equally true of the ex-Dorobo

18. von Höhnel, 1894, i, p. 398; Chanler, 1896, p. 121.

newcomers to the tribe and of the fully Samburu newcomers to the area.[19]

Lkerna: A branch of Lorogushu phratry who lost their stock during the great cattle plague and became bee-keeping and hunting Dorobo, associating closely with the Masula of Mount Ngiro and the Ndoto mountains. Today, they are brothers by descent of the Lorogushu, but socially and ceremonially are closer to the Masula.

Werkile: A group of Loimusi phratry who have also become Dorobo and the Ndoto mountains, but did not cultivate bees extensively. They have no close associations with the Masula.

Laidotok: A general name for the Dorobo living in the Ndoto mountains including the Lkerna and Werkile and also a few others who were Dorobo in the area prior to its acquisition by the Samburu.

*   *   *

Since 1900, there has been further migration between these groups and with neighbouring tribes, but there remain certain clusters of people who consider themselves to be the hard core of these earlier groups. The present disposition is as follows: Loliin, Olkerenye, Eremoto, Lorokoti, Lemarmar, Dondoli, and Lesupukia are all represented in the Dorobo reserve on Leroghi which consisted of 210 taxpayers in 1958 and was set up for those who had evaded the official removal of the Masai from the area in 1913 or had drifted back to it subsequently. There are a handful of families living in the areas they previously inhabited and these have been absorbed for tax-paying purposes into Samburu phratries, although socially they remain apart from these phratries. Presumably there are many others living with the Masai in the reserve to which they were removed.

The Leuaso, Lngwesi, Ndigiri, Mukogodo, and Mumonyot Dorobo now belong to the *Doldol reserve* (683 tax-payers in 1959), the Leuaso and Mukogodo alone having traditional territorial rights to live there. The others, since being confined there, have started to cultivate bees to some extent.

The Suiei Dorobo (190 tax-payers in 1958) and those Dorobo absorbed by the Samburu (Lanat, Lengiro, and Laidotok) still inhabit their traditional territories.

*   *   *

A definite pattern emerges from these notes and it suggests that for an indefinite period, many of these Dorobo groups:

19. See also p. 121.

(a) have formed reciprocal relations with certain neighbouring tribes.

(b) have spoken the same language as these tribes and observed some of their customs (e.g. loosely acknowledging their age-set systems).

(c) have to a certain extent intermarried and intermigrated with these tribes, albeit on a small scale.

It seems probable that these same general principles are true of the Dorobo groups further south in their relationship with the Masai, of the Okiek with the Nandi-speaking tribes, and of the Warta with the Boran. A number of changes of language have been reported (e.g. the Elmolo and Mukogodo to Masai).[20] A recurrent feature is that with the territorial advances and tactical withdrawals of the pastoral tribes, the Dorobo groups tend to remain closely associated with their traditional hunting grounds and to adapt themselves socially to their new surroundings. In this way they may be absorbed (e.g. the Lengiro, Lanat); they may retain a certain degree of separateness (e.g. the Suiei who still speak a purer form of Masai than the Samburu); or they may retain their Dorobo characteristics while entering into a new reciprocal relationship with their new neighbours (e.g. the Dondoli with the Purko Masai, the Ndigiri with the Kikuyu, the Lngwesi with the Meru, or various other families with countless European settlers as they moved into the area: each of these were previously associated with Laikipiak).

This general pattern suggests that ties to one particular area are more important for the hunting and gathering tribes than for the purely pastoral ones. This may be because an intimate knowledge of the countryside is more essential to their form of economy, because bees can only be cultivated in one spot over a number of years, or because the Dorobo, as suggested by Thomson, were to some extent immune from attack. In the past it is likely that after a tactical defeat, the pastoral tribes would prefer to migrate some distance in order to remain in a compact and strong tactical position, than to face a severer defeat by staying where they were. The Dorobo on the other hand tended to live in small inaccessible groups and offered no real prize for the raiders. When the Masai were removed from Laikipia to their southern reserve in 1913, it was the Dorobo who in general evaded this and returned to their former country. This has also been reported among the Nandi Dorobo (Okiek)[21] and is an example of a wider pattern. Whether the Dorobo

20. cf. the changes in language that Maguire reports among the Dorobo of Tanganyika (1948, pp. 2 ff.) and Lambert, 1950, pp. 58 ff.

21. Huntingford, 1953, p. 54, reports that the Okiek of the north Tindoret

were officially classed as belonging to the neighbouring tribes, or as illegal immigrants to an old area or as squatters on European farms, they persistently showed this tendency to remain in their former territories.

The Dorobo should not be confused with blacksmiths, in spite of the fact that both have a generally depressed status. Blacksmiths among many of the pastoral tribes, and certainly among the Samburu and Rendille (p. 118 and p. 63), formed a separate caste but they were fully accepted as integral members of these tribes both economically and socially. The various Dorobo groups, on the other hand, for all that they might intermarry with pastoralists, were essentially on the fringe of the societies they associated with. They were tied to neighbourhoods rather than to neighbours, and there was no pressing need for these nomadic tribes to foster a continuing relationship with any Dorobo group.

Dorobo Standards of Behaviour and Marriage

None of the groups mentioned here are officially allowed to hunt today, and they have all acquired herds of stock. They are nevertheless still regarded by their neighbours as Dorobo for other reasons than their recent history, and it is necessary to look further afield than the definitions suggested by von Höhnel and Donaldson Smith.

The term Dorobo may be defined with reference to social behaviour, which falls short of the standards that the Samburu (for instance) would expect of themselves. The Samburu delight in telling stories of the meanness, the crudeness, the discourteousness, the competitiveness, and the selfishness of the Dorobo. While they may acknowledge that age-sets of their neighbours, they do not follow the rigorous obligations to help an age mate, to respect members of more senior age-sets, or to avoid each others' daughters.

In discussing differences in attitudes and norms of behaviour between the Dorobo and the Samburu, marriage is a very important aspect. The Dorobo are widely regarded as marrying their own 'sisters'. In order to appreciate this view, it is necessary to examine more closely marriage and its relationship to recruitment into each society.

The Samburu (and Rendille) identify themselves as belonging to one of a number of exogamous clans. Any outsider who associates closely with one particular clan will only be accepted eventually as a member of it if he and his descendants observe its exogamous restrictions. If he marries into it, he confirms his position as an

---

forest crept back there after having been removed by the administration in 1937.

outsider. Only after a generation or so, when it has become clear
that neither he nor his descendants will ever contemplate marriage
with their adopted clan, will they be more or less accepted as
members and obtain the full benefits of clanship, including material
support in times of hardship and moral support in times of controversy.

Recruitment into a Dorobo group follows an altogether different
pattern. A man often consolidates his position in that group by
marrying the close kinswomen of the people he now associates with
and by giving them his daughters as wives. In this way he confirms
his membership of the group. And if it is one in which individual
lineage groups claim ownership to certain portions of land for
cultivating bees (e.g. the Suiei, Lengiro, and Mukogodo, but *not*
the Leuaso), he may be given concessions to use certain hillsides
or trees for his own bee-hives. The closest social ties are not
between clansmen who do not intermarry, as with the Samburu
or Rendille, but between cognatic and affinal kinsmen who live
close to one another and share in their daily tasks. These groups
often have fewer than 100 adult males and their exogamous groups
appear to extend no further than a shallow patrilineage of perhaps
three generations. Beyond this no relationships can be traced.

With their limited numbers, it is not altogether surprising that
intermarriage between Dorobo groups is very common. The following table shows all the marriages made by the present living generation of the Leuaso and the Mumonyot Dorobo and by their fathers:

Table 10
INTERMARRIAGE OF DOROBO GROUPS

| Tribe or Dorobo group of wives | Dorobo group and generation of husband | | | | Total |
	Leuaso Dorobo Present	Past	Mumonyot Dorobo Present	Past	
Same group as husband	44	17	46	10	117
Neighbouring Dorobo group	9	4	19	10	42
Distant Dorobo group	6	9	1	2	18
Neighbouring pastoral tribes	10	5	5	5	25
Others and unknown	1	4	1	1	7
TOTAL	70	39	72	28	209

According to these figures more than 40 per cent of the marriages
have been contracted outside the group and there is no obvious
change in the general pattern between the present and the previous
generation. It is interesting to note that the Mumonyot (the Laikipiak group who only became Dorobo after they lost their cattle

towards the end of the last century) have married more widely with neighbouring Dorobo groups than have the Leuaso and less widely further afield. In doing this, they appear to have been consolidating their ties in the area to which they have no traditional claims; their closest ties have been with the Mukogodo Dorobo and twenty of the twenty-nine marriages recorded with neighbouring Dorobo groups have been with Mukogodo girls.

In view of the extent to which the Dorobo are generally despised by pastoralists, it may seem incongruous that they should have been allowed to marry so many girls from pastoral tribes. There are two reasons for this. In the first place, within such tribes as the Samburu there are certain groups, such as Lengiro and Lanat, who still retain certain affinities and ties with other Dorobo. Secondly, at least ten of these twenty-five marriages—and probably many others—have been made with women who have previously run away from their husbands, and have gone to seek a living among the Dorobo in preference to returning to their own parents' homes. In one or two cases, this has led to a divorce and the present marriage to the Dorobo husband has been confirmed by the payment of bridewealth. But in other cases, probably the majority, the woman is living in concubinage, and sooner or later it is likely that her former husband or her father, having ascertained her whereabouts, will try to force her return. In other words, these are not marriages in the Samburu sense of the term, but temporary unions, where the woman has tried to evade any efforts by her husband and kinsmen to return to them by seeking an area where Samburu custom no longer prevails. More determined women even run as far afield as the Masai reserve in order to break their fetters. For the Samburu generally, these various Dorobo groups have a reputation for harbouring runaway wives, and they may at first be deterred from forcing the return of these wives by the further reputation of the Dorobo for sorcery (p. 116).

The differences between the two types of society may be summarized as follows: in so much as an institution (e.g. an age-set system or clan exogamy) does not limit the behaviour of its members, it can be said that this institution does not exist. The Dorobo who regard the age-set system as less important and who have fewer exogamous restrictions are despised by the Samburu for not observing the same strict rules of behaviour. The Masula of Mount Ngiro are regarded generally as Samburu: they belong to a Samburu phratry, they conform with the general restrictions of the age-set system, and intermarry with other Samburu phratries. On the other hand, they also marry to a very marked extent among themselves, they often try to avoid the obligations due to an age mate, their daughters are notoriously disrespectful leading to generally unstable marriages, and occasionally eldest sons are allowed to be circumcised prematurely while their fathers are still only firestick elders. To this extent, they are still regarded as Dorobo, and this general belief is reinforced by the fact that they still keep bees and regard themselves as having exclusive ownership of the land around Mount Ngiro. It is not that these Samburu Dorobo do not subscribe to the Samburu social system, nor that there are not among them men who are determined to conform to the ideals of Samburu society and are generally respected for this by all Samburu, but rather that there are a considerable number of men who are prepared to flout custom in many small ways, and the strength of public opinion in the area is consequently insufficient to curb them.

Dorobo, quite apart from any racial or economic considerations, can best be regarded as typifying those groups of people who fall far short of an ideal expressed by the term *Samburu*. In so much as certain Samburu clans fall more short of this ideal than others, they may loosely be referred to as Dorobo by other Samburu, and when there are specific connections with earlier Dorobo groups, as at Mount Ngiro, then this is seen as significant.

When the White Cattle moiety teasingly (and inconsistently) point out the close Dorobo associations of the Black Cattle moiety as compared with their own Rendille associations, it is, in effect, a way of overemphasizing their own dissimilarity from the Dorobo. For all the criticisms that the Samburu have of the Rendille, they would never suggest that they are in any sense Dorobo. They have too great a sense of respect.

The Dorobo under Administration

The Dorobo generally have been regarded by the administration with mixed feelings. On the one hand, as individuals, they have often shown a greater willingness to collaborate and to enter government service than their richer, more tradition-bound pastoral neighbours. On the other hand, as geographically remote, loosely organized groups without strong internal forces of cohesion, they have tended to respond less to indirect rule. In the 1930s, the Suiei and more recently the Leroghi Dorobo have proved more difficult to manage from an administrative point of view than the Samburu. In the Doldol reserve during the 1950s, the problem was acute.

In order to appreciate the Doldol situation, it is necessary to recall the recent history of the reserve. Today, it covers an area traditionally inhabited by the *Leuaso* and the *Mukogodo* groups. After the defeat of the Laikipiak, the *Mumonyot* survivors allied themselves with the Mukogodo, intermarried with them, and taught them cattle husbandry. And then, after the land to the south had been colonized by Europeans, the *Ndigiri* and *Lngwesi* groups also came into the area, and the Ndigiri learnt from the Leuaso how to keep bees. Table 10 shows the extent to which one of the oldest groups in the area and one of the newcomers to Dorobo society had intermarried and formed social ties with their neighbours over a period of time.

The reserve lay in difficult country and for many years was administered from the distant government station at Nanyuki where during the 1920s, 1930s, and 1940s the authorities had too many other problems on their hands to concern themselves unduly with an isolated pocket of minority groups. For the neighbouring tribes, whether pastoralists from overgrazed drought-ridden areas, agriculturalists from overcrowded locations, or simply Dorobo, the reserve appears to have offered an unadministered paradise, and individuals immigrated from near and far, consolidating any links they already had with the resident Dorobo and forming new links. Apart from the Mumonyot, the reserve also acquired other Laikipiak survivors, as well as Purko, Keekonyokie, Dalalekutok, and Enkidongi Masai, Samburu, Kikuyu, Meru, and Dorobo from many parts of northern Kenya. The process whereby during this period the Dorobo group acquired new members and adapted themselves to their new surroundings was, in fact, in the best traditions of Dorobo society.

Spasmodic attempts to administer the area were for several decades limited to seeking out intruders and returning them to their tribal reserves without regard for the links they had already formed locally. The deportees for their part simply filtered back to the Doldol reserve in their own time and took up their old associations until they were next deported. Samburu were deported in 1912, 1921, 1935, 1940, 1946, 1955, 1958, and 1959. Even the Mumonyot, who had no recognized tribal reserve elsewhere, were deported no less than seven times in 1912–13, 1929, 1935, 1935–6, 1939, 1940, and 1946. The Kikuyu who had established strong links in the area, especially as traders, were deported *en bloc* during the Mau Mau emergency in 1953.

Without any effective means of policing the area, no Nanyuki official could finally resolve the problem. Nor should the administrative work entailed by this policy be underestimated. Having found families or tribal groups to deport, it was necessary to confer with other administrations to ensure that they would accept the deportees; it was necessary to arrange for all the stock to be deported as well; and in doing this, it was necessary to choose moments and organize routes so that the endemic and sporadic quarantine restrictions of the area were not violated. Periodically, other administrations re-

fused to play what they sometimes regarded as the Doldol administrators' sport, especially when it involved accepting such groups as
the Mumonyot for which no other tribal area would accept responsibility.

From the mid-1950s, local administration was moved to Doldol
itself and an attempt was made to impose some form of grazing
control. To this end, the policy of expurgating intruders and their
stock was intensified, and the area was systematically depopulated
of Masai, Samburu, Kikuyu, etc., etc. For the Dorobo, this policy
now entered a new and sinister phase. It was based on the European
notion of ultimate Dorobo descent and aboriginal rights to live in
the district. On these terms, very few members of the reserve could
claim an indisputable right to remain. On the other hand, they could
claim that the close social links and multiple ties of marriage between all sectors bound them into one rather loosely structured
society, and that these current social relationships were more important to them than ultimate tribal origins.

Thus, the new policy threatened not only the newcomers, but
also the web of relationships that constituted Dorobo society. This
does not appear to have been a society which was particularly
prone to political wrangling and feuding—possibly because of its
loose structure; but under this situation of an imposed strain, the
rifts between different Dorobo groups and between different families
were exposed and morale was low. Individuals and groups would
inform to the administration on newcomers. One or two of the
informers were primarily thought to be trying to enhance the power
of their own groups and its accretions at the expense of others, while
others were themselves recent immigrants hoping to divert attention. Inevitably, the administration was faced with an erratic and
confused picture of allegation and counter-allegation, and had to
decide for itself what information was genuine and what was false.

Rumour and suspicion spread around the reserve. Should the
Purko Masai still among the Ndigiri be denounced to the administration? Or should the whole of the Ndigiri Dorobo be accused of
being Purko and belonging rightfully to the Masai reserve. What
about the Meru still living among the Lngwesi? And the Mumonyot
—when were they next going to be deported?

The situation came to a head when in 1959 some elders of the
Ndigiri group (including some of the immigrants) persuaded the
administration that the Leuaso were recent immigrants to the area
and belonged rightfully to the Leroghi reserve. In the sense that the
Leuaso had closer links with the Leroghi Dorobo than others of
the Doldol reserve, there was an element of feasibility in this. Moreover, the administration was very prepared to listen to this allega-

tion since the Leuaso in many ways presented the biggest problem of the reserve. They were stockpiling cattle from Leroghi because of the scheme imposed there,[22] they were the most notorious stock thieves of the area: in 1959, they owed fines of up to £600, and fifteen of their thirty-seven *moran* were in prison or awaiting trial for stock theft. But in so much as the Leuaso were one of the only two groups that could quite definitely claim some kind of aboriginal rights to remain in the area, the allegation was unfounded.

The Leuaso were by no means unpopular among the other Dorobo —even among the majority of the Ndigiri. But it is an indication of the extent to which communication had broken down between the administration and the people and of the extent to which morale was at a low ebb that no one spoke up for the Leuaso. There was a similar feeling of helpless inevitability as had occurred among the Samburu on Leroghi when faced with uncompromising control over their grazing (p. 185).

It was during this period that a curious rumour spread across the Doldol reserve. The wider reputation of the Dorobo for sorcery was largely based on the extent to which they themselves believed strongly in its existence. During the recent expurgation from the area, two Masai diviners (*laibonok*) had been sent to the Masai reserve. It was thought that in their spite they had left behind a number of evil charms which were having a malignant effect on those that remained. Impending misfortune was held to be hanging over the entire reserve, and it was felt that this could only be exorcized by calling in a Meru ritual expert to perform a purification ceremony with each of the five Dorobo groups.

In fact, there was no obvious evidence to suggest that the reserve had suffered *more* misfortune recently than at other times, and it seemed rather more likely that the feeling of impending misfortune reflected the insecurity and mistrust that pervaded the area as a result of the administrative policies. General anxiety concerning their future had led to the rapid spread of rumour and suspicion. Suddenly this rumour did not confine itself to impending administrative decisions over which the people had no control, but spread to impending mystical misfortune over which they felt they also had no control.[23]

22. Two counts revealed that their cattle had increased from 1,392 head in 1958 to 3,678 head in 1959. The Leroghi Dorobo had been within the Leroghi grazing scheme since 1952, but unlike their Samburu neighbours, they had no low-country kinsmen to send their surplus stock to. Instead, therefore, they sent them to the Leuaso (see pp. 183–4).

23. For a fuller discussion on the effects of stress and anxiety on local beliefs and individual credence, see *The Samburu*, p. 272, and Sargant, W. W., *Battle for the Mind*, p. 36.

At least a part of this generally unhealthy and unhappy state of affairs in the Doldol reserve appears to have arisen from the misconception that the Dorobo groups were specific and rigid tribes. This had led the administrators to look for certain groups which had a specific right to live in the area in order to expel everyone else. But the more they looked, the more people they found who had only recently migrated to join these groups. Such is the nature of Dorobo society. In trying to divide 'true Dorobo' from accretions, the administration were faced with the problem of where to draw the line and this led to apathy and an enhanced sense of insecurity among the people themselves and a hardening of attitudes on both sides. The way in which the imposed policy threatened the social fabric of the reserve appeared to have a number of secondary effects, ranging from a local cult which reflected the plight of the people to an impressive amount of stock theft and other crime (by no means confined to the Leuaso alone). At the same time, the fines imposed on the reserve steadily mounted as the Dorobo and the administration were caught up in a vicious circle. Ultimately, when the administrative axe hung over one of the only two Dorobo groups who *could* claim some kind of aboriginal rights to remain in the area, a point had been reached when the communication of essential information to the administration had completely broken down.

The Elmolo

The Elmolo have acquired a reputation in Kenya as the smallest tribe in Africa, and a number of other peculiarities about them have attracted considerable attention. Broadly, they may be classified as Dorobo, especially in their relationship with neighbouring tribes, but whereas other Dorobo traditionally hunted and kept bees, the Elmolo gained their livelihood through fishing on Lake Rudolf. In other respects, the Elmolo are an almost classic example of a Dorobo group who have remained attached to one area and one form of economy, while at the same time changing superficial aspects of their custom and culture as their pastoral neighbours have changed. During the nineteenth century, the Elmolo spoke a Cushitic language (as do the Rendille, see Table 7); today they speak Samburu (Masai) and have acquired a number of cultural features of Samburu society. Like the other Dorobo they have also begun to acquire small numbers of cattle and small stock, though to all intents and purposes their livelihood is still rooted in the traditional fishing economy.

Whether the Elmolo are in fact the smallest tribe in Africa or even Kenya must largely depend on one's definition of tribe: they do not appear to have been substantially smaller than some of the smallest Dorobo groups elsewhere. On the other hand, in recent years they were undoubtedly more cut off socially from their neighbours than other groups considered here. In 1958, the only newcomers to the Elmolo in living memory had been three Turkana men. No women had been married into the tribe from elsewhere, although one or two of their women had been married off to other Dorobo groups. Altogether there were 143 persons living in two villages 3 miles apart on the south-eastern short of the lake. They comprised 36 adult males, 40 adult females, 37 unmarried boys, and 30 unmarried girls. At other times, these two villages would merge into one.

Available evidence suggests that aspects of Samburu culture have been acquired over a period of time and are even still being acquired. Thus, while in the past the Elmolo did not circumcise their males or have *moran*, in 1958 three young men had of their own volition been circumcised (probably privately among other Dorobo) and a number of others had adopted the braided red-ochre hairstyle of Samburu *moran*.

A number of other features, however, were clearly acquired at an earlier stage, and logically one could assume that this was during the 1880s and 1890s when a considerable number of Samburu had turned to fishing in the area after losing their cattle during The Disaster. Thus, the Elmolo claim to belong to four Samburu phratries (Lokumai, Masula, Lorogushu, and Longeli) and their men of different ages claim to belong to the appropriate Samburu age-sets. The change of language also may have dated from this period: in 1958, the oldest living men only remembered words of their old language, middle-aged men only knew that there had once been another language, while a number of the younger men were not even aware of this fact. Today, the only remnants of this language are in the technicalities of their fishing jargon.

Regardless of this cultural borrowing, the structure of Elmolo society is altogether different from Samburu. While one can speak of named age-sets and phratries following the Samburu, one can hardly speak of an age-set system or a segmentary descent system. Among the Elmolo, association with any age-set or phratry does not regulate a man's behaviour towards others. There is no developed notion of reciprocity among age mates or of respect for seniors; membership of a phratry may be claimed through either parent and in no way does it regulate marriage. A number of Elmolo simply did not belong to any of the phratries.

Some Samburu practices, however, have been grafted on to something more fundamental to the society. Customs associated with marriage are an example. Thus the bridewealth given by the groom to his father-in-law, which at one time consisted of two fishing rafts, today consists of two or three cattle and some small stock. The custom whereby young men give beads to girls has also been acquired and possibly the custom of circumcising girls.[24]

Differences in the contexts of these customs are significant. Among the Samburu, a girl is given beads by her lover (of her own clan) who acquires sexual rights over her but no more, and pregnancy should be avoided; on her marriage to a man of some other clan, she is circumcised, he hands over the bridewealth and then acquires full rights over her as a wife. Among the Elmolo, on the other hand, the giving of beads is a first stage of marriage: it is not her lover who gives her the beads but her husband, and at the same time he gives her father some of the bridewealth. The couple then live together in their own hut, and while he has sexual and economic rights over her, in the event of divorce, she would retain any children born to them. Some four to ten months later, she is circumcised and he hands over the remainder of the bridewealth. From this point, divorce is less likely and the husband has rights to his wife in the fullest sense including the right to keep any children she bears. Of the forty women in the survey, three had been given beads but were not yet circumcised; the huts that they had built were known by the Samburu term for a hut built by some older girls to entertain their lovers (*senkeran*).

In comparing themselves with the Samburu, the Elmolo reckoned that their bridewealth was a relatively high price to pay, that marriages were stable (they would only admit to one instance of divorce), that adultery was an outrageous offence, and that sexual relations among the unmarried was deplorable; young lovers would exchange brass thumb-rings (cf. the Samburu giving beads) but their relationship was expected to be restrained. As compared with Samburu, the Elmolo were by tradition monogamous, and it was popularly held that the domestic squabbles caused by polygamy would undermine any economic advantages. In 1958, only one Elmolo had more than one wife; he had a rather forceful character and was a Turkana by birth.

In order to appreciate the diffusion of Samburu culture into Elmolo society, it would be necessary to know more of the relations between them. The fact that they were in close contact towards the end of the last century hardly explains the more recently acquired customs. During the present century, relations have been distant, with the Samburu showing little interest or respect for the

24. It is equally possible, though, that the Elmolo may have also circumcised their girls *before* coming into cultural contact with the Samburu.

Elmolo and the Elmolo mistrusting the Samburu. In 1921, Samburu *moran* killed six of their men, for which they were awarded 3,000 goats as compensation. More recently, Samburu have tended to give them empty promises of future payment when trading with the Elmolo. In addition, the Elmolo maintain that Samburu *moran* have from time to time pilfered their stock. Altogether, the Elmolo respect the Rendille more, since at least they are honest in their dealings. In this trading, the Samburu and Rendille exchange mostly small stock in return for leechcraft, cords, and ropes which the Elmolo have made from vegetable fibres primarily for their own fishing, and sandals and whips made from hippopotamus hide.

It is significant that the more recent cultural borrowing consists entirely of customs that affect the younger generation. Moreover the initiative appears to have been taken by young men who have visited the Dorobo elsewhere: possibly the homes of their married kinswomen. In discussing their customs, these younger Elmolo were very ready to point out the extent to which they have become Samburu superficially. It was only when this general topic had been exhausted that they would admit that in many other ways, their social obligations and general structure were not precisely those of the Samburu. It was as if these younger more impressionable Elmolo were reacting against the scorn that they knew the Samburu had for them by becoming partially Samburu.

To any visitor, the most noticeable feature of the Elmolo is their diseased appearance: their lips are blotchy and their teeth discoloured; apart from those born with deformities, younger men complain of weak legs, middle-aged men are distinctly bow-legged, and older people can no longer walk. The high degree of inbreeding may partly be responsible for this, but it is generally accepted that a major cause is their unbalanced diet. One theory is that because of the low calcium carbonate content of the lake, their bones suffer from a calcium deficiency; another is that the alkaline lake water has caused a disease called 'fluorosis'; and a third is that like the Eskimos, they have too much protein from their fish, but too little calories.

Whatever the cause of their condition, it has certainly given credence to the general belief in Kenya that the Elmolo have been a dying tribe. The belief is in fact due to a misreading of the early literature, and this appendix provides an opportunity to clarify the confused issue and to identify the different Elmolo groups that have been reported on Lake Rudolf.

Elmolo is a Cushitic term for people who fish on Lake Rudolf, in rather the same way as *Dorobo* is a general term. The Samburu term for Elmolo is *Ldes*. After The Disaster of the 1880s (p. 154) a number of Samburu turned to fishing on Lake Rudolf, north of Porr and in effect became Elmolo. In his account, von Höhnel *quite specifically* drew attention to the fact that the Elmolo in this region formed several separate tribal groups, numbering altogether two or three hundred.[25] Another group of Elmolo were also found fishing in Alia Bay half-way up the eastern shore of the lake. These were the Reshiat Elmolo who came down south to fish seasonally.

During the early days of exploration, different writers appear to have come into contact with different groups of Elmolo. Of the earlier writers, I would guess that only Neumann and Maud actually met the Elmolo of today:[26] Neumann's remarks on the distinction between these Elmolo and the Samburu Elmolo are probably correct in every detail, and his description of the Elmolo techniques of fishing is identical to their techniques today. The Elmolo described by von Höhnel and Donaldson Smith to the south-east of Lake Rudolf were almost certainly Samburu Elmolo.[27] From various sources, one gathers that the Elmolo of Alia Bay tended to migrate north to the Reshiat country to help in the harvest,[28] and to return to fish in the bay in times of famine[29] or cattle epidemic.[30] When Stigand passed along the shore in 1909 there were no Elmolo in Alia Bay[31] and none have been reported permanently living there since then. More recently, these have been regarded by the Kenya authorities as Ethiopian poachers with no right to fish or hunt in Kenya. Their excursions have tended to be with firearms, and it has largely been through fear of them that the Elmolo of today have remained at the southern end of the lake. Thus historically, there appear to have been three principal groups of Elmolo: the Samburu Elmolo who returned to the cattle economy at the turn of the century, the Reshiat Elmolo who have been banished from Kenya, and an earlier generation of the group known as Elmolo today.

In 1934, an expedition to Lake Rudolf included among their

25. von Höhnel, 1894, ii, p. 111. The fact that von Höhnel reported that these were Rendille, Samburu (Burkeneji), and Reshiat Elmolo does not at first sight clarify the issue, since the Rendille at that time had plenty of camels and today there is no suggestion that they have ever had to fish in the lake. On the other hand, in one or two other contexts, von Höhnel apparently confuses tribal identities.
26. Neumann, 1898, pp. 265 and 378; Maud, 1904, p. 577. Neither of these writers mention the prevalence of deformity among the Elmolo; the first brief mention of it appears in Lloyd Jones' account (1925, p. 242) after he had been in the area in 1913. Unaccountably, the Marsabit records in 1927 refer to their sound physique: possibly they too had found the wrong Elmolo!
27. von Höhnel, 1894, ii, p. 111; Donaldson Smith, 1897, pp. 332–3. See also Neumann, 1898, pp. 267–8.
28. von Höhnel, 1894, ii, p. 212.
29. Neumann, 1898, p. 274.
30. Donaldson Smith, 1897, p. 294.
31. Stigand, 1910, pp. 192–3.

research an investigation of the Elmolo of today. They found only eighty-four alive at that time, and concluded that these were the sole survivors of the far larger number reported by von Höhnel. Because they spoke Samburu, it was also concluded that they were the Samburu Elmolo and this in its turn raised the question of how they had acquired new artifacts and new techniques of fishing in less than fifty years.[32] The source of confusion, of course, is not that the Samburu Elmolo had acquired new artifacts and techniques of fishing, but that another group of Elmolo (whom von Höhnel never met) had acquired a new language.

Subsequently, other newspaper articles have referred to the findings of this expedition and to von Höhnel's estimates and have asserted that the Elmolo have been a dying tribe. It would seem, however, that while the Elmolo of today may be in need of medical help, there is no evidence to support the contention that they are or ever were diminishing in size. Indeed the fact that their population has increased from 84 in 1934 to 143 in 1958 suggests a rapid increase.

Conclusion

The Dorobo can more profitably be regarded as a residue of the existing peoples of the area than as the descendants of an aboriginal race. For as long as there has been historical record, there have been such groups, absorbing odd members of defeated and impoverished tribes, forming relations with neighbouring tribes and other Dorobo groups, and occasionally becoming members of the richer tribes with whom they associated.

This is rather different from the manner in which the Samburu have absorbed impoverished Rendille, which has derived from an essentially stable and well-defined relationship. At the same time, the fact that camel-owning Rendille have been able in times of hardship to turn to the cattle economy of the Samburu has meant that altogether they have only formed distant relations with the Dorobo. In other words, while the Dorobo provided an outlet in times of hardship for the Samburu, the Rendille already had their own outlet in the Samburu.

The stigma attached to being a Dorobo and having Dorobo ancestry is not simply a matter of being a pauper and, by implication, being forced to obtain a livelihood through hunting, fishing,

32. Dyson and Fuchs, 1937. This article gives a full account of the Elmolo material culture. The fact that some Elmolo alive in 1958 could be recognized from earlier photographs in 1934 makes it quite clear that the Elmolo studied then were the Elmolo of today and *not* the Samburu Elmolo of 1888 (some of whom were still alive in 1958—in the cattle economy).

and gathering—for some pastoralists at certain times this may have been a matter of sheer survival—it is also a matter of falling short of the norms of behaviour held, for instance, by the Samburu and Rendille.

Today, most of the Dorobo have stock. But bilateral and affinal ties are still basic to the society, the age-set system is still comparatively unrestrictive as compared with that observed by the Samburu, they still tend to live in small scattered groups with from 100 to 200 adult males, the strength of public opinion is still low and individual competitiveness still high. All this in the eyes of such tribes as the Samburu or Rendille suggests behaviour and social organization associated traditionally with Dorobo society, and they will not accept that through economic development they have transcended their Dorobo status.

BIBLIOGRAPHY

Arkell-Hardwick, A., *An Ivory Trader in Northern Kenya*, Longman, London, 1903.

Avanchers, Léon des, 'Esquisse Géographie des Pays Oromo au Galla', *Bulletin de Societies de Geographie*, series 4, xvii, Paris, 1859.

Beech, M. W. H., *The Suk*, Clarendon, Oxford, 1911.

Boyes, J., *John Boyes: King of the Wa-Kikuyu*, Methuen, London, 1911.

Boyes, J., *The Company of Adventurers*, 'East Africa', London, 1928.

Cavendish, H., 'Through Somaliland and around South of Lake Rudolf', *Geographic Journal*, 11.4, 1898.

Chanler, W. A., *Through Jungle and Desert, Travels in Eastern Africa*, Macmillan, London, 1896.

Christie, J., *Cholera Epidemics in East Africa*, Macmillan, London, 1876.

Dundas, K. R., 'Notes on the Origin and History of the Kikuyu and Dorobo Tribes', *Man*, 1908.

Dyson, W. S. and Fuchs, V. E., 'The Elmolo', *Journal of the Royal Anthropological Institute*, vol. 67, 1937.

Gulliver, P. H., *A Preliminary Survey of the Turkana*, sm. fol. School of African Studies, University of Capetown, 1951.

Handbook of Kenya Colony and Protectorate, 1920.

Hobley, C. W., *Ethnology of A-Kamba and other East African Tribes*, Cambridge University Press, 1910.

Höhnel, L. von, *Discovery by Count Teleki of Lakes Rudolf and Stefanie* (2 vols.), Longmans, London, 1894.

Höhnel, L. von, 'The Lake Rudolf Region: its discovery and subsequent exploration, 1888–1909', *Journal of the Royal African Society*, vol. 37, 1938.

Huntingford, G. W. B., *The Southern Nilo-Hamites*, Ethnographic Survey of Africa, International African Institute, London, 1953.

Huxley, E., *White Man's Country*, Macmillan, London, 1935.

Johnston, H., *The Uganda Protectorate*, vol. 2, Hutchinson, London, 1902.

Kenya Government (Economics and Statistics Division), *Kenya Population Census 1962. Advance Report of Volumes I and II*, 1964.

Kenya Land Commission: Evidence and Memoranda, H.M.S.O., London, 1933.

Lambert, H. E., *The Systems of Land Tenure in the Kikuyu Land Unit*, University of Capetown, 1950.

Leach, E. R., *Political Systems of Highland Burma*, Bell, London, 1954.

Leese, A. S., *A Treatise on the One-humped Camel in Health and Disease*, Haynes, London, 1927.

Lloyd-Jones, W., *Havash! Frontier Adventures in Kenya*, Arrowsmith, Bristol, 1925.

Macdonald, J. R. L., 'Notes on the Enthnology of Tribes met with during Progress of the Juba Expedition of 1897–99', *Journal of the Royal Anthropological Institute*, vol. 29, 1899.

Maguire, R. A. J., 'Il-Torobo', *Tanganyika Notes and Records*, 1948.

Maud, P., 'Exploration of the Southern Borderland of Abyssinia', *Geographic Journal*, 22.5, 1904.

Neumann, A. H., *Elephant Hunting in East Equatorial Africa*, Rowland Ward, London, 1898.

Patterson, J. H., *In the Grip of the Nyika*, Macmillan, London, 1909.

Peck, E. F., 'The Relationship of Salt Starvation to Contagious Necrosis and Lameness in Camels', *The Veterinary Record*, No. 14, vol. 50, 1938.

Peters, C., *New Light on Dark Africa*, Ward, Lock and Co., London, 1891.

Sargant, W. W., *Battle for the Mind: a Physiology of Conversion and Brainwashing*, Heinemann, London, 1957.

Seligman, C. G., *Races of Africa*, Butterworth, London, 1930.

Shackleton, E. R., *The Merille or Gelubba*, ms. Kenya Government, 1932.

Smith, A. Donaldson, *Through Unknown African Countries*, Arnold, London, 1897.

Smith, A. Donaldson, 'An Expedition between Lake Rudolf and the Nile', *Geographic Journal*, 16.6, 1900.

Spencer, P., *The Samburu, a Study of Gerontocracy in a Nomadic Tribe*, Routledge and Kegan Paul, London, 1965.

Spencer, P., 'Dynamics of Samburu Religion' (paper read at a conference at the East African Institute of Social Research, July, 1959 (cyclostyled)).

Spencer, P., 'The Function of Ritual in the Socialisation of the Samburu Moran', in Mayer, P., *Socialization: the approach from social anthropology*, ASA8, 1970, Tavistock.

Stigand, C. H., *To Abyssinia through an Unknown Land*, Seeley, London, 1910.

Tate, H. R., 'Journey to the Rendille Country, British East Africa', *Geographic Journal*, 23, 1904.

Tate, H. R., 'Nairobi to Samburu and Rendille', *East African Quarterly*, April–June 1904.

Thomson, J., *Through Masailand*, Samson Low, London, 1885.

Wellby, M. S., 'King Menelik's Dominions and the Country between Lake Gallop (Rudolf) and the Nile Valley', *Geographic Journal*, 16, 1900.

Wickenburg, Count, *Petermanns Geographische Mitteilungen*, 1903, Nos. 9 and 10.

INDEX

Key:
R   Rendille
S   Samburu
*   see *The Samburu* (Spencer 1965) for a fuller account on the entry

abortion, R 42, S 83–4
administration (*see* British administration)
administrative centres: established, 158, 160, 161, 196; siting of, 6–7, 192–3
adultery (*see moran*)
African District Council (A.D.C.), 173, 177; and grazing schemes, 189
affines, R 56, 105, S 75, 105, *
affrays: among R youths, 100; among S *moran*, 100, 123, 160
age grades, 73–4, *
age mates, **33**; avoid daughters, 34; forms of address, 88–9
age-set system: Ariaal, 130; Dorobo, 206, 208; Elmolo, 214
age-set system (*Rendille*), **33–6**, 73–4; age-set line (*teeria*), **33–5**, 45, 143; and *almhato festival*, 58–9; ceremonies, 29, 45–51; climbing, 34, 47, 130; initiation, 36, 45–6, 65, 66, 67, 68, 70–1, 114, 122; marriage of, 51, 52–3, 99; and warfare, 98; (*see* ritual leader)
age-set system (*Samburu*), 33, **73–5**, *; age-set line, 75; and British administration, 149, 160–4, 175–9, 196; ceremonies, 85–94; development during *moranhood*, **89–93**, 162–3; initiation, **85–9**, 97, 106, 114, 124–5, 126, 176; retiring to elderhood, 92–3, 162, 175–7; (*see* ritual leader)
agnatic kin, R 41, 43, 45–6, 54, S 77–8, *
allotted herds (S), **76–7**, 82, 103; and Ariaal, 132; competition over, 76–7, 107; inheritance, 77, 81; rights of affines, 75–6, 84, 139
almhato ceremony (R), **58–9**, 67, 70, 130
alternations, R **32**, 42, 46, 64, 72–3, S 72–3, 80, 92, *
ancestry: and age-set system, R 34, S 75, 151; belief in, R 29, 149; S 78, 149; and bond brothers, 111; bones of ancestors, 56; and clans, R 27, 65, 147, S 78; and Dorobo, 200, 211, 213; and Rendille immigrants, 131, 137
annual cycle (*see* cycles, dry season, rainy season)
Arbah Jahan, 20, 131, 132
Ariaal Rendille, 2, 12, 14, 20, 65, **130–6**, 142, 145, 153–4; immigration from Rendille *proper*, 130–2, 134–5, 137, 143; and Samburu, 130–7, 186
Arkell-Hardwick, A., 1–2, 156, 157, 158, 192
avoidances: affines, S 105; blacksmiths, R 63, 118; bond brothers, 30–1, 36; daughters, R 34, 36, 44, S 85, 206, *; and death, R 60, S 107–8, 116; and generational seniority, 32, 73; girls and elders, 44, 85; and homicide, S 109; *hosoop*, R 48; *moran* and certain foods (*menong*), S 90, 93, 94, 103; and totemism, R 61, S 117–18; wives, 30–1, 36, 94; women and *soriu* festival, R 58

bajo, R 44, 47
Baragoi, 5–6, 160, 169, 195
Baringo (*see* Lake Baringo)
barrenness, R 36, 66, S 82, 115
Barsalinga, 182, 203
Barsaloi, 7, 160, 181
birth, R 41, S 80–1, 128; averting misfortune, 82, 119; uncertainty surrounding, 57; unpropitious, R 42, 66, 71, 143, S 83, 91
Black Cattle moiety (S), 87, 108, **121–2**, 124, 209
blacksmiths, R 42, **63**, 65, 137, 206, S 83, **118–19**, 123, 206; and ceremony, R 55, 58, 60, S 82, 86, 124, 129
blessing: blacksmiths, 63; boys, 82; elders, R 59, S 82, 87, 88, 89, 92, 103, 104; *hosoop*, R 48, 49; *iipire*, R 61; *laisi*, S 116–17
bloodwealth, R 61, S 110–12
bond brotherhood, R **30–1**, 36, 64, 121, 123, S 72, 123, *; and cursing, 113; formal, 30–1; and homicide, 72, **109–12**; joking, 30, 50; and *nkiyu*, 90; and totemism, 61–2, 117–18

joking relationships; and alternate generations, 32, 73; and bond brotherhood, 30–1, 50, 56, 65; and man-of-the-feather, 50

Kenya Independence, 3, 174, 179, 189, 197
Kenya Land Commission, **161**, 163, 179, 193; Evidence, **9**, 152, 158, 180, 182
Kikuyu, 199, 202, 205, 211
Kiliako age-set, 33, 97, 122, 123, **160**–3, 175
Killing in warfare, *R* 43, 52, 69, 96–7
Kimaniki age-set, 33, 123, 125, 144, **164**–**5**, 176–8
King's African Rifles, 159, 163–4, 167
Kipayang age-set, 33, 150
Kipeko age-set, *R* 33, 35, 79, *S* 33, 149, **152**–**3**
Kirimani, 153–4
Kishili age-set, 35, **165**
Kiteku age-set, 33, **153**

lahaoloroge ceremony, 46, 69
laibon, see diviner
Laidotok Dorobo, 151, 204
Laikipiak Masai, 96, 147, 149, **152**–**8**, 202, 203, 209; Dorobo, 201–3, 207
laisi, 82, 83, **116**–**17**, 119, 121, 123, 126; (*see* iipire)
Laisamis, 9, 20, 151
Lake Baringo, 5, 86, 136, 150–3
Lake Rudolf, 7, 9, 20, 46–7, 71, 153, 155, 157, 213
Lamagaati, 12, 14, 20, 141
Lanat Dorobo, 151, 202, 203, 204, 205, 208
land ownership, 8–9, 121, 207, 209
launon (*see* ritual leader)
Lbarta Plains, 150–3, 158, 159, 182
Leese, A. S., 8, 12, 13
Lekerisia Dorobo, 151, 201
Lemarmar Dorobo, 151, 201, 204
Lengiro Dorobo, 151, 203, 204, 205, 207, 208
Leroghi: Dorobo Reserve, 204, 209, 211; Plateau, 5, 7, 9, 20, 24, 124, 150, 151, 163; and stock control, 160, 179, 182, **184**, 193, 196
Lesarge (*see* Saali Orare)
Lesupukia Dorobo, 151, 201, 203, 204
Leuaso Dorobo, 151, 202, 204, 207–8, 209, 211–12
Lineage group, *R* 27–9, *S* 72, 103, 150
Linguistic: classification of tribes, 1, 146–8; change, 148, 203, 205, 213, 218
Lipaale age-sets, 33, 49, 68, 144, 153
Lkerna, 151, 204
Lngwesi phratry, **122**, 123, 136, 202
Lngwesi Dorobo, 151, 202, 203, 204, 205, 210, 211
loans, 78, 139–40
Loiborkineji (*Burkineji, Samburu*), 1–2, **14**, 217
Loikop, 1, 109
Loimusi phratry, **123**, 135, 136, 204
Lokumai phratry, 20, 100, **123**, 135, 136, 157, 214
Loliin Dorobo, 151, 201, 204
Longeli phratry, 20, 31, **123**, 135, 136, 214
Lorokoti Dorobo, 151, 201, 204
Lorogushu phratry, 20, **122**, 131, 135, 136, 160, 204, 214
lovers, *R* 42, 44, 98–9, *S* **95**, 99, 215, *; Elmolo, 215
low country, **5**, 7, 13, 25, 124, **184**, 193, 197, 212
Lower Belisi moiety, 28, **29**, 41, 45, 47, 64–5, 126
Ltudaani Dorobo, 151, 203
lunar cycle (*see* cycles)

mal (*see* shared beast)
man-of-the-feather, 49, 50, 65
man-of-the-fire, 49, 61, 64, 117
man-of-the-horn, 50, 51, 61, 63, 64
Maralal: administrative centre, 1, 5–6, 161, 169, 192, 196; district, 169, 195